Magical Mushrooms,
Mischievous Molds

GEORGE W. HUDLER

Magical Mushrooms, Mischievous Molds

PRINCETON UNIVERSITY PRESS

PRINCETON AND OXFORD

✦ *To Dave French*

Fifth printing, and first paperback printing, 2000
Paperback ISBN 0-691-07016-4

*The Library of Congress has cataloged the cloth edition of this
book as follows*

Hudler, George W.
Magical mushrooms, mischievous molds / George W. Hudler.
p. cm.
Includes index.
ISBN 0-691-02873-7 (cl : alk. paper)
1. Fungi. I. Title
QK603.H79 1998
579.5—dc21 98-10163

This book has been composed in Baskerville
Designed by Jan Lilly

The paper used in this publication meets the minimum requirements
of ANSI/NISO Z39.48-1992 (R1997) (*Permanence of Paper*)

www.pup.princeton.edu

Printed in the United States of America

20 19 18 17 16 15 14 13
ISBN-13: 978-0-691-07016-2 (pbk.)

ISBN-10: 0-691-07016-4 (pbk.)

✦ CONTENTS

CONTENTS

Thirty years ago I found myself, as a senior in the College of Forestry at the University of Minnesota, seated in a classroom waiting to hear my first lecture in a course called "Forest Pathology." Unlike most of my other courses, which by their title gave me some idea of what to expect, pathology had me baffled. Surely there weren't enough diseases of trees to take up twelve weeks of lectures and labs! Maybe there was a typo in the course catalog, and I was really there to learn how to purify water in the wild, how to cope with a bad case of poison ivy, or how to recognize the early symptoms of Rocky Mountain spotted fever. In other words, it was forest*ER* pathology.

Then the professor strode to the front of the room. Unceremoniously he dropped his notebook on the lectern and proceeded to issue a stern warning to those of us who persisted to squander our meager funds at the local tavern: we were all doomed to short, excruciatingly painful lives. "It's not the beer that will get you," he said. "It's those free peanuts. They are loaded with a mold that makes one of the most potent carcinogens known to man. Your liver just can't take such abuse forever!" I felt relieved that I had had popcorn the night before.

He talked about the ineffectiveness of the foot bath at the university swimming pool in removing germs from sweaty feet. "The damn thing's a cesspool of pathogenic fungi," he proclaimed. "If you want a good case of athlete's foot, that's the place to wallow." I tried to imagine tiptoeing around on the lip of the gutter the next time I went to the pool, and decided that this year I'd get my exercise at the hockey rink.

He concluded his introductory remarks by telling us about a colleague and his wife who had recently hosted a dinner party. At some point in the evening, the wife excused herself to use the bathroom, which was on the second floor, just above the dining room. Shortly after her departure, a blood-curdling scream filled the air, plaster rained down on the guests, and the woman's leg was seen dangling through a hole in the ceiling. Fungi decaying the floor joists in that warm, moist room had finally had their day and left the woman hanging, so to speak.

The professor may also have said something about tree diseases in that first lecture. Frankly, I don't remember: what remains vivid in my mind is that the tone of his voice and his presence before the class left little doubt that not only did he have a message of the utmost importance to share with us, but he was looking forward to the opportunity to do so. For the first time in my college career—I had been at it for four years by then—I found myself looking forward to the next class.

That afternoon, the first lab meeting was scheduled. As I rounded the corner in the hall and eagerly strode through the door in anticipation of more stimulating discussions, my euphoric bubble burst abruptly: there on the tables—horror of horrors—were microscopes! These evil contraptions had plagued all of my previous efforts to study biology and had never yielded more than a mediocre reflection of my eyeball, and here they were again. Nuts!

Moved only by the positive experience of the morning lecture, I begrudgingly decided to give the 'scopes one more chance and dutifully followed along as the lab assistant explained how best to prepare a slide and what one could expect to see. At the moment of truth, I warily set my eye to the lens, and all was just as we were told it would be: not only were there spores in the view, but there were eight of them, all lined up in a row like eggs inside a balloon, surrounded by the thinnest of membranes.

At that moment, which is as vivid in my mind today as it was so many years ago, my life took on new meaning. I was completely captivated by the fungi and couldn't find enough time to look at them, identify them, and learn more about their natural history. Somehow, I knew, I would find a way to craft a career around them. Indeed, my previously untapped enthusiasm propelled me through two graduate degrees and into my present position as professor of plant pathology at Cornell University.

Throughout this adventure, I have fervently hoped that some day I would be able to repay my debt to the fungi and to the professor who introduced me to them. If my teaching and my writing changes the life of just one person the way mine was changed that memorable September afternoon, I will be gratified in knowing that I have at least begun to balance the ledger.

ACKNOWLEDGEMENTS

Over two thousand students have enrolled in Plant Pathology 201—Magical Mushrooms, Mischievous Molds—since its inception in 1989. Each one has brought to the classroom a keen mind, a curiosity about the natural world, and a sense of humor, and to each of them I extend my most sincere thanks for their contributions to my life and work.

Authors of several previous books popularizing the fungi also helped to shape my thinking in preparation of this tome. Other than those listed in the Notes, I was especially inspired by the writings of C. M. Christensen (*Molds, Mushrooms, and Mycotoxins*), W.P.K. Findlay (*Fungi: Folklore, Fiction, & Fact*), W. D. Gray (*The Relation of Fungi to Human Affairs*), Lucy Kavaler (*Mushrooms, Molds, and Miracles*), and R. T. and F. W. Rolfe (*The Romance of the Fungus World*).

In addition, many of my colleagues at Cornell University provided the emotional support and technical expertise I needed to see this project to completion. Special thanks are due to Bill Fry and Steve Slack for issuing the challenge and providing me with the resources to make a go of it. E. Bosley Jenkins did much of the first round of library research, providing a firm foundation for all that has followed. Sandra Tracy has been my assistant for the past 9 years in the lab, library, and classroom, and her enthusiasm, good judgment, and patience have helped to bring my sometimes chaotic work habits back into line so we could continue to move forward. Roxanna Barnum tactfully managed my calendar so I could have the occasional whole day to devote to reading and writing. Gary Bergstrom, Wayne Sinclair, Tom Zitter, Peter Mullin, and David Kalb—often unknowingly, I'm sure—offered just the right comments at just the right time to keep me from making potentially embarrassing misstatements. Kent Loeffler and Bob O'Brien prepared some of the illustrations, and their contributions are noted where they appear in the text. R. P. Korf, Kathie Hodge, and Pavel Lizon generously reviewed the entire manuscript, and their suggestions throughout the project helped me to stay on track when my energy would have had me go in a wrong direction.

This project was completed while I was on sabbatical leave at the University of the Orange Free State in Bloemfontein, South Africa, and I am indebted to my hosts there, Mike and Brenda Wingfield, for their gracious hospitality and free use of facilities so that I could close the door and wrap this up.

Jack Repchek, senior editor at Princeton University Press, approached me with the opportunity to undertake this project and has been unfailing in his support of the effort, even when I ran several months beyond the original deadline. He, Alice Calaprice, Charles Mims, and James Kimbrough also reviewed the manuscript and made numerous helpful suggestions.

Finally, I thank my family—Sandy, Jennifer, and Elizabeth— who put up with my long nights at the office, my frequent interruptions of dinner-table conversation to share a mycological tidbit, and my constant diversions of family outings to photograph or otherwise ponder a special fruit-body. Throughout it all, they've been real "fun guys"!

About twelve thousand years ago, a hapless Middle Eastern native struggled to make sense of a most peculiar situation. His mind was playing tricks on him, causing him at once to be fearful as the landscape relentlessly spun before his eyes, and calmed as the tension in his muscles effortlessly unwound. The dizzying sensation was reminiscent of the lightheadedness that came with standing up quickly after a midday rest, but it persisted, first for several minutes and then for an hour or so. The day had begun like any other, with a bit of food and some juice from wild grapes, and he had taken care to drink liberally afterwards as the temperature rose with the morning sun. Perhaps the gods were punishing him for stealing the juice from passersby several days earlier, but he had stolen drink before with no retribution. And this didn't really seem like punishment: in fact, the sensation was rather nice. H'mmm . . . quite nice. And he closed his eyes and fell asleep.

What this person didn't know was that his senses had been muted by ethyl alcohol, a waste product of microorganisms known as fungi. Upon waking up sober, he drank more of the juice and the sensations returned. Now there was little question but that the magic came from the gourd, and he drank more juice to see if he could keep the magic alive inside him. His discovery of the drink that would later be known as wine would forever change the course of human history.

• • • • • •

About six hundred years ago, a crowd gathered in the square of a small German town on the shores of the Rhine River. They cheered with glee as the trap door on the platform fell away and Frau Wilma Meyburg was left to dangle in mid-air from a rope fixed securely around

*her neck. As her lifeless body swayed in the breeze, a sense of relief over-
came the villagers. They were certain that her death would bring freedom
from the horror that had plagued their lives in recent months. Surely,
they thought, peaceful sleep would replace the long nights of listening to
neighbors screaming to be free of demons and burning limbs; the mysterious deaths of unborn children would cease; and the barren teats of precious livestock would be filled with milk. Surely, they thought, life would
return to normal. Of course, if it didn't, there was Frau Schwinkle to be
reckoned with . . .*

What those people didn't know was that they had been eating
rye that was contaminated with a fungus. And that fungus would
defy their attempts to mete out justice then and for hundreds of
years to come. Even the Salem, Massachusetts, witchcraft trials
would have fungus-infested rye as their root cause. Years later
the same fungus would be the source of the world's first doses
of lysergic acid diethylamide (LSD) and it, too, would forever
change the course of human history.

• • • • • •

*About 270 years ago, Filip Johann von Strahlenberg braved
the harsh climate and perilous terrain of Siberia to explore the land and
learn about the people who lived there. The very fact that he survived
the journey under such trying circumstances was remarkable. But what
was even more remarkable was what von Strahlenberg discovered about
the natives' customs. Particularly noteworthy was how they enlivened
their tenuous existence by eating hallucinogenic mushrooms. The experience was apparently worth a high price, as evidenced by a man who
gladly traded ten oxen for a single mushroom. Tribesman too poor to buy
the mushrooms would gather outside the party tent, waiting for the cel-
ebrants to come to the door to "make water." Then they would do their
best to catch the urine and drink it, because it also contained a goodly
portion of the hallucinogen.*

Later scholars would link the same mushroom to the forbidden fruit in the Garden of Eden, to the Soma of ancient Hindu

worship, and to Santa Claus, and this one, too, would forever change the course of history.

· · · · · ·

About ten months ago, singer/songwriter Bob Dylan was overcome with a hacking cough, chest pains, and general lethargy. Puzzled over the cause of his ill health and frustrated by its intrusion into his busy schedule, he sought the advice of a physician. She also was unable to make a positive diagnosis without ordering a battery of laboratory tests and consulting with other specialists. Meanwhile, Dylan's health deteriorated, his heart began to fail, and he was confined to the intensive care unit of a hospital. The answer to the famed musician's problems, it turned out, was blowin' in the wind, for he had contracted a potentially fatal fungus disease by inhaling airborne spores. After several months of convalescence, he recovered, with long overdue respect for the power of the fungi that lurk in every nook and cranny of the world around us.

Dylan's disease, histoplasmosis, is common in some segments of the human population, and many people apparently host the fungus without showing symptoms. For those whose lives are threatened by it, the course of their history is forever changed.

· · · · · ·

About eight hours ago, a young boy of Zulu ancestry stood on the side of a busy highway in Kwazulu-Natal, South Africa. In his left hand he held a bag of mushrooms that he had picked from termite mounds earlier in the day. A paper company executive heading north for a holiday spotted the boy and his treasure and pulled over. After a bit of skillful negotiation between the two, the deal was sealed: twenty-five rands for ten mushrooms. The paper company executive drove on, content in knowing that his evening meal would be garnished with one of the most flavorful of wild mushrooms. The Zulu boy went home, content in knowing that the sale of the mushrooms would allow his family to buy food for an evening meal.

INTRODUCTION

It is unlikely that the boy had any inkling that with his trans-
action, he had become part of one of the fastest-growing business ventures in the world—the collection and sale of wild mushrooms. In some locales, mushroom harvesters have become so
aggressive in their pursuits that fragile terrain has been dam-
aged and delicate ecosystems are threatened. But for those with
few alternative sources of income, the chance to tap into the
multimillion dollar industry is too good to pass up. Only time
will tell what impact *they* will have on the course of history.

• • • • • •

*About twenty seconds ago, you opened this book. The chances
are that before you did, you thought that the fungi were some of the most
disgusting organisms ever to grace your presence. But now you have
started reading, and before you are done you will learn about fungi as
decayers and recyclers of organic matter, as sources of beneficial medicines and treacherous toxins, as causes of disease in plants and animals,
and as sources of food. You will also find out how the fungi changed the
history of the biblical nation of Israel and the countries of Ireland and
Mexico. They played key roles in weakening opposing armies in two
world wars and were part of the arsenal developed to secure victory in
an anticipated third. You will learn that some of the most respected Greek
philosophers may have formulated their great thoughts while inspired by
fungus-induced hallucinations. And you will meet a few of the many
fascinating people who have strengthened our knowledge of the fungus
world through their dedicated exploration.*

Who knows? By the time you are done *you* may have learned
something that will forever change the course of human history.
Stranger things have happened. Welcome aboard.

Magical Mushrooms,
Mischievous Molds

CHAPTER 1

Classification and Naming

Every blink of an eye, every beat of a heart, every bloom of a flower, every bit of life in all but a few unusual bacteria is as it is on Planet Earth only because energy from the sun, in the form of photons, has been trapped and converted into chemical bonds. And when those bonds are broken in a truly astounding cascade of reactions, the energy from them is released and used to do the work needed to keep us all alive.

Green plants are crucial players in this scheme, for they are the Earth's primary solar collectors. Within their cells, the energy of light is trapped in the joining of carbon dioxide with water to make more complex compounds such as sugar and starch. And those compounds, together with small amounts of mineral elements from the soil—nitrogen, potassium, phosphorus, iron, calcium, and others—become increasingly more complex, forming amino acids and proteins and enzymes and nucleic acids. They, in turn, direct still more chemical reactions to make wood and flowers and fruits, and leaves and roots and all the other parts that go together to create more plants that are even bigger and better solar collectors.

Moreover, the energy captured by plants is not used only to ensure their own future; the survival of almost every organism that is not a plant also depends on the work that plants do. Many organisms eat plants, thereby "swallowing" the energy and releasing it for their own purposes through digestion and subsequent metabolic processes. Others eat animals that eat plants, and still others eat animals that eat animals that eat plants. No matter how long the chain gets, every link along the way uses some of the sun's energy, originally bound in plant tissue, to do the work needed for its own growth and development. So long as the sun shines and plants keep growing and trapping its energy and feeding the planet's herbivores, life ought to continue ad infinitum.

From the beginning of time, however, there have been several potential problems with this idyllic scenario. First, those great green solar collectors are perhaps a bit too good at what they do. They grow bigger and make more of themselves and feed the world, but as they do so they also trap mineral elements from the soil in such complex chemical webs that these elements are no longer available to aid the growth and development of other plants. Without some means to complete a cycle, the soil could eventually become so depleted that lack of essential elements could bring new plant growth to a screeching halt.

Second, as leaves and flowers and fruit reach the ends of their useful lives, they become nuisances. They're slippery, they smother other plants that are still trying to grow, and they just plain get in the way. Some people would even say they stink. One way or another, spent plant material has to be reduced to a tolerable volume or we would find ourselves, our houses, our roads, and our water courses totally overwhelmed by it.

Third, plant debris is not the only problem. One must also cope with the bodies of all those animals who, through natural processes of their own, have reached the ends of their useful lives. After all, they stink and take up space, too. And, having gotten where they have by eating plants, they have also amassed a significant store of essential elements in their cells.

Obviously, since life has been continuous on Earth for millions of years, a means of making room for future generations and of recycling scarce resources to nourish their growth has been essential.

ENTER: THE FUNGI

I will acknowledge at the outset that there are several different groups of organisms that help to break down complex organic matter into its essential elements. Notable among these are the unicellular—some say primitive—life forms known as bacteria, and the slightly more advanced organisms, though still microscopic in size, known as protozoans. But the fungi are arguably the most important of the lot, and because this book is about fungi they will hold center stage.

These seemingly fragile organisms possess a powerful array of chemicals known as enzymes that ooze out of the fungus body and, like two hands pulling apart Tinkertoys, systematically uncouple some of the bonds that hold atoms of organic molecules together. The reduced chemicals are then absorbed through the walls of the fungus cells, where they are further undone to provide nourishment for the organism's relentless growth.

Cellulose, pectin, and lignin—the stuff plant cells are made of—are particularly vulnerable to attack. But the fungus enzymes also go after flesh and bones, plastic and paint, gas and oil, and many other complex materials. And the best evidence indicates that they have been doing their recycling for a very long time—at least as long as the 400 million years or so that land plants have been around, and probably closer to 900 million years.

For most of recorded human history, the fungi were known largely because of the mushrooms that some produced. These mysterious earthly excrescences, springing up as they did—literally overnight—were viewed by many as the probable work of evil spirits, witches, or the devil, and most assuredly they were able to corrupt the minds and bodies of hapless souls who stooped to pick them. Such attitudes persisted among laypeople well into the nineteenth century, but the scientific community recognized much earlier that the fungi—at least the mushrooms—represented a life form comparable to plants. In fact, the earliest classification schemes devised by biologists in the 1700s listed the fungi on the plant side of a two-kingdom system—plants and animals. Members of the plant kingdom were rooted in place, had rigid cell walls, and could make their own food by way of the poorly understood and not-yet-named process of photosynthesis. Animals, on the other hand, could move around, had no walls surrounding their cells, and obtained food by eating either plants or one another. The differences between the kingdoms were obvious, and although the fungi were regarded as *unusual* plants, they were presumed to be plants nonetheless.

When Antony van Leeuwenhoek applied a primitive microscope to botanical study in 1665, and when Robert Hooke and others improved upon the instrument throughout the nineteenth century, biologists discovered a whole new world of tiny, living organisms that shook their previous perceptions of life on Earth. Among other things, microscopic examination of fungi made it quite clear that they were not plants. Not only were they without chlorophyll and unable to make their own food, but the food they did use was first digested outside of the fungus body and then absorbed through the cell walls. And the fungal cells themselves were very simple in structure and function. Each one had a clearly visible central body—a nucleus—and most were tubular in shape, connected end to end, and appeared *en masse* as circular growths of hairlike material. Roots, stems, leaves, and all of the other tissues that comprise typical plants were nowhere to be seen in the fungi. Thus it was decided that they were unique enough to deserve a kingdom of their own, and in 1784 that concept was proposed to the scientific world. Thus, a third kingdom of living organisms—the *Fungi*—was born.[1]

The three-kingdom concept for classifying life forms was used by the scientific community for almost two centuries until, in 1969, another system of "natural" classification was introduced. This one was devised by Cornell University ecologist R. H. Whittaker,[2] who proposed an evolutionary scheme involving five kingdoms. The *Monera*, including bacteria and other single-celled organisms without true nuclei, gave rise to the *Protista*—simple, often multicelled organisms with nuclei, and occasionally chlorophyll, in their cells. From the *Protista* arose the

Plantae, Animalia, and *Fungi.* Mycologists blanched a bit as Whittaker moved some of their prized subjects, such as the "fungus" that caused the Irish potato famine, out of the *Fungi* and into the *Protista,* but they agreed with his reasoning and were not about to stand in the way of progress. The five-kingdom system seemed to accommodate all of the shortcomings of previous classification efforts, and members of the scientific community heaved a great sigh of relief that finally the issue was settled.

Well . . . yes, most members heaved a great sigh of relief, but some remained skeptical, certain that there was still more to learn about the interrelationships of the major groups of organisms. Indeed, with the advent of the new technology that enables scientists to decode the genetic material that makes us all different from one another, still another classification scheme has arisen. This one, originating in the laboratory of Dr. Carl Woese and colleagues at the University of Illinois, suggests that the living world had evolved from the very earliest primordial slime into three domains: the Archaea, or primitive bacteria; the Bacteria; and the Eucarya.[3] Each domain contained any number of kingdoms, each arising independently from other kingdoms in that domain, most likely not in any orderly evolutionary succession. The new concept continues to be debated as I write these words, but the data are sufficiently convincing for most experts to view the arguments favorably. Some find it hard to believe that *Homo sapiens* may not be a higher form of life than fungi, but that they are instead equal partners on parallel roads. But those of us familiar with the nature of the fungi expected as much all along!

Evolutionary arguments aside, however, today's students of biological classification generally agree that the true fungi are uniquely different from other groups of living organisms in several major ways.

First, the fungus body is usually comprised of cells with nuclei and with walls made of chitin and other polysaccharides but rarely cellulose. These features contrast with the Archaea and

Bacteria, which have no clearly defined nucleus; animals, which have no cell walls; and plants, which have walls with cellulose as the major component.[4]

Second, fungi are heterotrophic. This means that they cannot make their own food as plants can, through photosynthesis. They obtain much of their nourishment by "digesting" the complex molecules in plants or plant products or in organisms that eat plants. The majority of that digestion takes place outside of the fungus body.

Third, the fungus body is structurally simple; there is no division of cells into various organs such as roots, stems, and leaves, or tissues such as xylem, phloem, and epidermis. As you will see later, fungi become more complex when they reproduce, but even the most elaborate are still much simpler than most members of the plant or animal kingdom.

Fourth, fungi reproduce by way of microscopic, seedlike propagules called spores. Each spore has the capacity to germinate and develop into a new colony of fungus cells. There are many different types of spores, but for purposes of this discussion, we'll consider just a few. One of these is known as a conidium (pl. conidia)—a spore that is little more than a fragment of the parent fungus. Many different species of fungi produce conidia; for each species they are unique in size, shape, color, and/ or generative cells. Some fungi even produce more than one kind of conidium. In all cases, these spores are produced without any cross-fertilization, and, except for the occasional mutation or other aberration in cell division, each is genetically identical to the parent.

Other spores worthy of mention here are ascospores and basidiospores. Each of these spore types is produced only after two compatible nuclei from the same species merge as one and then separate during the process of meiosis. In some fungi, the two nuclei may originate within one fungus body, and a process of self-fertilization leads to ascospore or basidiospore formation. Opportunities for evolution of such fungi are largely limited to genetic changes triggered by spontaneous mutations within the fungus culture or gene exchange during simple cell division, and both are relatively uncommon.

In other fungi, the nuclei must come from two separate but compatible mating types of the same species. For these, the capacity to adapt to environmental changes is far greater because they enjoy the advantage of outcrossing with relatives that have evolved in the face of various selection pressures. For plant pathogenic fungi, for instance, the pressures working against them might be toxic fungicides or resistant plant hosts. If those fungi are obligated to mate with other members of the same species, they seem to produce offspring with tolerance to fungicides or to disease-resistant hosts much more quickly. They are better pathogens, if you will—an issue to be revisited later.

Spores can be single- or multicelled, and they vary greatly in shape and wall ornamentation from one species to another (fig. 1.1). The only consistent feature of virtually all spores is that they are small. They rarely exceed a length of 100 micrometers in any one dimension, and most are less than 20 micrometers. (One micrometer equals one one-millionth of a meter; 100 micrometers equal about one-tenth of the thickness of a dime.) Some spores are borne singly on specialized generative cells, and the whole reproductive apparatus is visible only with a microscope. In other cases, however, spores are produced by the millions in "fruit-bodies" such as mushrooms and puffballs. Other members of the kingdom fall between these two extremes with a vast array of sizes, shapes, and colors.

Students of the fungi are interested in the structure of reproductive bodies and how spores are produced because these features form the basis for the classification and naming of fungi. For this convention, we are indebted to the Swedish botanist Carolus Linnaeus. Linnaeus's efforts, beginning with his *Species Plantarum* in 1753, brought order to a chaotic and frenzied era when describing and naming life forms were a biologist's main tasks. By focusing his attention on physical features of repro-

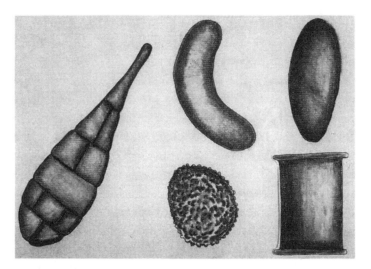

Fig. 1.1. Spores vary tremendously in size, shape, color, and surface texture but rarely exceed 100 micrometers in length or width.

ductive bodies such as flowers and mushrooms, Linneaus developed a system for naming plants—including, at the time, fungi—that was not only more logical but much simpler than preceding taxonomic schemes. For instance, before Linneaus, the common buttercup was technically known as *Ranunculus tripartitis foliis peltatis quinquangularibus multipartitis laciniis linearibus caule multifloro.* He shortened it to *Ranunculus acris.*

After Linneaus, two pioneers in the field of mycology, Elias Fries and Christian Hendrick Persoon, published the first extensive works on fungal taxonomy, which still stand as the foundations for all that has followed. Fries, a Swede, was most interested in fleshy fungi—especially mushrooms—and lichens. He became famous not only in his home country but well beyond its borders for his many publications that named and described new species. Perhaps his greatest contribution was the three-volume *Systema Mycologicum,* which still stands as a valuable, authoritative resource on shelves of botanical libraries throughout the world. Thousands of species described by Fries still have the name he gave them over 170 years ago. To colleagues in Sweden and elsewhere he was—and still should be—known as "the grand old man of mycology."

Persoon, on the other hand, was mired in obscurity and financial hardship throughout his life. Born in South Africa and raised as an orphan in the care of the Dutch government, he somehow became interested in—and then obsessed with—the study of fungi. Plant pathogens known as rusts and smuts were his forte, and at occasional times of good fortune he traveled to the far reaches of the world collecting and identifying various species. Unfortunately, Persoon's life was also fraught with times of illness and bad fortune, and it was indeed remarkable that he was able to contribute as much as he did to the scientific world. A friend visiting him near the time of his death noted that he "was startled to see a shrunken man with gray hair and a tangled beard. His eyes were watery, inflamed, and blinking." Shortly thereafter, he sold his herbarium of 14,000 specimens to the Dutch government. In tribute to Persoon's life, one admirer penned these words: "Thus lived and died perhaps the greatest genius Mycology has ever known, for Persoon was a builder. He began the work with practically nothing and left a system of which others have availed themselves with much too little acknowledgement."[5]

Many others followed in the footsteps of Fries and Persoon, and students of the fungi quickly learn the names of the major contributors. Early experts on North American fungi were L. D. von Schweinitz (1780–1834), J. B. Ellis (1829–1905), C. H. Peck (1833–1917), J. C. Arthur (1850–1942), J. N. Dearness (1852–1954), W. A. Murrill (1869–1957), F. J. Seaver (1877–1970), E. S. Luttrell (1916–1988), and R. Singer (1906–1994).

Of the American mycologists, perhaps one of the most colorful was Curtis Gates Lloyd (1859–1926). Lloyd was educated to be a businessman and, together with his two older brothers, made a tidy fortune in pharmaceuticals. Unfortunately, his aptitude for business didn't match that of his brothers, and when he was thirty-six, they convinced him to retire. This he did with pleasure, because he knew he would then have time to pursue his lifelong hobby of collecting and identifying fungi. Lloyd favored the larger fungi and in a relatively short time he became one of the leading experts of his day in the identification of puff-balls. He had the resources to support occasional expeditions to add new specimens to his large personal herbarium and to publish his own private notes. At one time he even purchased the inventory of a failing shoe store just to get some boxes for storing his burgeoning herbarium.

In addition to the contributions he made to taxonomy, Lloyd was well known for objecting to the practice of adding the name of the discoverer of a fungus after its Latin name. To Lloyd, this was "advertising," and he contended that such labels were the chief causes of careless work, meaningless splitting, and what he called "name-juggling." As part of his satirical attack on the publication of authors' names, Lloyd created Professor N. J. McGinty, through whom he named several fungi, including the fictitious *Lycoperdon anthropomorphus.*

In what was perhaps his final act of distinction, Lloyd prepared his own tombstone with this epitaph:

> Curtis Gates Lloyd
> Monument erected in 1922 by
> himself, for himself during his
> life to gratify his own vanity.
> What fools these mortals be.[6]

✦ Classification of Fungi

Historically, fungi within the kingdom have been further separated into lesser groups with similar characters according to the following hierarchy:
    Kingdom
    Phylum

Class
   Order
     Family
       Genus
         Species

Plant pathologists interested in fungi as pathogens of plants
also use classifications such as "forma specialis" and "race"
to describe fungi that are morphologically similar but have
different hosts or different reactions on the same hosts,
respectively.

Most recently, the kingdom *Fungi* has been considered to be
divided into four phyla based on differences in the morphology of reproductive structures, as follows.

Chytridiomycota. With a single class, Chytridiomycetes.
There are about 100 genera and 1,000 species in the phylum.
They are the only true fungi with swimming spores, or
zoospores. Each vegetative colony is a single cell with many
nuclei but with no crosswalls to separate the colony into individual cells except when spores are produced. For some
species in the group, sexual reproduction has been described. In these species, fusion of compatible nuclei results
in a zygote in which meiosis occurs and swimming spores are
eventually produced. Mostly, chytrids are decayers of aquatic
vegetation, but some parasitize plants, other fungi, and
animals.

Zygomycota. With two classes, Zygomycetes and Tricho-
mycetes. This phylum has about 175 genera and 1,050
species. Asexual reproduction is by sporangiospores, at first
contained within a membrane at the tip of a generative cell.
When the membrane ruptures, the spores are blown away.
Sexual reproduction, if it does occur, is typically by fusion of
nuclei from compatible colonies followed by formation of a
zygote—a zygospore—then by meiosis and the production of
uninucleate spores. Many members of the Zygomycota are decayers of dead organic matter, but some are pathogens of
arthropods—with promise as biopesticides—and others form
symbiotic relationships with roots of higher plants.

Ascomycota. With at least 3,200 genera and about 32,000
species. Fungi in this phylum are usually referred to as ascomycetes. The approximate number of classes within the phylum is uncertain, and some authors are reluctant to delineate

classes at all. Vegetative cells of ascomycetes do have crosswalls that divide the hyphae into many cells, each cell containing one or more nuclei. Asexual reproduction is by production of conidia on generative hyphae that may or may not be contained in or on a fruit-body.

Sexual reproduction, which occurs in most members of the phylum, is by fusion of compatible nuclei to yield a zygote that undergoes meiosis, often followed by a mitotic division, to yield eight spores, ascospores, contained in a saclike cell, an ascus (pl. asci). There are several variations on this general theme. One has compatible nuclei arising from the same colony in what is called homothallic sexual reproduction, while another has compatible nuclei obligately originating in different mycelia, called heterothallic sexual reproduction. Compatible nuclei may also coexist in the same mycelium without fusing for many hours, days, or weeks until environmental conditions suitable for sexual reproduction occur. Asci may be produced directly on the substrate on which the fungus is feeding, but more often they are contained in a cup- or flask-shaped fruit-body. There are numerous variations in shapes, sizes, and colors, each unique to a particular species. Many ascomycetes decay organic matter, but others are important pathogens of plants and animals. In addition, most lichens are associations of ascomycetous fungi with algae or blue-green algae. Some yeasts are ascomycetes, uniquely different from others in the phylum in both physical and physiological properties.

Basidiomycota. With three classes—Basidiomycetes, Teliomycetes, and Ustomycetes—and approximately 22,300 species. As with the Ascomycota, the delineation of higher levels of classification, above orders, is currently being reviewed and debated. Vegetative cells in the Basidiomycota have septa and the formation and structure of those septa is diagnostic for some taxa. Sexual reproduction is by fusion of compatible nuclei followed by meiosis and production of (usually) four basidiospores on the outside of a generative cell, the basidium, which may or may not have crosswalls of its own. Compatible nuclei may coexist in the same cell or spore for many weeks or months before fusing to allow continued progression of sexual reproduction. Asexual reproduction is highly variable within this phylum. Some species produce conidia like those of the Ascomycota, but many others are not known to produce them at all. Members of the Basidiomycota occupy a broad range of ecological niches. They decay organic matter, cause diseases in plants and animals, and form symbiotic relationships with higher plants. Some, particularly those known as "rusts," are obligate parasites and must have a living plant host if they are to complete their life cycles.

In addition to those organisms in the kingdom *Fungi*, there is one other phylum, the Oomycota, in the relatively newly proposed kingdom *Stramenopila*, that deserves mention here. The Oomycota contains organisms that look very much like fungi on both macroscopic and microscopic levels but have some fundamental structural and biochemical differences from them. They were long thought to be true fungi, and are still considered to be legitimate subjects for teaching and research by mycologists. In addition, some members of the Oomycota are serious plant pathogens. Most Oomycota have hyphae without crosswalls, they reproduce asexually by way of zoospores and they reproduce sexually by fusion of compatible nuclei, meiosis, and production of oospores. Oomycota are largely soil- or water-borne fungi, but one, *Phytophthora infestans*, played an important role in precipitating the legendary Irish potato famine.

◆

CHAPTER 2

What Fungi Do and How They Do It

So a fungus has no chlorophyll, its physical structure is relatively simple, its cells have nuclei, and it reproduces by way of spores. But how does it go from its relatively meager beginnings—often a single cell—to become an active decayer of whatever source of food it chooses, and eventually to produce more of its own kind?

Development of a new fungus culture usually starts with a spore. In the presence of a little free moisture, the spore swells with water in much the same way that a germinating seed does. Then the cell wall expands through a preformed weak spot, the germ pore, to create a thin, balloon-like protuberance. This first extension of growth is called the germ tube. At some ill-defined point in the elongation of the germ tube—for plant pathogens, when penetration into the host is achieved; for molds, when the germ tube is at least half as long as the spore—it becomes known as a hypha (pl. hyphae) (fig. 2.1). With continued growth, the hypha will likely branch, giving rise to more hyphae and soon to a visible colony. A large collection of hyphae is called "mycelium." Mushroom growers also call masses of hyphae "spawn."

One of the features of the fungi that distinguishes members of the kingdom from other multicellular organisms is that virtually all growth occurs by way of elongation of hyphal tips. Somehow, the cell wall at the growing end of each hypha must remain elastic enough to allow for wall extension and yet rigid enough to contain protoplasm and allow for the streaming of nutrients to other parts of the fungus body. Exact mechanisms by which this phenomenon occurs are not entirely understood

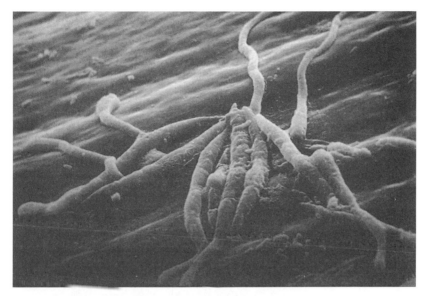

Fig. 2.1. Spores of *Ascocalyx abietina* shown here on the surface of a pine needle have germinated.

at this time and continue to be the subject of scientific investigation.

Within a few minutes to a few hours of spore germination, growing hyphae begin to exude some of the powerful enzymes needed to digest food for the fungus. Cutinases digest leaf surface waxes, cellulases destroy plant cell walls, and other enzymes dismantle other pieces of the complex organic architecture that was once plant or animal. At the same time, mycotoxins, which are fungal by-products that are poisonous to animals, or antibiotics, which are metabolites that inhibit growth of microbes, may also permeate the substrate. The purpose of these by-products is apparently to discourage potential competitors from getting more than their share of the available food. Even the best of chemists with all the tools that science has to offer looks with envy upon the ease with which the fungi produce chemicals that have long defied laboratory synthesis.

17

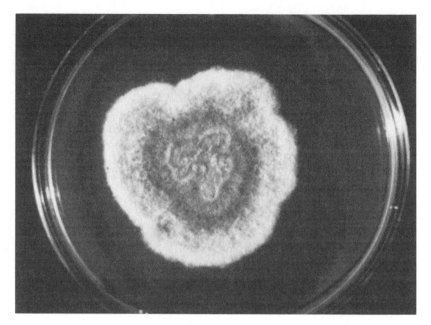

Fig. 2.2. Fungus cultures typically grow in circular patterns to maximize their chances of finding nourishment.

Because the supply of enzymes packaged with each spore is limited, the spore must germinate on or very close to a suitable food source. If it doesn't, it will perish. If it does, growth continues, with the unobstructed colony usually expanding in a circular fashion (fig. 2.2). Where growing space is limited, the colony readily assumes whatever shape will allow it to occupy the greatest available area. Eventually, food supplies near the origin become exhausted and older cells die, leaving a ring of actively feeding and growing hyphal tips. Inside the ring, where the substrate has already been exhausted, the fungus is unlikely to be present, or just barely so. Outside, it has yet to claim its juicy morsels. Fairy rings on lawns are good examples of this annular growth habit. Fungus infections of people, known as ringworm, are, too, although those infected with the pathogen may choose a word other than "good" to describe the colony they are hosting.

✦ The Humongous Fungus

Just how big can fungus cultures get? In a 1992 issue of *Nature*, results of work on the genetic analysis of a fungus identified as *Armillaria bulbosa* appeared.* The investigators were trying to resolve taxonomic questions about the species, and had collected mushrooms from a 35 acre woodland in northern Michigan for subsequent nucleic acid analysis. Much to their surprise, results of these analyses showed that some mushrooms from throughout the area were identical in every way. They also concluded that the mass of mycelium from which the mushrooms originated must be one of the largest and oldest (1,500 years) living organisms on Earth. Perhaps even more surprising was the enthusiasm with which the nation's media picked up on the story. National Public Radio, the *New York Times,* and *People* magazine were a few of the many who brought mycology to the masses, if only for a few brief moments.

* M. L. Smith, J. N. Bruhn, and J. A. Anderson, "The fungus *Armillaria bulbosa* is among the largest and oldest living organisms," *Nature* 356 (1992): 428–431.

Sooner or later every fungus culture—whether in your refrigerator, in the foundation of your house, on the oranges in your fruit bowl, or between your toes—must produce more spores in order to ensure the survival of its kind. These spores may be little more than fragments of the parent culture (conidia), or they may originate through a process of sexual reproduction. The latter allows for much more rapid evolution of new strains of a given species and can present formidable challenges to those trying to breed disease-resistant plants or develop antifungal chemicals for plant and animal disease management.

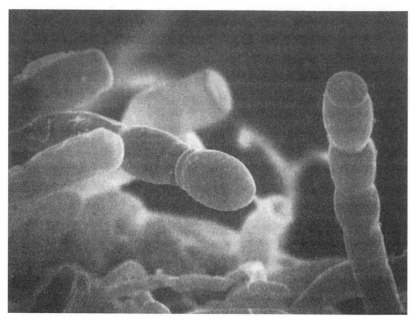

Fig. 2.3. Windblown conidia of *Microsphaera alni* are often produced in chains of spores.

Many fungi produce specialized, spore-bearing hyphae upon which clusters or chains of spores grow. Such spores are usually dry and powdery at maturity and are easily whisked away by the next breeze, with their fate thereafter left to chance (fig. 2.3). If the fungus is involved in the crude degradation of organic matter—let's say it rots leaves on the forest floor—then its requirements for growth are not likely to be particularly stringent, and chance alone may be adequate for its survival. If the fungus occupies a special niche, however, then most of the spores—if windblown—will probably perish, with only a small percentage landing in a suitable spot.

Other fungi have far more elaborate structures for spore production. And these fruit-bodies, as they are called, involve some remarkable mechanisms to ensure that spores produced in or on them have the best possible chances to leave their origins and find suitable sites for starting new colonies. For starters, consider the meadow mushroom. It is commonly found on lawns in temperate climates, it's a close relative of the button mushroom that Campbell's puts in its soups, and it's a tasty treat. If you pick a meadow mushroom and turn it over, you will see that the underside is lined with hundreds of thin, pink to chocolate-brown slices or gills of fungus tissue (see plate 2C). And if you view the surface of one of those gills through a microscope, you will find yourself looking down on the ends of hundreds of thousands of cells, each shaped somewhat like an elongated balloon. Some of the cells will have smooth surfaces because they're either not yet old enough to be producing spores or they are special spacer cells to help keep everything else from getting too crowded. Others, however, clearly identifiable as basidia, will have four (occasionally, two) spikelike projections on their surfaces (fig. 2.4). And resting very precariously on each of these spikes there will likely be a basidiospore. When basidiospores are mature and ready to start a new colony, they fall free from the basidia and drift slowly down between neighboring gills until they are out from under the mushroom cap and able to be blown clear of it (fig. 2.5). At that point, then, their fate is left to chance. But with ever increasing acreage dedicated to lawns, golf courses, and parks, I would say the chances are pretty good.

Before you leave this mushroom to consider other fungi, stand back for a minute and look at it again. Aren't those gills awfully close together? Can you imagine how many spores, once detached from their mother cells and falling toward the open air, might accidentally get stuck on adjacent gills if all aren't perfectly vertical? I suspect a lot. Fortunately, the meadow mushroom, and most others like it, can adapt to slight changes in the angle of the fruit-body by reorienting their gills accordingly. If the mushrooms get tipped too far, however, few if any spores will escape. Mushrooms with thinner stems will actually continue to grow if they are tipped over. Cells on the lower side of the stem

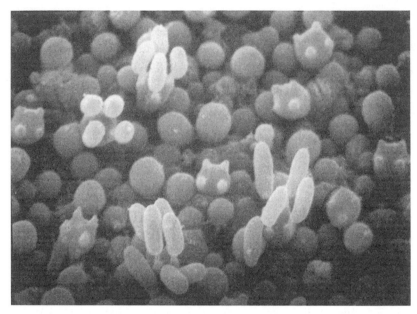

Fig. 2.4. The surface of a mushroom gill viewed with a scanning electron microscope. Note that generative cells—basidia—are in various stages of development. Several have all four basidiospores ready for dispersal.

will grow more rapidly, thus causing the stem to bend upward to ensure vertical orientation of the gills.[1]

✦ Sclerotia

At times, environmental conditions do not favor reproduction or mycelial growth, even if the food supply is plentiful. The two most common limiting factors are temperature and water. Fungi will not grow if they are too hot or too cold, and they can't grow if the substrate is so dry that their enzymes have no medium in which to act. To survive those difficult times, hyphae may aggregate into a roughly spherical body called a sclerotium (pl. sclerotia). Cells on the outside of a sclerotium typically have thick pigmented walls to form a protective shell over the living tissue within. When conditions favorable for

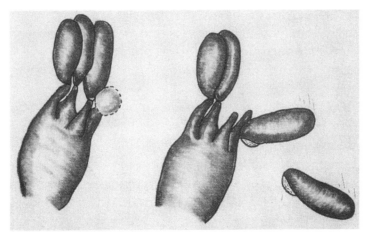

Fig. 2.5. Each basidiospore is released when the weight of a
water droplet formed at its base detaches it from the basidium.

fungal growth return, the sclerotium may either germinate
with hyphal growth, functioning like a gigantic spore, or it
may produce a spore-bearing body.

The shaggy mane is also a kind of mushroom that produces
its spores on gills, but it faces a unique challenge in releasing its
spores into the wind. Look at the shaggy mane in plate 3A, and
I think you'll appreciate the dilemma. The cap is so large and so
long that it seems impossible for any spores other than those on
the very bottom edge ever to see the light of day. The rest must
surely be forever trapped within.

Not to worry! The spores produced on the edge of the cap are
the first to mature, and they are indeed whisked away by the
wind as they fall. But as these basidia shed their spores, the
shaggy mane uses self-made enzymes to digest the spent tissue,
which drips away as a slimy, black liquid. This process then exposes the next generation of spore-bearing cells. When they are

done, they also drip away, and the process continues until the once photogenic mushroom is reduced to little more than a fibrous stem surrounded by black goo (plate 3B).[2] Is it any wonder that this group of mushrooms and its relatives are known as "inky caps"?

Most of the other fungi that fruit as mushrooms, brackets, or other large woody or fleshy bodies disperse their spores as the meadow mushroom does. Some produce spores on the insides of tubes, some on the outsides of teeth, and some on smooth, horizontal surfaces. But in all cases, the spores are released from the mother cells in a way that maximizes their chances for transport. *Ganoderma applanatum,* a wood rotter with a perennial, platelike fruit-body goes so far as to grow new shelves from the old ones if a once-standing host tree falls over (fig. 2.6).

Through a complex series of chemical reactions that yield light as a by-product—the process is called bioluminescence—some mushrooms literally glow in the dark. Fruit-bodies of *Omphalotus olearius, Panus stypticus,* and *Mycena illuminens* are typical examples. Although a functional value of the glow has yet to be demonstrated, it is suspected to attract insects that help to dislodge spores from the mushroom gills so they can be blown away.[3] Other fungi have mycelia that bioluminesce, but their advantage for the fungi is not known. However, glowing bits of fungus-colonized wood have been used by people to light trails at night, identify friendly from not so friendly soldiers in time of war, and brighten the hair of young maidens on tropical isles. Luminescent mycelium is also the foxfire of contemporary lore.

Many ascomycetes have cuplike fruit-bodies, and they also depend on wind to carry spores to new sites (fig. 2.7). The very nature of their structure presents an obvious dilemma, however. Somehow, the spores must get out of the cup and into the wind. But how? A microscopic exam of the interior surface of a cup fungus provides the beginning of the answer. Spores here are not borne outside of a balloonlike mother cell but rather inside

Fig. 2.6. *Ganoderma applanatum* produces a new shelf with
the correct orientation if its perennial fruit-body gets tipped
over.

of it, in a sac. And there are usually eight spores instead of four.
Furthermore, the exposed end of the sac has either a hole in it
or a loosely hinged cap. Thus, the mother cell is able to contain
the spores until water pressure within causes the weakest part—
the tip—to give way. As pressure within the sac is relieved, the
spores are literally shot out through the end. Sacs at the bottom
of the cup shoot their spores straight up, while those on the
edges bend toward the light or open such that the ejected spores
may ricochet off the lid and then go up and into the breeze.[4]
People lucky enough to wander onto a crop of cup fungi just as
dispersal occurs are astonished to see thick clouds of spores
shoot several inches into the air (fig. 2.8).

If, by now, you have visions of clouds of fungus spores that are
released into the air from any number of fungus fructifications
and are carried away by the whims of a passing breeze, you've
got it right. In fact, many fungus spores depend solely on wind
to transport them to untapped sources of food. However, the un-
certainty associated with such a random means of dispersal must

Fig. 2.7. The spore-producing cells of a cup fungus line the interior surface of the cup.

be countered with additional survival strategies, and most fungi with windblown spores have them.

The first strategy is simply a matter of numbers. Fungi depending on wind for dispersal produce a lot of spores. In only a few cases has "a lot" actually been counted, but when it has, the results are impressive. For instance, the fungus causing a disease known as "smut" of corn produces about 25 billion spores per average-sized ear of infected corn. The fungus causing stem rust of wheat generates about 10 billion spores from an acre of moderately diseased plants. And the wood decay fungus, *Ganoderma applanatum*, has been estimated to produce spores at the rate of 350,000 per second. It does that for up to six months a year—thus 5.4 trillion spores—and it may continue at that pace for ten years or more.[5]

Fig. 2.8. Cup fungus spores are literally shot into the air, to be floated away with the next gust of wind. (Drawn by Robert O'Brien.)

The second strategy is that the spores are very small and therefore they can stay aloft for a very long time. Even in still air, an average-size spore of 20-micrometer diameter is likely to fall at a rate of about 7 feet per minute. But that's in very still air. The fact of the matter is that spores are lifted up by the slightest of drafts and could conceivably stay aloft indefinitely. When they finally do settle out on downdrafts or in falling rain, they are likely to be far from their origin. Professor C. M. Christensen reported once using a marker fungus—one of distinctive color, not normally found in his area—to measure spore dispersal within his office building. Five minutes after the culture dish was opened on the first floor, some spores of the fungus were trapped on the fourth floor. Five minutes later, they were falling on the fourth floor in amounts of thousands per square yard.

Outside, conditions for long-distance dispersal are even better. Wheat rust spores were once collected in amounts of millions per square yard in springtime in North Dakota, where the nearest source of the fungus was hundreds of miles away. And on another occasion, they were trapped out of air being sampled north of the Arctic Circle, again thousands of miles from their nearest possible source.

A third feature of airborne fungus spores is that most are physically able to survive long periods of flight time. They usually have thick cell walls, a feature that keeps their vital contents from drying out, and their (usually dark) pigmentation shields them from damaging ultraviolet light. In addition, some have spiny cell walls that cause them to remain clumped together as they are carried aloft.[6] Apparently there is safety in numbers.

While the majority of fungus spores are carried by wind, by no means are they all. A second important vehicle is falling rain, and no fungi depend on it quite so much for spore dispersal as the bird's nest fungi (fig. 2.9). These wood decay fungi produce packets of spores (eggs) in cups (nests) that may be up to a third of an inch in diameter. Each cup contains four to ten spore packets, and at first glance there appears to be no way for the relatively large and weighty packets to escape. But wait a while . . . until it rains. Then, when a bird's nest fungus cup is hit dead center by a falling raindrop, the water splashes up the sides, and as it does, it can carry one or more packets of spores with it. In some cases, a tetherlike filament with a sticky end trails the spore packet and helps to fasten it to a nearby stick or blade of grass. There it remains until the shell weathers, releasing the spores.[7]

Other fungi use water in a more subtle but, to them, an equally important way. Some causing disease in woody plants produce spores in tiny, flask-shaped bodies embedded in the bark; only the necks of the flasks protrude. When the bark is moistened, spores ooze out of the flasks in a sticky, gooey matrix reminiscent of toothpaste oozing out of a tube. When these spore tendrils are hit by drops of water, each drop breaks up into hundreds of smaller droplets, and each of those, laden with spores, may remain suspended for several minutes or several

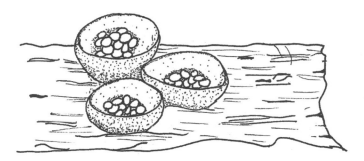

Fig. 2.9. Bird's nest fungi produce packets of spores in cups on decaying wood. (Drawn by Robert O'Brien.)

hours, depending on relative humidity, temperature, and wind.[8] Insects, birds, and other animals also pick up spores produced in sticky masses, but their role in spore dispersal often tends to be haphazard. Insect transmission of the Dutch elm disease pathogen (see chapter 4) and blue-stain fungi (see chapter 12) are notable exceptions.

Other fungi that need help from animals to disperse their spores have evolved simple but effective mechanisms to attract them for that purpose. Perhaps the best known is a large group of fleshy fungi called "stinkhorns" (fig. 2.10). The fruit-bodies of these organisms have some of the most unusual shapes among the fleshy fungi. They are also topped with spores contained in a sticky, foul-smelling matrix that turns the noses of most civilized folks, but is eagerly sought by flies and other insects used to eating rotting flesh.[9] Hundreds of flies typically descend on fresh specimens of these fungi and remove the spores in a few hours of frenzied activity. Some of the spores are eaten, and pass through in feces. Others simply rub off the insects' bodies during subsequent foraging. In either case, homeowners whose grounds are hosting stinkhorns are glad to have the odor removed.

Other fungi produce their spores in matrices with little odor but attractive taste. Over one thousand different plant parasites

Fig. 2.10. Stinkhorn spores are in a gooey mass that smells like rotting flesh. This specimen will soon attract hoards of hungry flies.

known as rusts and several dozen or so that cause a plant disease known as ergot produce spores in droplets of nectar with high concentrations of sugar. The sweet taste of these solutions serves to encourage insect foraging, and in the process spores are successfully moved from one portion of a plant to another, or to another plant altogether. In some cases, new infections result. In others, the spores serve to fertilize existing colonies and allow sexual reproduction to occur.

Some fungi, apparently not content to rely on nature's elements to spread them around, seem to have taken matters into their own hands. Those in the genus *Pilobolus*, the cap throwers, are good examples. These fungi live on herbivore manure. You can observe them readily by incubating fresh—the fresher, the better—droppings from a horse, deer, rabbit, or other four-legged herbivore in an almost closed container for two to five days. A tin can with a piece of window glass to cover all but a small part of the top works as well as anything.

Spores germinate in the dung soon after it is dropped. The hyphae grow in the dung for a few days, and then the fungus produces new fruit-bodies that are unlike anything described so far. They vary in size (usually an eighth to two-thirds inches long), and are single-stalked and almost colorless. A shiny black packet of spores sits atop the swollen upper portion of each stalk (fig. 2.11). As the fungus nears spore-dispersal time, careful observers will note that the stalk is aimed at the brightest light. Outside, in a natural setting, it follows the sun as it rises in the

Fig. 2.11. *Pilobolus* spp., the cap throwers, shoot packets of spores off the dung they grow on. (Drawn by Robert O'Brien.)

morning. Sometime between 9 and 11 A.M., with the angle of the stalk at about 45 degrees from the horizon to achieve maximum trajectory, water pressure inside the swollen portion becomes so great that the stalk explodes, hurling the spore packet for distances of up to 12 feet.[10] From the perspective of the fungus, this elegant mechanism ensures that its spores will be shot far enough from a dung pile to land on fresh grass, where they will be eaten by a grazing animal. From the perspective of the mycologist, this is just another piece of evidence that part of the modern military establishment was based on mechanisms used for thousands of years by the microbes coming from the south end of a horse going north.

Another fungus with a novel means for spore dispersal is the artillery fungus, *Sphaerobolus stellatus*. This fungus decays wood. In a forest environment, the fruit-bodies are often difficult to find because they are small (about $\frac{1}{16}$ inch in diameter), light-brown cups that blend readily with the color of the wood they are on. However, with the vastly increased use of waste wood chips to decorate and mulch landscape plantings, the fungus has become a frequent visitor to one's front yard.

The unique spore dispersal mechanism in *Sphaerobolus* centers on the nature of the cup. Each one is lined with a translucent slimy substance upon which a packet of spores sits. The cup is rigid and will not yield readily to external forces. But the slime is hydrophilic: it absorbs water readily. On the day that *Sphaerobolus* is ready to disperse its spores—usually a rainy day—the slime absorbs water and swells, pushing against the sides of the cup. It tries to expand . . . anywhere. But the cup doesn't yield, and the pressure builds. Finally, the slimy lining turns itself completely inside out in a violent reversal of pressure that hurls the spore packet, with some slime still attached, out of the cup at speeds of up to 27 feet per second, for distances of over 18 feet. You can actually hear the spore-packet ejection mechanism when it goes off.[11]

Many home and car owners wish that were all there is to the

Fig. 2.12. *Sphaerobolus stellatus* has the loudest, and one of the most powerful, spore dispersal mechanisms.

Sphaerobolus story, but unfortunately for them there's more. The small bit of slime surrounding each spore packet is a powerful adhesive, and wherever the packets land, that's where they will stay for several days—at least. Efforts to wash them off right away are usually futile, and even later, when the packets do finally flake off, a tenacious brown stain remains. A typical foundation planting bed that is 6 feet wide and 30 feet long, mulched with wood chips, may yield several thousand *Sphaerobolus* spore packets in a good year, and they effectively ruin the appearance of the houses and cars to which they stick. Insurance adjusters in the northeastern United States have received many claims to have spotted houses or cars refinished, and many landscape professionals are rethinking their use of wood-chip mulch.

In addition to the many thousands of fungi for which spore transport is overland in one way or another, there are a few hundred more that live in water or moist soil and produce swimming spores. These spores are driven by the whipping action of one or two filaments that extend from the spores. Their movement in pure water seems to be erratic and without direction, but some eventually find a suitable substrate. Species of some root pathogens are attracted to root exudates and literally swarm to the roots once they pick up the right chemical signals.[12]

CHAPTER 3

Fungi as Pathogens of Food Crops

DESPAIR IN IRELAND

When Spanish explorers first ventured into South America in the mid-1500s, they learned of many new and unusual plants, some of which were important sources of food. One plant of particular interest grew in the Andes Mountains, where it had become a mainstay in the natives' diets because of its high yields despite cool, short growing seasons. In fact, the Incas who ruled the region so revered the plant that harvest time was cause for extraordinary celebration. Extraordinary, indeed! One Spanish visitor reported on a remarkable harvest ceremony he attended, where after a great feast all the men assembled in the plaza and divided into two groups. They began to fight fiercely; some fell wounded or dead, prompting the women to rush into the fray and collect blood from the bodies. This they sprinkled over the fields to insure a good crop the following year. In another report of a particularly fierce fray, the victorious males split open the skulls of the vanquished and ate the brains while the women dipped pieces of the cherished plants into pools of blood and ate them.

Despite the barbaric customs associated with the cultivation and harvest of this mysterious plant, the Spaniards found it good enough to take home to try on European soil. There it grew well but was met with mixed reactions—most of them bad—because it was so different from anything else in the diet of the times.[1]

Legend has it that when Sir Walter Raleigh gave a basketful of these plants to Queen Elizabeth I, her kitchen staff cooked and served the leafy tops of the plants as they would lettuce or spinach. The hapless souls who ate the meal were stricken with excruciating indigestion. The diners should, instead, have eaten the "roots," but these, it was said, had a bland, starchy taste and caused uncontrollable flatulence. Furthermore, parts of the plant resembled the grotesque tumerous growths common in humans afflicted with a lymph-node disease known as scrofula, making some people fearful that the new plants were a cause of this awful disease.

Despite these misgivings, the plant did have some nutritional value, and peasants throughout Europe, especially those living in areas with short growing seasons, eventually began to cultivate it for food. Clearly one of its most attractive features was that so much could be grown on so little land. For instance, one acre of average farmland could produce 6 tons of the crop annually, and it stored well over winter, bringing stability to an unstable food supply.

So what was this plant with such a colorful history? Botanists know it as *Solanum tuberosum*. The rest of us know it as the potato, and once people learned how to prepare the tubers properly—they are not roots at all—it quickly became a dietary staple, especially among those of meager means. Oppressed Irish peasants, trying to eke out livings on small plots of land for which they paid exorbitant rents, were especially receptive to the new food. In fact, they were so receptive that by the late eighteenth century, a typical tenant family of husband, wife, and four children consumed about 250 pounds of potatoes each week! It wasn't the best food one could hope for, but it was far better than anything the Irish had seen for many, many generations. And with appetites sated and in reasonably good health, they found time to turn their attention to the more pleasurable aspects of life. They married earlier, had larger families, and were able to nurse more newborns through an otherwise precarious infancy. From 1800 to 1845, the population of Ireland nearly doubled— from 4.5 to 8 million people.

Not everyone in Ireland was enthusiastic about the prominent role played by potatoes in the health of the country. One author, writing about the situation in 1843, saw things this way:

For about a century and a half, the potato has been the only food of the peasantry of Ireland. A very limited portion of the land, a few days labour, and a small amount of manure will create a stock upon which a family may exist for twelve months. . . . Nearly every soil will produce potatoes; they have been seen growing from almost barren rock on the side of a mountain and in the bog where the foot would sink many inches in the soil. . . . On the whole, it is perhaps to be lamented that the use of "Ireland's root" has been so universal in the country, and that the people have been so well contented with it that they have made no exertion to mix the potato with varied food.[2]

Two years later, the first signs of impending disaster appeared. They were reported to English audiences by Dr. John Lindley, the distinguished editor of *The Gardener's Chronicle and Agricultural Gazette*, on August 23, 1845:

A fatal malady has broken out amongst the potato crop. On all sides we hear of destruction. . . . There is hardly a sound sample in Covent Garden Market. . . . The disease consists in a gradual decay of the leaves and stem, which become a putrid mass and the tubers are affected by degrees in a similar way. The first obvious sign is the appearance on the edge of the leaf of a black spot which gradually spreads; the gangrene then attacks the haulms (stems), and in a few days the latter are decayed, emitting a peculiar and rather offensive odour. When the attack is severe, the tubers also decay. . . . As to cure for this distemper, there is none. One of our correspondents is already angry with us for not telling the public how to stop it; but he ought to consider that Man has no power to arrest the dispensations of Providence.[3]

In field after field and store after store, throughout Europe, potatoes turned to putrid, black mush. Irish peasants were particulary hard hit by the turn of events because for most of them, potatoes were the only source of food, and by the end of the year about a third of the potato crop was lost. The people made do with considerably fewer rations and emerged from the winter of 1845–46 hungrier and weaker than usual but looking forward to a bountiful harvest the following year.

Alas! The blight was worse in '46. At first the fields looked as if poised to atone for the previous year's malady, but in mid-July the plants suddenly began to whither. Wrote one clergyman: "On July 27th I passed from Cork to Dublin and this doomed plant bloomed in all the luxuriance of an abundant harvest. Returning August 3rd I beheld with sorrow one wide waste of putrefying vegetation. In many places, the wretched people were seated on the fences of their decaying gardens wringing their hands and wailing bitterly at the destruction which had left them foodless."[4] Think about that: in only seven days, from July 27 to August 3, a flourishing crop collapsed completely. Clearly, a powerful force was at work.

The following winter (1846–47) brought unparalleled misery. Food was gone and the winter was one of the coldest and wettest of the nineteenth century. Those lucky enough to be able to leave Ireland did so. But hundreds of thousands of others stayed, and starved. Recollections from survivors were so vivid half a century later that it seems certain the image of the famine will live forever in Irish history. A parish priest remembered the following:

> [Father Kinney] pointed out to me a spot on the road just outside of the church gate where he found a poor man sitting one Sunday morning. The man had a small loaf clutched in his hand and was making attempts to raise it to his mouth. He was so weakened from hunger and exhaustion that he had not sufficient strength to lift the bread to his mouth. Then he [bent] his head down, holding the loaf between his knees, to try to get a bite in that way but the result was that he simply toppled over. The priest then annointed him and he died there tearing the dough with his nails.

And the child of a shop owner had this to tell: "On one occasion a mother came in with a baby in her arms. The poor little thing was gaunt and thin and kept whining for something to eat. The mother would persist in putting its lips to her breasts which were milkless in order to stop it crying. A drink of milk was given to the baby and its mother and later the same day the mother was seen dead by the roadside with the baby still alive in her arms."[5]

Not all who went hungry from the blight died of starvation. The weakened population was beset by other diseases including typhus, dysentery, and cholera. In the ten years that followed, one million additional people died from these secondary causes.

The English government was slow to respond to the plight of its colony. Tragically, exports of dairy products, grain, meat, and vegetables from Ireland to traditional European markets continued as they always had. Government officials fearful of jeopardizing a favorable balance of trade argued successfully against importation of foodstuffs to save the starving masses. And the plight of the peasants became ever more desperate.

Finally, in 1846, conscience and fear of international scandal overcame greed. The government relaxed its import laws, and corn from the United States found its way to Irish ports. There it was greeted with little enthusiasm because the proud Irish were loathe to receive free handouts of "chicken feed." Furthermore, transport of the corn to rural areas was difficult, no one knew how to prepare it, and for people whose digestive systems had been so conditioned to potatoes for so long, changing to another staple required some weeks of painful adjustment. Eventually, these hindrances were overcome, but not in time to save the thousands who starved in the interim.[6]

For those able to do so, escape from the doomed island became an attractive option. Over two million people took that course of action in the years during and immediately after the famine. Many headed for North America, hoping to leave the horrors of their homeland behind them. But it wasn't that easy. Many, like the 90,000 Irish emigrants who boarded ships for Canada in 1847, carried the legacy of their plight with them. Of those, 15,000 died at port or during the passage or at quarantine stations on the other side. Those who survived left a trail of typhoid behind them as they ventured into the Canadian interior. A great mound in Montreal covers the bodies of 6,000 Irish who died there.

Despite their desperate plight, the immigrants who did survive the crossing were far from welcome as they put ashore in North America. Their poverty, their disease, and their reputation for ill temper and hard drink caused most other folk to keep their distance from the "Paddies." Only employers who needed manual laborers seemed to welcome the Irish. They worked in factories, on railroads, in forests, and elsewhere for long hours and little pay, building the foundation on which America would rise to world power. When the American Civil War broke out, Irish regiments joined the fight, and their courageous contributions finally helped to break the social barriers and get them "over the tracks."[7]

Perhaps the greatest legacy of the famine was to make emigration an Irish tradition. It is estimated that one of every two people born in Ireland between 1830 and 1930 left the country to make a permanent home elsewhere. In fact, only recently, in 1996—150 years after the famine—has Ireland reported a net gain in population.

While famine ravaged the land, sowing the seeds of discontent that still complicate relationships between Ireland and Great Britain today, controversy of a different sort was embroiling those who tried to determine just why the potatoes were dying. The starving were willing to lay blame anywhere they could. Some said it was "the little people." Others suspected static electricity generated in the atmosphere by puffs of smoke emitted by those newfangled things called locomotives. And some blamed "mortiferous vapours" or "miasmas rising from blind volcanoes in the interior of the earth."

But the scientific community tried a more rational tack. Dr. Lindley blamed the problem on plants becoming "overladen with water." He theorized that they had been growing so fast and furiously during the good weather that when rain came, they soaked up too much water. The Reverend M. J. Berkeley, on the other hand, "a gentleman eminent above all other naturalists of the United Kingdom," was convinced that a mold was involved. He and Lindley debated the issue in print and at scientific meetings, and these debates touched off what would eventually become a hotly contested issue of the nature of disease in plants and animals of all kinds.

Finally, Anton DeBary settled the issue in 1861 by demonstrating that only when potatoes were inoculated with a fungus did they succumb to the frightful disease. To that fungus DeBary gave the name *Botrytis infestans.* Today we know it as *Phytophthora infestans,* the terrible plant destroyer.[8] DeBary determined that *P. infestans** spent the winter as dormant hyphae in previously rotted tubers or in other diseased plant parts. Debris cast aside during the previous year and laying in cull piles on the edges of fields was particularly hazardous because it provided inoculum for the next epidemic. In spring, as temperatures warmed and new sprouts from potato seed pieces began to poke through the soil, *P. infestans* also resumed its growth and produced asexual spores on the infected debris. The spores were formed during wet weather in minute transparent capsules that were easily dislodged and blown for short distances by the wind (fig. 3.1). If they landed on potato plants while the plants were wet, the capsules ruptured, each yielding six to twelve swimming spores.

* A convention among biologists is to abbreviate the Latin name of a genus with its first letter after the first reference to it in a chapter or section of a manuscript. Thus, e.g., *P. infestans* after the previous *Phythophthora infestans.* Similar abbreviations are used elsewhere in this book.

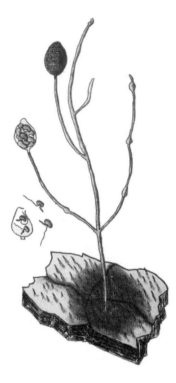

Fig. 3.1. *Phytophthora infestans* produces swimming spores in minute capsules on infested leaves or tubers.

They, in turn, could swim an inch or two at best, because they were propelled only by two tiny threadlike projections called flagella. But they did move far enough to find a place on the plant surface where their chances for germination and penetration into the leaf were best. There they drew in their flagella and germinated, and the germ tubes found their way into the plant by growing through stomata. Once inside the plant, *P. infestans* secreted enzymes that digested the potato tissue, thus providing nourishment to the fungus and eventual death to its host. Tubers were usually protected as long as they were underground, but as soon as they were dug and exposed to the air, they were subject to infection by spores from nearby plants.

Weather in the summers of 1845 and 1846 was particularly favorable for potato blight in Ireland and much of the rest of Europe because it was unusually cool and wet, especially early in the season. By 1847, however, the summer weather had become a bit less favorable for the fungus, and by then the surviving Irish peasants had learned to use imported crops to supplement their potato stores. The ravages of the blight subsided.

Significant epidemics occurred again in 1872 and 1879, but by then, peasants who formerly depended solely on potatoes had found other foods to sate their appetites and fill their bellies. In 1890, it was discovered that the disease could virtually be eliminated from potato fields with several applications of copper sulfate. And with that, the threat of late blight to potatoes and thus to the people who depended on them for food almost disappeared.

However, the social upheaval begun by the Irish potato famine continues to impact world history to this very day. Nowhere has this been more true, perhaps, than in the United States, where approximately 40 million Americans (20 percent of the total population) claim at least partial Irish ancestry. Before the massive influx of the Irish in the mid-nineteenth century, the Catholic Church had held a minor place in the spiritual and political life of American citizens, but since then it has become a major force. Moreover, the influx has given birth to some of the best in college football: Notre Dame's Fighting Irish!

Contrary to popular belief, the Irish weren't the only ones to have the course of their history changed by *P. infestans*. In Germany, blight wiped out a bumper crop of potatoes in 1914, when during the war the Kaiser's High Command foolishly ordered all surplus crops moved to the cities for safe-keeping. A few blighted tubers were mixed in with an otherwise sound crop that was being stored in the warm, humid basements of city buildings, and things quickly went bad. The odor alone was so nauseating that schoolchildren were excused for "stench vacations" while the mess was cleaned up. A government trying to win a war was suddenly confronted with an unexpected crisis on the home front.

In 1915 and 1916, the blight hit in the field, but this time the Germans faced a different challenge. Military strategists bent on winning the world through war had diverted most of their copper reserves to manufacturing shell cases, leaving little or none for fungicides. *P. infestans* ran rampant in both growing seasons, crucial foodstuffs were lost, and over 700,000 Germans starved. Some historians argue that by the time the United States and Britain entered the fray in 1917, blighted potatoes had already so weakened German resolve that Allied victory was assured.[9]

For many years, in Ireland and in the rest of western Europe and North America, *P. infestans* lacked a compatible mating type and reproduced only asexually. This simplified the challenge to the agricultural community to develop and implement disease management strategies because the pathogen's capacity to change was limited to spontaneous mutations, and those were relatively rare. With little chance for the fungus to evolve through sexual means, disease-resistant varieties and appropriate fungicides were more than adequate to protect the potato crop.

In 1984, however, a second strain of *P. infestans* was discovered—first in Europe and then in North America. The second strain, apparently introduced from South America, was a compatible mate for other strains in the Northern Hemisphere, and with that, sexual reproduction became a possible means for rapid change in the fungus. Resistant varieties of potatoes were no longer resistant, and fungicides once capable of suppressing the pathogen lost their effectiveness in the face of a now rapidly changing adversary. Tomatoes were also good hosts for the new strains, and backyard gardens became breeding grounds for an increasingly diverse fungus population (fig. 3.2).[10] Today, plant scientists and farmers find themselves once again locked in a battle they thought they had won a hundred years ago. But *P. in-*

Fig. 3.2. Tomatoes rotted by *P. infestans* are increasingly common in home gardens in the northeastern United States.

festans, with its diminutive form and elegant structure, is a formidable adversary—not to be outdone by the mere efforts of more advanced life forms.

THE WRATH OF GRAPES

Potato blight was not the only catastrophic disease to strike crops in nineteenth-century Europe. Two other blights hit the grape crop and caused considerable economic loss before they were brought under control.

The first showed up in 1845, the same year that potato blight made its first strike. A Mr. Tucker, who worked as a gardener for an English clergyman, noticed that his grapes were beset with a peculiar malady that he had not noticed before. A powdery white substance appeared on the vines and fruit, giving off a moldy smell and causing young grapes to shrivel and die (fig. 3.3). Older grapes just rotted. At first, Tucker suspected that the problem was the same as the one plaguing potatoes, but he

Fig. 3.3. Severe infestations of powdery mildew leave few usable grapes. (Photo courtesy of the Department of Plant Pathology, University of the Orange Free State, Bloemfontein, South Africa.)

quickly dispelled that notion when under a microscope he could see that this was one of a large group of diseases collectively called "powdery mildews." In fact, he not only identified the disease but was also able to control it by spraying the plants with a mixture of lime and sulfur.[11]

Despite Tucker's success in coping with the fungus in England, powdery mildew sprang up in France and then in Germany, Spain, Portugal, and Italy. Vineyard owners reported losing up to 80 percent of their crops, and some abandoned their lands completely to reestablish plantings in North Africa. Fortunately, by 1855, use of sulfur to control the disease was perfected, and powdery mildew joined a growing list of manageable crop diseases.

Where had the grape powdery mildew come from? This time it appeared that the disease originated in North America, where it was common on wild grapes. In all likelihood, it was inadvertently shipped to Europe on diseased stock imported for hybridization experiments.

The second grape disease appeared in 1865, scarcely ten years after powdery mildew had been tamed. This one also came to Europe on plants from North America, and again the plants had been purposely introduced for breeding experiments, this time for insect pest resistance. Unfortunately, a fungus pathogen of little consequence to the North American grapes grew on the breeding stock and quickly moved onto European plants in experimental vineyards. The fungus, *Plasmopara viticola,* caused a leaf and fruit disease known as "downy mildew." If left unchecked, downy mildew promised to be every bit as damaging as powdery mildew, and the situation once again plunged grape growers into the depths of despair. But a fortuitous sequence of events spared them prolonged agony.

It so happened that in 1882, Professor Millardet was strolling through the French countryside lamenting the severity of the mildew and its damage to the grape crop. He suddenly found himself surrounded not by the typically diseased plants but rather by beautiful, lush green ones. Upon inquiry, he learned that the farmer in this area was so angered by people stealing his grapes as they walked down the road near his vineyard that he sprayed the plants with a concoction intended to discourage such freeloading. The substance was a mixture of copper sulfate and lime, and Millardet soon determined that it was very effective in preventing infection by the downy mildew fungus.[12] He dubbed the material "Bordeaux mixture" because Bordeaux was the nearest sizable city. The mixture also proved to be effective against a wide range of other plant pathogenic fungi, and it quickly became the first broad spectrum fungicide used in food production. Bordeaux mixture is still used in agriculture today, having enjoyed some renewed popularity in recent years because organic gardeners view it as natural enough to be an acceptable pesticide when nonchemical disease control measures fail.

THE RUST OF THE STORY

25Then Joseph said to Pharaoh, "The dream of Pharaoh is one; God has revealed to Pharaoh what he is about to do." 26The seven good cows are seven years, and the seven good ears are seven years; the dream is one. 27The seven lean and gaunt cows that came up after them are seven years, and the seven empty ears blighted by the east wind are also seven years of famine. 28It is as I told Pharaoh, God has shown to Pharaoh what he is about to do. 29There will come seven years of great plenty throughout all the land of Egypt, 30but after them will arise seven years of famine, and all the plenty will be forgotten in the land of Egypt; the famine will consume the land. (Genesis 41: 25–30)

Students of the Bible know well that following Pharaoh's dreams, the lands of Egypt, Sinai, and Canaan were, indeed, blessed with seven years of plenty followed by seven years of famine. But only the Egyptians—warned of impending trouble by Joseph's visions—stored enough grain to get through the lean years, and averted disaster. The tribes of Israel to the north were not so lucky, and as one year's crop failure led to another, they eventually moved south—to Egypt—in search of food. At first they were welcomed, but the hospitable tenor of their Egyptian hosts lessened as the years passed. Eventually, the Israelites were scorned and then subjected to such brutal oppression that escape into the desert under Moses' leadership became an attractive option. And so the story goes.

Students of the fungi are drawn to the same passage by its reference to the famine being carried on an east wind. That bit of information, together with the knowledge that climate in the Middle East four thousand years ago was cooler and wetter than it is now and that east winds were (and still are) harbingers of rain, is enough for some to suggest that plant pathogenic fungi were most likely responsible for the wasted crops.[13] The fungi involved would have been species we now call *Puccinia graminis, P. recondita,* and *P. striiformis* (see plate 1A). They cause diseases known as stem rust, leaf rust, and stripe rust, respectively, on cereal grains such as wheat, barley, rye, and oats. These are plants native to the Middle East and were some of the first to be cultivated by civilized people. By the time of the Pharaohs, cereals would have been such important dietary staples that loss to disease could indeed have caused a famine of the magnitude described in Genesis.

People who grow the world's food still find the cereal grain rusts to be formidable adversaries. Plant breeders are constantly challenged to develop grain varieties resistant to the ever-changing rust population, and seed producers struggle to multiply these varieties in time for the next planting season. Farmers, meanwhile, cast anxious eyes toward the heavens, hoping that spring winds and rains won't work too much in the rusts' favor.

From a biological standpoint, the grain rusts and many of their relatives on other plants are unique in that they grow and reproduce on two completely unrelated plant hosts. In the case of *Puccinia graminis,* species of barberry (*Berberis*) host the fungus just as well as wheat does, although the fungus develops entirely different reproductive bodies on the two hosts. Because barberry leaves are cross-fertilization sites of *P. graminis,* they are also sites for the rapid evolution of new races of rust. Eradication of barberry plants, a once common practice mandated by

Fig. 3.4. Wheat with bunt spores in the kernels yields flour that is gray and stinky. (Photo courtesy of the Department of Plant Pathology, University of the Orange Free State, Bloemfontein, South Africa.)

law in both the United States and Canada, did much to slow the evolution of virulent races of rust, but crop surpluses of recent years have lulled many people into thinking that continued barberry eradication is not necessary. As the staff at the USDA Cereal Rust Research Lab in St. Paul, Minnesota, are quick to point out, complacency about barberry and rust and their potential impact on the world's food supply sets the stage for serious crop losses and higher food prices if the right weather and the right races of rust converge on a crop at the same time.

The fungi, especially the troublesome ones, just do not give up. And with increased numbers of people traveling the globe, inadvertently carrying exotic microbes with them, the threats to plants and plant health and planet health remain worthy of continued study. Let us hope that plant pathologists don't give up, either, for the fungi would most certainly come out on top.

✦ Lip-Smacking Smut: Who'd Have Guessed?

Not all plant pathogenic fungi have tales of woe associated with them. In fact, when left to the devices of the right spin doctor, some of the most grotesque diseases are grist for some of the best stories. Take bunt or stinking smut of wheat, for instance. This disease is caused by *Tilletia foetida,* a fungus that spends the winter as dormant spores on the surface of the previous year's seeds. In the spring, the spores germinate to produce secondary infectious spores, and these attack wheat flowers just as pollination is occurring. Not only does each infected flower become a site for fungus growth rather than the desired seed growth, but, what's worse, the infected plants smell like rotting fish. So it came to be that, as legend has it, a miller in the English (some say the French) countryside was faced with a shipment of gray, foul-smelling flour made from smutted wheat, and he experimented with ways to save his investment. The fruit of his labor is still with us today. By adding molasses to darken the flour (thus masking the "smut gray"), and a pungent new spice from India to cover the fishy odor, he produced the first generation of ginger snaps.* Who knows? Without smut, we might still be without these flavorful sweets.

* Carefoot and Sprott, *Famine on the Wind.*

CHAPTER 4

Fungi as Agents of Catastrophic Tree Diseases

Chestnut Blight

[In the past year, the disease] has spread to such an extent that to-day it is no exaggeration to say that 98 percent of all chestnut trees in the parks of this Borough are infected. The spread of the disease is so sudden that unless some radical measures are taken, or a natural enemy of the [causal] fungus develops, it is safe to predict that not a live specimen of the American chestnut will be found two years hence in the neighborhood of the Park.[1]

These were the words of Hermann W. Merkel, chief forester at the New York City Zoological Park in the Bronx in 1905, just a year after he first noticed dead branches on some of the American chestnuts in the park. The disease Merkel was writing about was one we now call "chestnut blight," caused by the fungus *Cryphonectria parasitica*. It had apparently been introduced in the zoo on infected Oriental chestnut trees several years earlier, and soon found American chestnut to be an ideal host. Mr. Merkel obviously realized that he had a serious problem on his hands, but it's doubtful that he could ever fully grasp that what he was reporting in 1905 was the beginning of the end for the American chestnut as a dominant tree in North American forests.

Before the blight struck, the American chestnut was the dominant tree in the eastern hardwood forest. In many sites, up to 25 percent—one in every four—of the trees were chestnuts. And they were big! The average diameter of the stems was 3 to 4 feet, and trees 100 to 150 feet tall were not uncommon. As raw material for construction, chestnut wood was ideal because it was straight-grained, easy to work with, and resistant to decay. It was so good for both indoor and outdoor building projects that many of the houses, barns, bridges, and other structures erected in nineteenth-century America were framed and sided with it.

In addition, its nuts were an important source of food for wildlife and people. Unlike most other species of nut-bearing trees, a female chestnut tree produced a crop of nuts every year. Their flavor was so much sweeter than Asian or European counterparts that boxcar loads of them were shipped to big-city markets on the East Coast, and some found their way to Europe. For many rural mountain families, sale of chestnuts represented their only source of income, especially during the era of the Great Depression. Indeed, the impending disappearance of American chestnuts promised to be nothing short of an economic and ecological catastrophe.[2]

For all the potential of C. parasitica to destroy such majestic members of the eastern hardwood forest, the fungus grew only on a relatively small portion of its host trees. Living bark and adjacent layers of wood were affected. The fungus didn't decay wood or spot leaves or rot roots. But it killed the cells in the bark that would normally carry food made in the leaves to other parts of the tree. And it plugged the cells in the wood that were needed to carry water and nutrients from the roots to the top.

On young branches or stems, where the bark was normally smooth and dark green, diseased regions—called cankers— were bright yellow-orange and readily visible (fig. 4.1A). On older stems or branches, however, the cankers were not always quite so apparent (fig. 4.1B). Their color was more like that of healthy bark, and often they were discernible only by the slightly swollen, split bark that was a typical symptom of the disease.[3]

The pathogen itself, like many of its relatives in the kingdom Fungi, produced two kinds of spores. Asexual reproduction was by conidia, which were produced in flask-shaped fruit-bodies embedded in the bark. These spores would ooze out of the fruit

Fig. 4.1A,B. Chestnut blight cankers on young sprouts (A) and older stems (B) enlarge to eventually girdle and kill infected stems and branches.

bodies in sticky, gooey masses, much like toothpaste squeezed out of a tube. A single fruit-body—a single flask, if you will—could produce up to several thousand spores. Rainsplash was the primary means for dissemination of these spores over short distances, but squirrels, birds, and other forest animals probably helped to spread them farther. In fact, the results of an early analysis of the spread of the disease implicated the pileated woodpecker as a major vector because chestnut blight seemed to be spreading along the same routes used by the woodpeckers during their annual fall migrations.

   C. parasitica also produced sexual spores, or ascospores, in sacs in flask-shaped bodies, similar in appearance to those described for conidia but structurally quite different. Their spores were puffed into the air, to be blown about by the wind. While such means of dispersal would seem to favor long-distance dissemination of the pathogen, it's unlikely that this was actually the case. The haphazard nature of spore movement through the air and the high probability that spores would land somewhere other than on chestnut bark probably negated much of the advantage afforded by the wind.

Unfortunately, growth of *C. parasitica* was not limited to dead and dying chestnuts. The fungus also parasitized other species of forest trees, including post and live oaks, and it grew and reproduced on dead shagbark hickory, red maple, and staghorn sumac. Thus, there was no hope that when chestnuts were gone from a particular area, the fungus, too, would disappear for lack of other food.

With so much in its favor, chestnut blight literally raced across the range of American chestnut, killing hundreds of thousands of trees in its wake. In the fifty years following the first report of the disease, it reduced this once majestic giant to little more than a forest shrub.[4]

As if to add insult to injury, the disease teasingly spared the root systems of its hosts. Thus, as trees were killed, the surviving roots would produce additional sprouts, most of which would also be killed by the blight within five years of their emergence. Occasionally, one would live long enough to produce nuts, and some even got to be 5 inches or more in diameter and up to 30 feet tall. Eventually, though, all succumbed to the disease. It's still that way today. *C. parasitica* is a formidable adversary.

While there seems to be little hope that American chestnuts will ever dominate eastern forests as they once did, scientists have invested considerable effort into trying to find ways to cope with the disease. One approach has been to breed blight-resistant Oriental chestnuts with American chestnuts in hopes of getting hybrids that grow like American chestnuts but have blight resistance. Early efforts yielded resistant trees, but unfor-

tunately they had the low, bushy growth of the Oriental parent
and were not hardy in cooler climates. More recently, however,
through application of a proven plant-breeding technique
known as backcrossing, there is renewed hope of joining disease
resistance with desirable growth habit in the same tree.[5]

Another ray of hope lies in a phenomenon called hypovirulence.[6] This was first discovered in a stand of European chestnuts in Italy in the 1930s. There, the trees began to show signs
of blight and were thought to be doomed. But, much to the surprise of scientists observing them, the cankers slowed in growth
and eventually stopped, and the trees recovered. Further investigation into this unusual happening revealed that *C. parasitica*
in these trees was infected with a pathogen of its own, a virus.
The fungus was sick. Unable to cope with the defense reactions
of the chestnuts, it was eventually overgrown by the tree and pre-
vented from causing further damage. Plant pathologists immediately seized upon the notion that if this virus disease of the
chestnut blight fungus could be spread to other sites, perhaps
all strains of the fungus would become sick and it would cease
to be a serious pathogen.

Unfortunately, after over twenty years of research on the subject and discovery of more than a dozen viruses, hypovirulence
has yet to find its way into the realm of viable management tools
for chestnut blight. Two significant stumbling blocks are (1) the
hypovirulent strains don't produce very many spores, thus limiting their ability to spread to new sites; and (2) when hyphae of
a hypovirulent strain meet those of an aggressive one, the two
don't readily grow together. Thus, there seems to be no quick
way to transfer the viruses. Despite these obstacles, research on
hypovirulence continues in the hope that advances in biotechnology will eventually help to bridge the gaps.

In the meantime, one can't help but marvel at the prophetic
wisdom of Robert Frost, who alluded to hypovirulence in the
chestnut blight fungus many years before its discovery.

Evil Tendencies Cancel

Will the blight end the chestnut?
The farmers rather guess not.
It keeps smoldering at the roots
And sending up new shoots
Till another parasite
Shall come to end the blight.[7]

DUTCH ELM DISEASE

As chestnut blight raced across the North American continent, another catastrophic tree disease reared its ugly head as a killer of elms in war-torn Holland in 1918 and 1919. Elms were crucial components of European landscapes, and affected trees died so quickly after first showing symptoms that elm disease, as it was called, became the subject of much concern (fig. 4.2).

Just as would happen today, self-proclaimed experts sprang up out of nowhere, and everybody had an idea about what was happening. Dr. Dina Spierenberg, one of the first people to bring the scientific method to the problem, had this to say about the public debate surrounding her work:

It is a mystery to us on what psychic basis many people who never have had anything to do with the agri-, horti- or forest-culture professions, people who otherwise certainly have not involved themselves with plant diseases, have judged the elm disease worthy of their attention. . . . This much is certain: . . . no plant disease has ever brought about so much interest and writing by unqualified people in the area of plant disease science in the Netherlands. The most peculiar opinions, all sorts of strange views, are reported to us in writing or orally as causes of the elm disease. A few of these have, more or less, a right to exist.[8]

Fig. 4.2. Dutch elm disease left millions of dead trees in its wake as it raced across Europe, then North America. (Photo courtesy of Cornell University Plant Pathology Herbarium, Ithaca, N.Y.)

Some of the causes not to be taken seriously by the scientific community included air pollution from motor vehicles; electric cables that, when broken, touched the ground and shocked the trees; poison gas from the World War I front; poor soil trucked in to shore up dikes in some areas of the country; and salt brine either dumped by ice trucks or left over from the cooking of salt potatoes.

But dead and dying elms were everywhere. They were not confined to sites where soil had been brought in, they were not only in areas where wires were broken, and they did not die only where salt had been dumped. Rational minds knew that something far more insidious was at work.

The persistence of five distinguished Dutch scientists—all of them women, by the way—paid off, and soon after they began work on the problem in earnest, the true cause of the disease

Fig. 4.3. Conidia of *Ophiostoma ulmi* are produced in a sticky matrix on stout black stalks. (Photo courtesy of Cornell University Plant Pathology Herbarium, Ithaca, N.Y.)

was discovered. Dutch elm disease, as it would be called, was caused by a fungus—a very curious fungus with two different types of conidia and occasional sexual reproduction, as well. The most common spore stage to be found in culture was the first to be described, and it was called *Cephalosporium ulmi*. Shortly thereafter, a second conidial stage was reported, and this one was called *Graphium ulmi* because it so resembled a brush (fig. 4.3).[9]

Finally, the sexual stage was discovered by pairing compatible strains, and it was eventually assigned to the genus, *Ophiostoma*. Today we know the fungus as *Ophiostoma ulmi*, with a second, apparently newly evolved species, *O. novo-ulmi*, also responsible for many elm deaths in North America and Europe.[10]

The fungi that cause Dutch elm disease are even more limited in their ability to colonize plant tissue than the chestnut blight fungus. While the tree is alive, the hyphae live only in the tubular cells that make up the outermost wood in elm trees. There they cause the cells to become plugged with chemicals of both fungus and host origin. As more and more plugging occurs, a diseased tree eventually runs out of ways to get water from the roots to the top, and it dies. Then the fungus will grow on previously live bark as well as wood.

Symptoms of Dutch elm disease are like those one might expect to see on any elm tree that has had a restricted supply of water and nutrients. First, leaves on individual twigs droop and turn yellow, a symptom tree pathologists call "flagging." Within a few days to weeks, the leaves turn brown and die, and additional flags appear in other places in the crown. Soon, large branches die and most trees are completely dead within two years.

Another diagnostic symptom of Dutch elm disease in a tree is the presence of a brown ring of discolored wood in the outermost portion of a branch, just beneath the bark. The brown color is evidence that plugging of cells has occurred; trees dying from some other cause would not have such a ring.

All elms are susceptible to Dutch elm disease to some extent, but some are more resistant than others. For instance, elms of Asiatic origin such as Chinese and Siberian elms are highly resistant, and some European elms are resistant as well. Elms native to North America, however, are highly susceptible. Foremost among these is the American elm, a tree that had become the cornerstone of urban forests throughout the continent by the mid-1900s.

Dutch elm disease was first identified in North America in 1930 in Cincinnati, Ohio. It had apparently been introduced through several eastern ports, presumably on elm saw logs coming in from Europe. By 1940, the disease had spread to nine states; by 1950 it was in seventeen states and southeastern Canada; and today it occurs throughout North America wherever American elms grow. Hundreds of thousands of trees have been killed, and the expense of removing them has run well into the millions of dollars.[11]

One factor weighs heavily in the efforts to manage Dutch elm disease: the interaction of the pathogen with several species of insects known as elm bark beetles.[12] Adult females of these insects lay eggs in elms that have recently died. The cause of death is of no importance to the insects, but it is vital to the fungus. When the eggs hatch, the young larvae tunnel out from the egg gallery, feeding on the inner bark and outer wood and growing as they go (fig. 4.4). When the larvae have reached maximum development, they stop feeding, settle down to pupate, and emerge from the tree as adults. If the female beetle chooses to lay her eggs in a tree that has recently been killed by Dutch elm disease, the fungus will sporulate in the beetle galleries. And when the adult beetles emerge from the trees, their bodies will be covered with the sticky spores of the fungus. But, with or without spores, the adults emerge from their host trees with only two things in mind—eating and mating—and not necessarily in that order.

Where the beetles eat is important. They seem to prefer the bark and wood of tender, young, healthy elm twigs. In the spring, just a few bites by the beetles create a wound that exposes the tree's vascular cells, and if the beetles are covered with spores, some invariably get deposited in the sap stream of the tree. Once inside the tree, the spores germinate and produce hyphae that can utilize elm sap for food. Soon more spores are produced and they are quickly carried throughout the tree. Elm bark beetles, then, through no fault of their own, have become unwitting vectors of this dread disease.

Millions of dollars have been spent in efforts to understand the biology of Dutch elm disease well enough to devise effective control measures and then to implement them. Some management strategies have been more effective than others, but there is no single silver bullet. Successful Dutch elm disease manage-

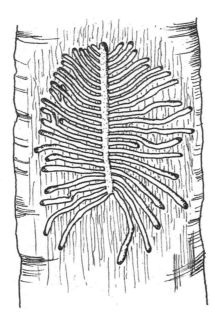

Fig. 4.4. Galleries like these made by the smaller European elm bark beetle are common on dead and dying elms. Eggs were laid in the vertical (egg) chamber, then larvae tunneled out away from the chamber and from each other. (Drawn by Robert O'Brien.)

ment programs must attack the problem on several different fronts, and the efforts must continue year after year for the lives of the trees.[13] Activities common to all successful programs include the following:

- Regular, thorough examination of each elm in the management program. The purpose of this is twofold. First, it enables one to detect dead and dying branches and direct their removal before they become infested by elm bark beetles. Second, it improves the chances for trees that do contract the disease to be identified early enough to give them the best chance for survival with curative measures.

- Sanitation. Whenever dead or dying elms are found, they must be removed and debarked or buried so they can no longer serve as beetle breeding sites. All dead elms or parts of them must be included in this effort, otherwise beetle populations can quickly escalate to unmanageable proportions.

- Timely applications of insecticides to protect the trees from beetles. Wholesale spraying of large trees in urban environments is viewed with disdain by many people, but there is little choice when elm preservation is the objective. Some success has been achieved by injecting elms with insecticides rather than spraying them, but most pest managers still view spraying as the most reliable course of action.

- Preventive or curative injection of trees with fungicides. Several fungicides have been formulated for injection into trees by certified pesticide applicators. Equipment used for actually inserting the fungicides may vary from one tree care specialist to another, as much of it is homemade, but several general principals should be followed. Injection should be into the roots or root collar area, application should be made through small shallow holes, and the chemicals should be introduced with as little pressure as necessary to push the chemicals into the tree. High-pressure injection forces large quantities of fungicide into a tree, much of which ends up in wood that is so old it no longer carries material to other parts of the tree. Fungicide deposited there never does the rest of the tree any good.[14]

- Disruption of roots between adjacent elms if there is reason to suspect the roots may have grafted and will serve as conduits of the fungus. Trees up to 30 feet apart may have such common root systems.

Failure to sustain a commitment to protect elms seems to have led to the downfall of many programs as states, cities, or individuals simply run out of money or enthusiasm to keep up the fight. But *O. ulmi* and *O. novo-ulmi* are tenacious in their resolve. The resources saved today by not preserving the remaining living elms will surely be spent tomorrow to remove dying or dead trees.

As to the future of elms in North America, there is little question that the genus will persist, albeit with considerably less stature. Highly susceptible American elms produce so many seeds so early in their lives that if they can grow for a just few years before contracting the disease, it will be sufficient to make more of their kind. Other species of elms, especially those native to other continents, are even better able to cope with the disease. And tree breeders are hard at work developing disease-resistant American elms as well as European and Oriental hybrids. Many selections are already on the market, with the promise for more choices in years to come.[15]

Other Noteworthy Tree Diseases

Chestnut blight and Dutch elm disease are the two most catastrophic tree diseases of recent generations. In both cases, the pathogens were unwittingly introduced into North America on plant material from other parts of the world. Unfortunately, these pathogens have found North American flora especially favorable for growth and reproduction, and in the process of trying to do little more than insure their own survival, they have changed our landscape forever.

There have been other such cases, however. *Cronartium ribicola,* the cause of white pine blister rust, invades branches and trunks of five-needled pines such as eastern and western white pines and limber pine, eventually killing its hosts (fig. 4.5). The disease is a major reason why eastern white pine in the northeastern United States and southeastern Canada is now rarely

Fig. 4.5. The white pine blister rust fungus
kills pines by girdling them.

managed for commercial timber production. Western white
pine sites in Montana and Idaho have also sustained significant
losses and are rarely replanted to white pine after logging or
fire.[16]

Nectria coccinea var. *faginata,* a pathogen of beech bark, together with the beech scale insect have killed tens of thousands
of American beech in forests from Nova Scotia south to West Vir-
ginia and west to Ohio. Both the fungus and the insect were introduced from Europe, presumably in the early 1900s. The disease they cause, beech bark disease, is viewed by forest
pathologists as a slow-moving but inexorable plague that will
eventually find its way into all stands of American beech in the

Fig. 4.6. Tar spot of maple leaves causes much alarm among home owners whose trees are affected. (Photo by K. Loeffler; courtesy of Cornell University Plant Pathology Herbarium, Ithaca, N.Y.)

eastern United States and kill thousands of additional trees. Fortunately, beech trees grown in landscapes can be protected with pest management programs designed to reduce scale insect infestations.[17]

A disease of little consequence to tree health but cause for considerable alarm among urban residents in an expanding area in the northeastern United States is tar spot of maples. The pathogen (*Rhytisma acerinum*) forms large—up to almost an inch in diameter—black spots, often with bright yellow margins, on the leaves of its host, Norway maple (fig. 4.6). In years with especially favorable weather for infection, the disease will cause premature defoliation. This disease is common on Norway maple in Europe but was unknown on the same host in North America until 1940. In August of 1986, it caused near complete defoliation of Norway maples in several upstate New York communities and since then has spread throughout the state and well into adjacent states. Damage to tree health is minimal because defoliation occurs late in the growing season, after the

Fig. 4.7. The dogwood anthracnose fungus begins its attack on leaves and twigs of susceptible trees. As the disease intensifies within the crown, whole trees may be killed.

leaves have nearly completed their useful lives. A closely related but apparently different fungus occurs on red and silver maples in North America. Severity of that disease also varies from year to year but even in the worst of times, it rarely defoliates its hosts.[18]

The most recently introduced tree disease occurs on dogwoods, especially flowering dogwood in the eastern United States and Pacific dogwood in the West. It is called dogwood anthracnose and was reported on both coasts of North America at about the same time in the mid-1980s. On the East Coast, two foci of infection were identified. One was on Long Island and the other about 20 miles north of New York City. Since then it has spread along the eastern seaboard as far north as Massachusetts, as far south as Georgia, and as far inland as eastern Tennessee. Hundreds of thousands of flowering dogwoods in landscapes and forests have died.[19]

The fungus causing dogwood anthracnose, *Discula destructiva,* infects leaves and, more importantly, the current year's shoots. By progressively killing all the growing points over several years, it either kills trees outright or predisposes them to lethal attack by other pests. Fortunately, as the first "wave" of disease seems to have passed through parts of the Northeast, individual trees with some apparent resistance to the disease have survived. Those should continue to produce seed for the next generation of natural trees and for systematic crosses by plant breeders.

There is little doubt that other potentially catastrophic fungus pathogens of plants will find their way to North American shores, and we, in turn, may send some abroad. Increased efforts to prevent movement of plant material through international ports serve to prevent accidental introductions. We can only hope that increased education about fungi as possible hitchhikers on our travels will raise public consciousness and help to slow the pace of these migrations.

CHAPTER 5

Ergot of Grain Crops

There had been no signs of trouble in Pont-St. Esprit until August 12 when Dr. Jean Viou was summoned to treat a patient for food poisoning. In three days there were a few more cases and by the weekend, anguished calls from all over town kept three doctors sleepless trying to soothe the burning feelings, the chills, and the violent pains all the patients complained of. The mass poisonings could be traced to one source: bread made by Maurice Maillot. The bakeries were closed and scientists were brought in but before they arrived one townsman already lay dead. The epidemic seemed to let up. Then on August 24, the mad panic seized Pont-St. Esprit. All through the night, the narrow streets shook with shrieks of madness and fright and the frenzied sound of feet fleeing unearthly adversaries. One man plunged out his window screaming hysterically that he was a jet plane. From her third floor hospital room, a 68-year-old woman leaped to the ground to escape the flames that she imagined engulfed her. A barge sailor shrieked "My head is on fire! There are snakes in my belly!" and tried to destroy himself.[1]

The cause for the terror that gripped the residents of this otherwise quiet little town in southern France in 1951 is still open to question. Some argue that the poisoning was due to contamination of the local grain supply with an insecticide. But there is compelling evidence to suggest that this was the most recent chapter in a long list of bizarre and tragic events associated with a peculiar fungus, *Claviceps purpurea*.

C. purpurea is an ascomycete, one of the sac fungi.[2] It spends the winter on or slightly below the soil surface in the form of

Fig. 5.1. Germinating ergot sclerotia (*C. purpurea*) produce up to a dozen spore-bearing stalks. (Photo by K. Loeffler; courtesy of Cornell University Plant Pathology Herbarium, Ithaca, N.Y.)

cylindrical, compact masses of mycelium, with each mass surrounded by a black rind. Many species of fungi produce such resting structures, called sclerotia (sing. = sclerotium). Those of *C. purpurea* range in size from one-fourth to one inch long and one-eighth to one-fourth inch wide.

In the spring and early summer, the sclerotia germinate to produce as many as a dozen stalks. Each stalk is swollen at the tip, making it vaguely resemble the end of a drum major's baton (fig. 5.1). Ascospores produced in flasklike structures embedded in the swollen tips are shot from the ground into the air, to be whisked away by a passing breeze. A few of the spores will be lucky enough to land on the only place where they can continue to grow—in the flowers of grasses or cereal grains. There they behave somewhat like normal pollen in that they germinate and send germ tubes into the ovaries of the host. But that's where the similarities with anything healthy end, because where the plant had intended a seed to develop, the fungus takes a different course. It quickly colonizes the host tissue, and within two weeks of infection more spores—conidia—are produced at each of the infection sites.

Unlike the wind-blown primary spores, the secondary ones are contained in droplets of nectar—just the kind of thing pollinating insects like to find. They visit the nectar, pick up some of the spores, and then move on to real flowers where they inadvertently inoculate them with the fungus. *C. purpurea* infects host tissue with both primary and secondary inoculum, eventually producing a sclerotium at each one. In autumn, the sclerotia fall to the ground, there to wait for winter's end and a new crop of host plants the following spring.

Sclerotia protruding from infected plants look vaguely like the spur on a rooster's leg. Because of this similarity, the French word for spur, *ergot,* has also been adopted to refer to the sclerotia and the plant disease caused by the fungus (see plate 1B). Host plants include such important staples as wheat, barley, oats, and rye, and the disease occurs worldwide, wherever susceptible hosts grow.*

Because of the way that sclerotia are lodged in the seed head, it is easy for them to get mixed in with good grain during the harvest. In fact, records from medieval times indicate that in years when weather conditions for ergot were especially favorable, up to 30 percent of harvested grain was not really grain at all but rather fungus sclerotia. If they weren't culled in the field or in storage, the sclerotia would be ground into flour and eventually find their way into foods eaten by people and livestock. And that's where the problems began.

* Some older European literature and literature from Third World countries refer to small grains as "corn" and list corn as a host for ergot. Readers should be advised that the plant that North Americans know as corn (*Zea mays*) is not susceptible to ergot.

Ergot sclerotia contain a wide variety of chemicals known as alkaloids, many of which are hazardous to the health of humans and other animals.[3] One such chemical is ergotamine, a vaso-constrictor powerful enough to completely restrict blood flow to some parts of the body, thus causing a condition known as gangrenous ergotism. Extremities are particularly sensitive, and ergotamine may cause symptoms ranging from the shedding of nails to the loss of hands and feet. In the latter cases, blood-starved limbs simply dry up, turn black, and fall off, with no pain or bleeding. However, the stench associated with the rotting limbs is reported to be overwhelming.[4]

Feelings of intense heat often precede the complete loss of sensation in diseased limbs by several weeks. Thus, some of the earliest references to gangrenous ergotism referred not so much to loss of limbs as to a "plague of fire" or "holy fire." When the staff of a hospital in Vienna dedicated to the memory of Saint Anthony undertook a successful campaign to treat patients afflicted with ergotism, the disease became known as St. Anthony's Fire. In churches throughout western Europe, wood-cuts, paintings, and drawings depicting the ministry of St. Anthony often show his followers with missing or burning limbs.[5]

A second alkaloid of note in ergot sclerotia is ergonovine. This chemical causes spontaneous abortions in human females as well as other animals. It may have had its greatest impact on human welfare not so much by causing the death of unborn children but rather by reducing the reproductive activity of livestock used for milk and meat.

Two other alkaloids produced by *C. purpurea* are ergine and lysergic acid hydroxyethylamide. Both are apparently capable of causing a condition known as convulsive ergotism, with symptoms ranging from vomiting, diarrhea, and general lethargy, to a sensation of ants crawling over the body (formication), vivid hallucinations, twitching, grotesque distortion of limbs, and seizures similar to those associated with epilepsy.

The historical record is replete with evidence that ergotism in all its forms was a major factor affecting the physical and mental health of people throughout much of the Middle Ages.[6] Residents of central Europe were especially vulnerable, and historians suspect that this was due to the prevalence of cereal grains, especially rye, in their diets. Unlike wealthier folk who could afford to sort and discard "dirty" grain, peasants unaware of the threat posed by ergot opted to eat every bit of meal gleaned from their fields.

The first documented epidemic of ergotism in Germany occurred in 857 A.D.: "A great plague of swollen blisters consumed the people by a loathsome rot, so that their limbs were loosened and fell off before death."[7] Almost a century later a report of a "plague of fire" in the vicinity of Paris contained the first indications that proper medical care might reverse the course of the disease. Victims taken to the church of St. Mary who were fed nutritious, presumably ergot free, food had a remission of symptoms and were eventually able to leave the hospital. But, alas! Upon returning home to their own stores, which included ergot-laden grains, the hapless folk were soon stricken again and on their way back to St. Mary's.

In 994, an epidemic of ergotism gripped south-central France, evoking descriptions reminiscent of those from Pont.-St. Esprit nearly 950 years later: "And when a plague of invisible fire broke out, cutting off limbs from the body and consuming many in a single night, the sufferers thronged to the churches and invoked the help of the Saints. The cries of those in pain and the shedding of burned-up limbs alike excited pity; the stench of rotten flesh was unbearable; many were however cooled by the sprinkling of holy water and snatched from mortal peril."[8]

From then on through the the mid-1800s, many other epidemics of ergotism were recorded. Most occurred in central Europe, especially France, but there were also occasional reports from England, Germany, and Russia. The numbers of people afflicted in each episode varied from one or two members of a family—with the rest usually suffering nonlethal but nonetheless unpleasant symptoms—to 40,000 during the aforementioned epidemic of 994.

Children seemed to be far more sensitive to ergot alkaloids than adults. In one epidemic, 56 percent of victims affected but not necessarily killed were under ten years old, while in another 60 percent were under fifteen years of age. In yet a third episode, 50 percent of children under age ten died from the disease, while most adults suffered debilitating convulsions but eventually recovered.

In virtually all cases, the incidence of ergotism in humans was extraordinarily high after growing seasons in which the weather conditions were especially favorable for the infection of plants by spores of *C. purpurea*. Extended periods of cool, wet weather in the spring prolonged flowering and encouraged production and successful transport of spores to new infection courts. If winter conditions following a year of high ergot incidence were also harsh, people were more likely to exhaust their best food supplies early and turn to lower quality stores—often ergoty, unbeknownst to them—just to stay alive. Only several weeks later did the hapless folk begin to suffer the dire consequences of their fallacious decisions. By then their deteriorating health was usually not associated with grain products but was erroneously blamed on a contagious germ, especially when symptoms were confined to certain families or persons in a specific area.

For some still unknown reason, gangrenous ergotism was most prevalent west of the Rhine River, especially in France, while convulsive ergotism occurred more frequently in the rest of Europe and in North America. Early students of the disease hypothesized that convulsive ergotism was simply the first stage of the condition, induced by a certain—presumably low—dose of fungus sclerotia. Gangrenous ergotism, they reasoned, was the consequence of a higher dose. However, too many records of symptom occurrence and expression included only one or the other type, regardless of the dosage. Furthermore, gan-

grenous ergotism was more likely than not to occur sponta-
neously, with no prior indications that a problem was in the off-
ing. Today it is generally agreed that the two types are, in fact,
caused by different chemicals in the sclerotia. Different strains
of the fungus are likely to vary in the relative amounts of the toxins they produce, with effects of different hosts, climate, and
plant fertility also contributing to the final formulation.

Modern-day historians trying to explain the hows and whys of
certain past events have compiled good evidence to indicate that
"bewitched" people in central Europe between the sixteenth
and nineteenth centuries may very well have been exhibiting
symptoms of ergotism. Some have even suggested that the principals in the Salem witch trials of 1692 were victims of this dread
disease, and the extensive written record of these events seems
to bear them out.[9] Although the symptoms of the people in the
Salem affair varied from one place to another and from person
to person, the spectrum compiled by historian Mary Matossian
in her book *Poisons of the Past*—including sensations of pricking
or ants crawling on the skin, distortions of the face, paralysis,
hallucinations, convulsive seizures, and dementia—is consistent
with those of ergotism. While most accused witches were older
adults, those actually "bewitched" and exhibiting overt symptoms were most often adolescents, the same age group known
from subsequent research to be the most sensitive to effects of
toxic alkaloids. In addition, bewitched people occasionally suffered loss of limbs. That animals as well as people became bewitched was a fact used by many to discount mere hysteria as the
root cause of Salem's troubles. Cows failing to produce milk and
other domestic animals exhibiting unusual behaviors, including
the occasional shedding of one or more limbs with dry gangrene, make the case for ergotism ever more convincing. As with
their human counterparts, some livestock even died.

Other evidence to implicate ergotism as a major factor in bewitchment on both continents focuses on the geographic distribution of witch trials, the diets of those afflicted, and the climate

associated with the frenzy. Historical records show that most trials in Europe were held in communities located in river valleys in southwestern Germany and southeastern France. These were places not only where rye was a staple food but where weather was typically cool and wet, even in a year when continental temperature averages were above normal. Peasants in these areas would consume up to three and a half pounds of bread a day if given the chance. The corollary of this analysis is that trials for bewitchment were virtually nonexistent where either rye was not a prominent food or the climate was sufficiently hot and dry to discourage development of most plant pathogenic fungi. The Irish, for instance, with their steady diet of potatoes, had virtually no problems with ergotism and only one record of a witch trial. On a smaller but equally significant scale, where actual homesteads of bewitched people in Salem colony could be located, all were on soil marginal for growing rye. Most were either near streams or swamps or on north-facing slopes, the sites most favorable for occurrence of a fungus-caused plant disease.

Insofar as the overall climate during the time of the witch trials is concerned, tree ring analyses indicate that in years when springtime temperatures were so cold that tree growth was slowed, the number of trials for witchcraft conducted during the following fall and winter increased. This was true for the European continent as a whole in the 1560s, from 1560 to 1689 in southwestern Germany, and again from 1650 to 1700 in Russia. The Salem affair was also preceded by two years of unusually cold spring weather.

Eventually, people became more aware of the consequences of eating ergot-contaminated grain, and greater effort was made to avoid it. In addition, agricultural scientists learned that if the sclerotia were buried more than a few inches beneath the soil surface, they would be unable to produce stalks tall enough for the spore-bearing bodies to reach open air. Thus, the deep plowing of fields soon after harvest became a plant disease management strategy. And, if fields were left fallow or planted to nonhost crops for one or two years, a susceptible crop could subsequently be planted with little threat of disease.[10]

By the middle of the nineteenth century, ergotism as a human disease had ceased to evoke much concern except for occasional cases of animal poisoning. Alkaloids associated with *C. purpurea,* however, continued to attract attention from the medical community, because decoctions made by boiling ergot sclerotia in water had become routine prescriptions for inducing labor in pregnant women. Ergot decoctions had been used for such purposes by midwives at least since the mid-1700s, and by 1808 the administration of ergot as a means to hasten delivery was described in the Medical Repository of New York as a legitimate technique. In fact, it was so effective that an upstate New York physician was moved to include the following note with a sample of the potion that he sent to a colleague:

> In compliance with your request I herewith transmit you a sample of the Pulvis parturiens, which I have been in the habit of using for several years, with the most complete success. It expedites lingering parturition, and saves to the accoucheur a considerable portion of time, without producing any bad effects on the patient. . . . Previous to its exhibition it is of the utmost consequence to ascertain the presentation . . . as the violent and almost incessant action which it induces in the uterus precludes the possibility of turning.[11]

Ergot decoctions with alkaloids causing constriction of blood vessels were also used in childbirth after the baby was born to lessen the chances for postdelivery hemorrhaging in mothers. Apparently this prescription met with good success.

Obviously, some by-products in ergot sclerotia were of enough reputed value in human medicine to have caught the attention of eighteenth- and nineteenth-century practitioners. Astute chemists and pharmaceutical manufacturers suspected there were more where those came from, and so it was that in the early 1930s, the chemistry of ergot derivatives attracted a young chemist named Albert Hofmann. Hofmann worked for a Swiss firm, Sandoz Pharmaceuticals, and his assignment at the time was to learn what he could about isolation and purification of ergot alkaloids. In the course of his work, Hofmann found himself focusing attention on derivatives of just one compound—lysergic acid. He assigned a number to each of the derivatives: LSD-1, LSD-2, etc. Eventually he got to LSD-25, and it was while working with that material one April day in 1943 that he began to feel unusually lightheaded and dizzy and became careless in his laboratory. He managed to get home on his bicycle, and after a deep night's sleep, awoke rejuvenated yet perplexed. Hofmann suspected that his bizarre experience was caused by the LSD-25, probably absorbed through the skin, and he began a series of self-experiments with regulated dosages under medical supervision. It wasn't long before he realized that he had stumbled onto a psychoactive drug of immense power at very low dosages.[12] As Hofmann's colleagues at Sandoz learned of his work, they, too, shared in his excitement for the promise of the new drug, and they enthusiastically joined in the "research" by taking the LSD themselves. A business trip at Sandoz took on a whole new meaning.

Soon, LSD-25 was patented and thereafter made available to the medical community for experimentation. Psychiatrists were particularly excited because it promised to open the deepest recesses of the human mind and to shed new light on how a healthy brain worked in comparison to a disturbed one. The potential for treatment of various mental illnesses was immense, and papers detailing experimental use of the chemical for such purposes appeared in the scientific literature with increasing regularity.

One group of specialists who found reports about LSD research particularly interesting were on the payroll of none other than the United States Central Intelligence Agency.[13] The CIA, at the time, was searching for a mind-control agent that would allow them to more effectively interrogate suspected spies, preferably without their knowing that such interrogation had occurred. LSD-25 looked like it had some possibilities, and, in preliminary tests, it worked just as the experimenters had hoped it would. An officer was given some secret military information and told not to divulge it to anyone else under any circumstances. After being unwittingly dosed with LSD, he not only told the secrets to unskilled interrogators, but when the drug wore off, he had no recollection of having spilled the beans.

Further experiments were not so successful, however. Too often, LSD either caused such anxiety or such distortions in time and space that test subjects were unable to convey information that was the least bit complex in nature. Eventually, the CIA product development branch gave up on the potential use of the drug as an interrogation agent, but they continued to explore other possible applications for LSD as a defensive or offensive agent. In fact, one such option that received serious consideration was to make it available to American spies so they could take it if they were caught and thus be completely incapable of disclosing meaningful information even when being tortured by their captors.

At another time, potential use of LSD as a battlefield agent, to be added to enemy water supplies or dusted over attacking troops, was considered. Imagine, the argument went, how ineffective an hallucinating soldier would be in combat! For whatever reason, further experimentation on that use of the ergot derivative was also abandoned, but the specter of what kinds of plans the Soviet Union might be making to use LSD against the West loomed ominously over many a Cold War strategy session.

By 1953, Allen Dulles, the director of the CIA, had become convinced that the next great battle between the world's superpowers would be for the control of people's minds, so he authorized funding for the supersecret mind-control program, Operation MK-Ultra. Under the auspices of this project, experimentation on mind control continued at full steam, with LSD being given to knowing and unknowing subjects in clinical settings, in mental institutions, in military barracks, in college dormitories, in jails, and in bedrooms. In the latter case, drug-addicted prostitutes were given an ample supply of whatever substance they needed to sate their own habits if they would lure unsuspecting clients into their rooms, dose them with LSD, and allow CIA officials to observe from behind one-way mirrors. Ironically, the most powerful of several governmental agencies charged with protecting U.S. citizens from threats to their freedom had quickly become one of the biggest suppliers of mind-altering drugs in the country.

In the meantime, legitimate research into the use of LSD as a psychotherapeutic tool was also under way. When combined with conventional counseling, it provided a rapid means for exposing long-repressed events and emotions, thus enabling clients more quickly and clearly to see the history associated with their current ills.[14] Results of this work were extremely promising, and significant progress was made in treating some mental problems that had defied previous efforts or were otherwise destined to take a long time to treat—and a considerable amount of money—without certain resolution.

Unfortunately for psychotherapy research, use and abuse of LSD by intelligence agencies eventually reached the public stage when several test subjects either died or suffered permanent emotional damage and their families sought redress from the government. Coincidentally, reports of LSD as the recreational drug among increasingly rebellious youth of the 1960s were daily fare in the nation's press, and the U.S. electorate demanded that their legislators reexamine the threat the drug posed to the nation's moral fiber. Governments around the world ceased to sponsor outside research with LSD, Sandoz quit manufacturing it, legislation was enacted to outlaw LSD in any form, and scientific experimentation ground to a halt.

Today, LSD is so easy to synthesize if one has the raw materials and a modicum of laboratory apparatus that it continues to be a commonly abused recreational drug. And some people of national and international prominence in the musical and literary worlds continue to champion its use. But for every one of today's satisfied customers there are veterans of the 1960s and 1970s who still reel from unexpected flashbacks and who nurse debilitating emotional scars from their ordeals. Clearly, in the case of *C. purpurea* and its metabolites, there are far better and safer ways to probe the depths of being human.

In the meantime, there is renewed interest in other ergot alkaloids within the medical community. Foremost of these is ergotamine, sold under the trade names Cafergot®, Ergate®, and Migril®. The drug has brought relief to many who suffer from migraine headaches.

◆ Great Thoughts?

Some ethnobotanists and mycologists propose yet another role for ergot-laced potions. If their hypothesis is correct, then the legacy of ergot may be that it has had a far greater impact on our perceptions of the human condition than most people could ever imagine.[a]

The foundations for this intriguing notion were laid thousands of years ago in the roots of Greek mythology when Persephone—daughter of the goddess of agriculture, Demeter—was kidnapped as she was playing with friends. After nine frantic days of searching, Demeter learned that with the consent of almighty Zeus, Hades had kidnapped Persephone to be his wife and she now dwelled in the Underworld.

Angered with Zeus and even more distraught over the knowledge of her daughter's fate, Demeter took the form of an old woman and wandered among mortal humans seeking some comfort for her grief. When her true identity was eventually exposed by a couple who had befriended her, she was furious and set a famine upon the Earth that almost destroyed the human race. Only a last-ditch arrangement by Zeus whereby Persephone would live a third of the year with Hades and the rest with Demeter saved the day. The goddess showed her pleasure by allowing the earth to yield crops for eight months, then returning it to barrenness for the four months that her daughter spent with Hades.

For hundreds of years afterwards, the Greeks celebrated Demeter's reunification with Persephone and paid homage to their blessings of good crops by reenacting the story in a celebration known as the Mysteries of Eleusis. In October of each year, the faithful would gather in Athens to begin the festivities with the Lesser Mysteries. Brotherly love and good will were the order of the day, and a large and raucous crowd gathered in the city. For several days, participants would purify themselves by proclaiming their debt to Demeter, cleansing themselves in the Aegean Sea, and sacrificing pigs. Then they began a festive pilgrimage to the small town of Eleusis, about 10 miles away.

Once there, only a select few were allowed to cross the Kephisos River and enter the temple of Eleusis, where the Greater Mysteries were unveiled. On paper (papyrus?), the requirements were "clean hands and intelligible speech," because the purpose of the Greater Mysteries was to "teach knowledge." However, it has also been recorded that a sizable amount of money changed hands, and it is most likely that the Greater Mysteries were at least as much a privilege of wealth as of intellectual strength.

In preparation for the Greater Mysteries, initiates would fast and rest and make additional unspecified sacrifices. They also pledged never to reveal the nature of the experiences they had during the Greater Mysteries. Then they would break the fast by drinking *kykeon,* a sacred potion colored purple and made of meal, water, and mint, and they would begin their journey into the unknown. Most honored their pledge of secrecy, and there are few reliable accounts of what happened once initiates left the larger crowd. Most stories recount great terrors that caused shuddering, sweating, and fear. One poet claimed that he had seen the beginning and ending of life. He learned that the whole process was in the form of a circle starting and ending in the same place and given by God.

What happened during the Greater Mysteries that caused such profound revelation to attract the likes of Socrates, Plato, Sophocles, Euripides, and Homer? We'll never know for sure, but R. Gordon Wasson, Albert Hofmann, and others have suggested that ergot alkaloids were likely to have been important contributors to the terrors, hallucinations, tremors, and sweats that continually reappear in descriptions from Eleusis. The fact that *kykeon* was purple and that water with ergot sclerotia immersed in it turns purple was the first clue. In addition, *kykeon* apparently had intoxicating properties that far exceeded traditional wine. Distilled wine might have enough alcohol to evoke some of the reported sensations, but there is nothing in the historical record to indicate that the ancient Greeks knew anything about distillation. Thus the case for *kykeon* being something else is strengthened.

Wasson and colleagues also studied artwork recovered from the ruins of Eleusis and concluded that they not only implicated some potent drink as a major factor in the Mysteries but that a grain of some sort was included in the drink. Rye was not a common crop in that region of the world, but barley was, and it could have been the source of enough ergot to enable people to become aware of its effect on the psyche. Also, the wild grass *Papusalum distichum* could have been identified as another host and provided greater quantities of the alkaloids.

The Mysteries of Eleusis will likely remain just that—mysteries. And scholars will continue to debate their nature and cause for a long time to come. For those of us who champion the place of the fungi in the world, the mere thought that a fungal by-product—even if it was a crude form of LSD—might have played such an important role in shaping the visions of some of the civilized world's greatest philosophers is particularly intriguing.

ª See R. G. Wasson et al., *Persephone's Quest* (New Haven: Yale University Press, 1986).

✦

✦ Bookshelf: Acceptable Risk

Discussion of the possible role of ergot alkaloids in the Salem witchcraft affair is not confined only to literature for academicians. The idea recently found its way into science fiction through the pen of prize-winning author Robin Cook. His heroine in *Acceptable Risk,* Kim Stanton, not only learns that one of her ancestors was persecuted as a witch during the Salem trials but also that ergot may have been responsible for her bewitchment. As if that's not revelation enough, she also stands by with some anguish as her boyfriend, an adventuresome biochemist, tries to make even more potent alkaloids by modifying those produced by *C. purpurea.* To assay the fruits of their labors, he and his colleagues test their new finds out on themselves. Unfortunately, changes in their personalities, which seem so positive at first, take a deadly turn, leaving the survivors with more respect than ever of the hazards of tinkering with the fungus world.

CHAPTER 6

Mycotoxins: Toxic By-Products of Fungal Growth

The toxic alkaloids produced by the ergot fungus of the previous chapter are called mycotoxins because they're produced by a fungus and they're toxic to humans and other animals.

Unfortunately, ergot alkaloids are not the only mycotoxins produced by members of the kingdom *Fungi*. In fact, there are hundreds, if not thousands, of such chemicals, and many will cause severe physical as well as mental distress, sometimes leading to death. The poisons in poisonous mushrooms are properly classified as mycotoxins, but here they will be deferred to a later chapter. Instead, think now about the molds that commonly grow on and in organic material—especially edible organic material—if environmental conditions are favorable. Think about the blue-green mold on bread that is left too long in your cupboard. Think about the greenish yellow mold growing on the leftover spaghetti that has remained hidden, sometimes for weeks, behind the more accessible treasures in your refrigerator. Think about the pink mold growing on ears of corn standing uncut in a field because it's too wet to harvest. Think about these and hundreds of others that have grown on stored foods for thousands of years.

In the earliest civilizations, such molds may have posed little threat to public health simply because large amounts of food weren't produced at any one time. Foodstuffs were either eaten soon after they were gathered, or they were dried. In the latter case, quantities were presumably small enough to be spread out on a level surface and dried quickly in the late summer sun.

Thus, opportunities for molds and their toxins to find their way into the diets of the earliest peoples were probably relatively slim.

As cultures advanced and made improvements in agricultural productivity, the need to store larger and larger quantities of food for longer and longer periods of time arose. Shipment of food from rural production areas to population centers became an integral part of the food distribution system. With little fanfare, the fungi emerged as important factors in human welfare by decaying that food in transit or storage. The rotted stores were likely either discarded or fed to animals, but if they were eaten by people, sickness or death resulting from them may very well have been blamed on one or more of the many other diseases plaguing earlier civilizations.

ASPERGILLUS FLAVUS

But all that changed in 1960 when 100,000 turkeys died on a farm in England. The magnitude of the loss was unprecedented, at least in recent recorded history, and animal scientists at the time were anxious to find the cause. Early in the investigation, it was discovered that the turkeys had been fed peanut meal that was heavily infested with a common storage mold known as *Aspergillus flavus*. When that mold was grown in pure culture and fed to a test population of healthy turkeys, they also died.[1]

Obviously, *A. flavus* posed a serious threat to the health of these animals, and shortly after this particular episode, chemists determined why. The fungus produced at least four different toxic chemicals. They were collectively called "aflatoxins" and they remain, today, some of the most potent toxins produced by any life form. Autopsies of the turkeys indicated that the primary site of action by aflatoxins was the liver, where they either killed tissue outright or induced formation of cancerous tumors.

Because *A. flavus* was such a common fungus capable of growing on so many different crops, its connection with the disaster at the English farm touched off a flurry of research. Officials associated with the United Nations Children's Fund (UNICEF) were particularly concerned with the unfolding investigation because they had undertaken a major campaign to encourage children in underdeveloped countries to eat more peanut meal. Its high protein content and ready availability made it an ideal food—or so they thought. With the discovery of aflatoxins, however, they feared that the well-intentioned UNICEF recommendation might actually be a time bomb just waiting to go off. They needed to know more about this fungus and its toxins, and they needed to know *now*.

There was also concern about aflatoxins in east Asian countries where *A. flavus* was purposely cultivated on soybean extracts to make soy sauce and some other kinds of soy food and drink. Might those people, too, have inadvertently adopted life-threatening practices for preparing their foods?

One of the first things to come to light from the ensuing research was that *A. flavus* was not just a single species.[2] Mycologists studying the morphology of cultures and the means by which the fungi produced spores determined that at least eleven different species of fungi were included in what became known as the *A. flavus* species complex. For the sake of simplicity, I will refer to the whole species complex just as *A. flavus*.

Second, it was learned that a number of different environmental factors affected the amount of aflatoxin any given culture would produce. One important variable was whether or not other fungi were also growing on the substrate. They usually were, for if conditions were right for *A. flavus* to grow on feed stored in a bin or silo, then they would also be right for many other fungi. And if many different molds were at work, then *A. flavus* produced relatively little aflatoxin. Without any competitors, however, it could produce significant amounts. Fortunately, pure cultures of *A. flavus* would only occur under somewhat unique circumstances, which is probably why aflatoxicosis hadn't reared its ugly head earlier.

Third, the nature of the substrate also turned out to be an important variable. *A. flavus* grew well on soybeans but produced relatively little aflatoxin, thus posing little threat to the preparation of Far Eastern foods. It also grew well on peanuts, and when that substrate was adequately moistened and held at a favorable temperature, abundant aflatoxin was produced. Pepper and nutmeg also turned out to be good substrates for growth of *A. flavus* if they were warm and moist. Fortunately, spices were typically kept as dry as possible to preserve their flavors, and this reduced the threat of aflatoxin production in these materials to virtually nothing.* Finally, pasta was found to harbor high quantities of the fungus. *A. flavus* apparently didn't come from the wheat used to make pasta, but was rather introduced at some other point in the manufacturing process.

A fourth discovery, made in tests of aflatoxin on other animals, was that different species reacted with varying degrees of sensitivity. Rainbow trout were highly sensitive. Half of a population of test animals had definite liver tumors and most of the rest had suspect tumors within a year of eating feed containing 20 parts per billion (ppb) aflatoxin. Rats were apparently less sensitive, but when white rats were given a ration containing only 15 ppb aflatoxin, nearly all of them eventually developed liver cancer. Young pigs were very sensitive, pregnant sows a bit less so, and calves even less. Cattle and sheep were most tolerant. However, in all of these animals, consumption of aflatoxin in concentrations too low to cause overt symptoms resulted in stunted growth or lack of normal weight gain.[3]

A fifth area of exploration addressed concerns that even if cows weren't directly affected by low-level exposures to aflatoxins, the toxins would be passed into the milk and eventually find

---

* In the case of pepper, investigators also found that it was contaminated with rodent droppings and insect parts, and *A. flavus* was just one more disgusting ingredient. Fortunately, today's standards are higher.

Plate 1A. Stem rust (*Puccinia graminis*) has plagued grain growers since the beginning of recorded history. The colorful spores of the fungus give rise to the name "rust." (Photo courtesy of the Department of Plant Pathology, University of the Orange Free State, Bloemfontein, South Africa.)

Plate 1B. Ergot of rye (*Claviceps purpurea*). The fungus sclerotia emerge where grain should normally form.

Plate 1C. Shiitake mushrooms (*Lentinula edodes*) are often produced commercially on compressed sawdust "logs."

Plate 1D. This look-alike (*Ganoderma tsugae*) of the reishi mushroom is purported to have a vast array of medicinal properties.

Plate 2A. *Morchella angusticeps*,
a delectable morel.

Plate 2B. *Gyromitra caroliniana*, one of the false morels.

Plate 2C. *Agaricus rodmanii,* a meadow mushroom.

Plate 2D. *Amanita virosa,* the "Death Angel."

Plate 3A. *Coprinus comatus,* shaggy mane.

Plate 3B. A shaggy mane near completion of spore dispersal.

Plate 3C. *Calvatia gigantea,* giant puffball.

Plate 3D. *Laetiporus sulfureus,* chicken-of-the-woods. (Photo courtesy of Cornell University Plant Pathology Herbarium, Ithaca, N.Y.)

Plate 4A. *Amanita muscaria,*
red variety (Colorado).

Plate 4B. *Amanita muscaria,*
yellow variety (New York).

Plate 4C. *Cladonia* sp. fruticose lichens known as "British Soldiers."

Plate 4D. Multiple lichen colonies showing fruit-bodies (cups) of several fungus partners.

their way into the diets of people that way. In fact, not only did cows pass the toxin on in milk, but so did human females.

Of course, there are no studies where people have voluntarily exposed themselves to aflatoxins and allowed scientists to observe their deterioration, so we don't know for sure just how sensitive humans are to the chemicals. But in comparison to other carcinogens, aflatoxins are generally considered to be the most potent ones known to humankind.[4] People afflicted with the hepatitis-B virus are apparently at even greater risk, for studies have shown them to have a 900-fold increase in the incidence of liver cancer when aflatoxin was likely to have been a regular contaminant of their diets.[5]

One fact not to be overlooked in the legacy of the aflatoxin disaster in England was the impact it had in changing the way many common agricultural commodities were grown, harvested, and stored. Prior to 1960, there was very little in the scientific literature to suggest that molds, other than antibiotic producers (chapter 8), had such power to destroy or alter other life forms through the production of toxic chemicals. Afterwards, the scientific community began a rigorous search for other potential mycotoxin producers, and the agricultural community instituted a whole new set of standards for producing foodstuffs for human consumption. Some of these have caused significant increases in food costs, and these costs persist.

THE GENUS *FUSARIUM*

Among other molds able to make potent toxins are members of the genus *Fusarium*. They have a long and sordid history in the annals of mycotoxicology because they produce three distinct types of toxins:

1. Zearelenone, a chemical that mimics the action of the hormone estrogen and causes malformation of female reproductive organs in livestock.

2. Trichothecenes, a group of structurally related chemicals with the ability to induce a variety of clinical symptoms depending on level of acute or chronic dose.
3. Fumonisins, compounds able to cause serious and often irreversible damage to mammalian organs.

Of these, the trichothecenes are arguably the most notorious. One, T-2, is produced by *Fusarium tricinctum*, a mold commonly found on cereal grains that either have not been dried properly after harvest or that have been left unharvested in the field because of unfavorable weather. As the fungus colonizes its grain hosts, it produces T-2 as a metabolic by-product, perhaps to discourage rodents from consuming the grain before the fungus does. T-2, in turn, causes a condition known as alimentary toxic aleukia (ATA) in humans and other animals. The disease is characterized by multiple, subcutaneous hemorrhages, bleeding from the nose and throat, low leucocyte count, exhaustion of the bone marrow, and deterioration of throat tissue.[6]

In 1944, an outbreak of ATA in the Soviet Union caught the attention of Russian biologists, who relatively quickly associated the human disease with *F. tricinctum*, T-2, and moldy grain. Apparently, residents in the affected area occasionally had to delay their normal harvest of millet until spring because autumn rains left the fields too wet for machinery and draft animals. Such was the case in 1943. The harvest of overwintered grain in the spring of 1944 was a meager one, but by that time there was little else to eat in the war-torn Soviet Union. Unfortunately, moldy millet was part of the fare, and the consequences were grotesque. Approximately 10 percent of the people in one district of the Soviet Union died outright from ATA. One third of them died of strangulation because their throats were so inflamed and swollen that they couldn't breathe. Others were left so weakened that they suffered crippling secondary illnesses. Quick and careful efforts of Soviet scientists enabled them to identify the cause of the 1944 outbreak and aid residents in preventing another one. Unfortunately, the work went virtually unnoticed by researchers outside of that country until about twenty years later. Then the aflatoxin episode in England stimulated greater interest in the overall subject and caused scientists to review the literature from around the world with greater scrutiny.[7]

Subsequently, it was determined that a wide variety of crops including rice, corn, oats, sorghum, wheat, rye, and hay would support growth of *F. tricinctum* and be potential sources for T-2 production. Milling, cooking, and storage had little or no effect on the toxin. The only way to avoid it was to prevent *Fusarium* from growing on the grain in the first place. That meant harvesting when moisture levels were low and keeping the grain dry and in anaerobic conditions, if possible.

Another trichothecene of significance to people who produce our food—and eventually, to the rest of us—is deoxynivalenol (DON), a trichothecene produced by *Fusarium graminearum*. DON is also known as vomitoxin in some circles, in obvious reference to one of the symptoms it induces in afflicted animals.

In most years, DON contamination is not a serious problem, but if weather is unusually rainy in spring and early summer when corn and cereal grains are being pollinated, the mold and its mycotoxin can reach intolerable levels. Even these levels aren't very high, though, since DON will cause feed refusal in pigs at concentrations as low as 0.7 ppm. Other animals also either refuse feed or eat so little that they lose weight and are predisposed to secondary infections. Because of the potency of this mycotoxin, most North American feed processors won't buy contaminated grain. In a four-year period in the 1990s, farmers in the midwestern United States and eastern Canada lost $3 billion worth of wheat and barley because of *F. graminearum* and its noxious by-product. And in 1996, Ontario's winter wheat growers lost $100 million and New York farmers lost $12 million because of extensive vomitoxin contamination of their grain.[8]

Trichothecenes have another place in history besides the one described above. Following World War II, as victorious Russian soldiers left Germany and headed back to the motherland, they found themselves without food and hungry as they trod across the wasted countryside. Often, their only source of food was grain that had not been harvested from German-occupied lands during the previous autumn. Some was still standing and much more was lying in the fields. With no other alternatives before them, famished Russian soldiers ate the grain and the mycotoxins therein. It is estimated that as many as a million of them suffered from mycotoxicosis, and many of the million died. And they had *won* the war!

YELLOW RAIN

Another episode in human history is also linked to trichothecene poisoning. It began in the mid-1970s, when the U.S. government began receiving reports of chemical attacks being launched by the invading Vietnamese on the Hmong peoples of Laos and Kampuchea. The following account by a Hmong refugee was typical of the stories that were heard:

> I was up on a hillside across a stream from the village tending my poppies. My children came with my wife to give me some food and while we were all on the hill across from the village, the MIGs came. We saw the colored gas, and the people in the village began to lie down and go to sleep. Then the MIGs came back and dropped the bags. When the bags burst, the powder inside turned into a yellow gas-like a cloud. When it came down it was like yellow rain.
>
> We were frightened, but we had many relatives in the village so we went back. Most of the people were already dead. Blood was coming from their noses and ears and blisters appeared on their skin. Their skin was turning yellow. All the chickens, dogs and pigs were also dead. The people who were

not dead were jerking like fish when you take them out of the water. Soon some of them turned black and they got blisters like the others. Blood came from their noses and they died.

I took my wife and children away to another village and we drank none of the water before we left. But we all felt short of breath and sick in our stomachs.[9]

The term "yellow rain" became associated with the reports because a yellow powder or liquid was associated with most attacks, and the material sounded like rain as it landed on the roofs of buildings and leaves of trees.

The U.S. government immediately suspected that the Soviet Union was involved in whatever was being done to the Hmong tribesmen of Southeast Asia and dispatched army medical teams to investigate. Unfortunately, because the villages were so remote, reports of attacks took anywhere from four to six weeks to find their way out to someone who could notify government officials. By the time the medics reached the site, there was no evidence to indicate what might have happened. They remained baffled until sometime in 1980, when a Defense Department research chemist recognized that the symptoms expressed by victims of these aerial attacks in Southeast Asia were similar to what one might expect from the exposure of humans to massive doses of trichothecene mycotoxins. Samples from living and dead victims and from surrounding vegetation were submitted to various laboratories for analysis and, sure enough, trichothecenes were found in some samples.

With this evidence in hand, President Ronald Reagan and his key security advisors began openly accusing the Soviet Union of violating the terms of both the 1925 Geneva Convention and the 1972 Biological Weapons Convention. The Soviets denied everything, but the Reagan administration persisted with its accusations for the following three years. The examples of atrocities associated with yellow rain, together with some other incidents, were used to great effectiveness by the president to solicit and obtain vastly increased budgets for development of defensive chemical and biological weapons for the U.S. arsenal.

In the meantime, the press and the scientific community began a critical dissection and analysis of the evidence that yellow rain was indeed comprised of mycotoxins. They were not convinced by what they saw.[10] The whole thesis that trichothecenes were being used was based on the analysis of one leaf, allegedly collected from an area where one of these chemical attacks had occurred. That leaf had been submitted to a plant pathologist at the University of Minnesota who confirmed the presence of the toxins. A few subsequent samples submitted to the same lab also tested positive, and a food scientist at Rutgers University found trichothecenes in yellow powder collected by an ABC news team in Laos.

But there were problems with the data. A leading critic of the government's case noted that in all the samples, the ratios of the various trichothecenes differed and some were absent in some samples. She argued that if the chemicals were really being produced in some controlled environment to be sprayed over the countryside, they should be more uniform in their content. Critics also pointed out that the U.S. Army conveniently glossed over a report from its own laboratory, which had found no trichothecenes in over one hundred samples analyzed.

Finally, the reports from the Hmong people were brought into question. Despite what government charges had implied, all of the 150 to 200 reports actually came from just one refugee camp in Thailand. And even these reports were shown to be unreliable, as demonstrated by the case of a refugee who reported that 230 villagers were killed the first time he told his story, thirteen the second time, and forty the third time.

The government case for implication of mycotoxins was further eroded when a Yale University professor of entomology and an expert in Southeast Asian bee populations noted that the yellow rain samples he examined were loaded with the pollen of native plants. The shape and texture of the droplets resembled the feces of bees. Additional research into the natural history of Southeast Asian bees revealed that members of one species tended to fly in swarms and to defecate *en masse* while in flight, giving the illusion of yellow rain. Clearly there was a second plausible interpretation of the data, weakened only—but significantly in the eyes of some people—by the refugee reports from the field. However, these too became less credible as time passed.

As the episode drew to a close, many civilian scientists seemed to be convinced that the yellow rain issue was a hoax perpetrated upon the American people by the U.S. military establishment to increase funding for defense-related activities.[11] The Central Intelligence Agency held fast to its original allegation and contended that the reason no further reports of yellow rain came forward was because they had so elegantly exposed the Soviet plot.

The chemical attacks, if they ever did occur, finally stopped in Southeast Asia, but similar allegations resurfaced in the mid-1980s in Afghanistan, where the Soviet Union was engaged in another kind of war. Of course, that episode in human history is also over, for now, and the truth may only be known if the world is allowed access to the secret files of the old Soviet government.

FUMONISINS

Another potentially serious problem with mycotoxin poisoning has shown up in recent years in corn-growing regions throughout the world. *Fusarium moniliforme* and its close relatives grow on feed corn, sometimes as pathogens and sometimes as symptomless residents in healthy tissue. They produce several closely related chemicals known as fumonisins that cause various, often deadly, diseases in the vital organs of domesticated animals and, perhaps, esophageal cancer in humans.[12] The most grotesque of fumonisin-induced diseases in North America is a condition known as equine leucoencephalomalacia, or "hole in-the-head disease" of horses. As the toxin kills horses' brain cells, the membranes deteriorate and the contents flow together into a watery mess. Feed with as little as 10 to 20 ppm fumonisin can induce symptoms.[13]

When researchers became aware of the potential threat of fumonisins to the horse population of the eastern United States, they began a rigorous effort to test samples of feed for toxin content. Fumonisins turned up in minute amounts in over 60 percent of samples tested. The best guess was that some amount of the mycotoxin was in almost all feed corn, but it had not been detected because it was there in such small amounts. Now, however, buyers of seed corn who are fearful of potential lawsuits from horse owners are reluctant to purchase any fumonisin-contaminated seed. And the U.S. corn trade with other countries may be in jeopardy.

OTHER mycotoxins cause other problems in domesticated animals and, occasionally, in people. Slafframine from fescue grass infected with species of *Acremonium* causes uncontrollable drooling in horses, cows, and sheep. Spores of *Pithomyces chartarum* contain sporidesmin, a toxin able to cause facial eczema and jaundice when eaten by grazing animals. *Phomopsis leptostromiformis* on lupines causes severe liver damage in sheep, cattle, pigs, and horses worldwide wherever lupines are grown as a forage crop. In sweet potatoes, *Fusarium solani*—acting on chemicals produced by the plant only when the plant is stressed by external factors—produces a toxin lethal to cattle. And in fungus-infected celery, a toxin causes photodermatitis, an extreme sensitivity to sunlight, in people who harvest the crop. There are many more.

Despite the foregoing discussion, documented episodes of life-threatening mycotoxin poisoning in the developed world are relatively uncommon. Aside from the occasional case of animal poisoning or, less often, human poisoning from careless consumption of obviously moldy food, most food scientists, veterinarians, and toxicologists argue that the food supply is safe. There are no data to justify unreasonable concern about mycotoxin contamination except in developing countries with poor storage facilities. Nonetheless, people are urged to discard moldy food rather than risk exposure. Rigorous government inspection programs, sophisticated new grain-storage facilities, and a small amount of chemical and/or heat treatment of potentially contaminated feed lots seem to have minimized the incidence of these compounds. And plant breeders are actively engaged in efforts to develop plants that either resist fungus attack or don't support mycotoxin production if they are colonized.

Furthermore, agribusiness leaders and some scientists have publicly expressed concern about the worth of increasingly sensitive assay procedures for identifying concentrations of these toxins in parts per billion. Detectable levels are far below those known to threaten human or other animal health, and reports of their presence may raise undue alarm if made without adequate interpretation.

✦ *Sick Building Syndrome*

Scientists who study mycotoxins typically focus their attention on toxins produced as liquids or solids. However, recent years have brought increased knowledge about the number and variety of gaseous toxic metabolites that molds produce, as baffled building contractors and environmental engineers try to explain the often perplexing issue of "sick building syndrome." Molds in the genera *Acremonium, Aspergillus, Cladosporium, Paecilomyces, Penicillium,* and *Phialophora* grow freely in air conditioning systems and, sometimes, on fiberglass insulation.[a] In one assay of gases liberated by five common molds, the following were recovered: 8 hydrocarbons, 9 alcohols, 9 ketones, 7 ethers, 12 esters, 3 sulfur compounds, and 10 terpenes. Some were demonstrated mammalian toxins; others were suspect.[b] Clearly, volatile mold by-products must be considered as possible contributors to the health problems suffered by workers in some office buildings.

[a] I. M. Ezeonu, D. L. Price, R. B. Simmons, S. A. Crow, and D. G. Ahearn, "Fungal production of volatiles during growth on fiberglass," *Applied and Environmental Microbiology* 60 (1994): 4172–4173.
[b] A. L. Sunesson, H. J. Vaes-Wouter, C. A. Nilsson, and G. Blomquist, "Identification of volatile metabolites from five fungal species cultivated on two media," in ibid., 61 (1995): 2911–2918.

✦ Bookshelf: Graham Greene and Mycotoxins

Mycotoxins are little known outside the agricultural community and it is unusual, indeed, for them to find a place in contemporary fiction. Nonetheless, author Graham Greene chose aflatoxin as his weapon of choice for the elimination of his character Arthur Davis by compatriots in his story, *The Human Factor.* To his credit, Greene used aflatoxin in the "right" way, feeding small amounts to his victim over the course of several weeks, thus causing a gradual decline in health, eventually leading to a death that would not attract undue attention from his family or the coroner.

✦

CHAPTER 7

Mycoses: Fungus Diseases of Humans

As travel to remote regions of the world, especially to the Tropics, increased at the beginning of the twentieth century, many people brought home with them small but lasting mementos of their perilous adventures. These unexpected hitchhikers, nestled neatly between the fourth and fifth toes of their hosts, were destined to change forever the course of human history. Millions of residents of north temperate climates who had never even set foot outside of the confines of their hometowns would become so intimately acquainted with these tropical "souvenirs" that they would bathe them in the morning, carry them to their workplace during the day, and tuck them neatly into bed at night, often without even knowing they were there. The visitors were cultures of a fungus known to mycologists as *Trichophyton rubrum*. The disease it caused in humans would become known as athlete's foot.[1]

T. rubrum is one of several hundred fungi with enzymes capable of utilizing human flesh or body fluids to nourish their own growth. Such fungi cause diseases called "mycoses." While many mycoses are little more than nuisances to those who contract them and are successfully treated with readily available pharmaceuticals, some previously rare or misdiagnosed fungus diseases have become far more serious agents of human suffering and death in the last fifty years or so. In fact, while health statistics show mortality from all other infectious agents is on the decline, mortality from fungi is on a steady, sinister increase.

But enough of that for now. Let us begin at the beginning, which, for our purposes, is 1839, the year David Gruby, an Austrian-born scientist studying in Paris, proved for the first time that a human disease was caused by a microorganism. Gruby identified the species *Trichophyton schoenleinii* as the cause of a disease known as *favus* or ringworm. In so doing he preceded the much ballyhooed pioneering work on the germ theory of disease by Lister, Pasteur, and Koch by forty years. But, alas, as luck so often has it, this landmark contribution to biological science, advanced through knowledge of the fungi, has been overshadowed by work on lesser microbes deemed more newsworthy by medical historians.[2]

Today, a typical medical mycology compendium lists about one hundred different human pathogens. In addition, many more species trigger allergic reactions when spores are inhaled by people with a special sensitivity to them. Curiously, most of the fungi that cause diseases of humans are classified as "mitosporic fungi." They either have no sexual stage, or, if one exists, it simply hasn't been discovered yet. Where the sexual stage has been found, the fungi usually belong to the ascomycetes. Only a few significant mycoses caused by fungi related to the mushrooms have been identified, but there are unconfirmed reports that other such diseases have occurred. Some respiratory pathogens are also members of the primitive Oomycota.

The field of medical mycology and the list of mycoses have expanded so rapidly in recent times for several reasons. First, people in the medical community are simply more aware of the role of fungi in the cause of disease, and they have better tools to use in their search for them. When faced with a puzzling diagnosis today, a diagnostician is more likely to consider fungi as the culprits than she might have been ten or twenty or fifty years ago. In addition, the once laborious processes of culturing a suspect pathogenic fungus from diseased tissue, identifying it, and proving its pathogenicity have been supplemented and in some cases replaced with more accurate, rapid, and reliable assays.

A second cause for steadily increasing rates of incidence of fungal diseases as well as deaths due to them is that increased international travel has allowed humans and pathogens to be more readily transported into new areas. Developing countries, especially those in the Tropics, seem to harbor more fungal pathogens of humans, and increased travel to and from these countries has enabled more people to come in contact with more pathogenic fungi.

A third factor contributing to increases in mycotic diseases has to do with drug therapy used to manage some of the most pressing human health problems of our time. Modern chemistry has provided an array of powerful compounds that help transplant patients to accept their new organs and to prolong the lives of cancer patients by depressing their immune systems. An unfortunate side effect of using these drugs is that the body's normally effective defenses against fungal pathogens are weakened, and the likelihood of contracting a mycotic disease is increased. Thus, such therapies are often accompanied by one or more antifungal drugs as well.

The relentless spread of AIDS through the world's population has also left a trail of frail, weakened bodies that are highly susceptible to infections by fungi that might otherwise have little or no effect on the human system. In fact, many AIDS-related deaths are due to one or more fungus diseases. Dr. Michael Rinaldi of the University of Texas aptly describes the situation this way: "Given the right immunocompromised host, virtually any fungus can kill a human being. In a real sense, such individuals become living petri dishes."

Finally, as people live longer, even if they are in otherwise good health, their immune systems generally start to deteriorate, and they are, as with people on immunosuppressive drugs, more likely to contract fungal diseases. Those predisposed by a congenital condition such as diabetes are at even greater risk. Some of the more common mycoses are described below.

DERMATOMYCOSES — DISEASES OF SKIN

The most common mycoses, those best known and most frequently contracted by people, are the dermatomycoses—diseases of the skin and other keratinized tissues. Athlete's foot, mentioned at the beginning of this chapter, is one good example. It is actually caused by one of three closely related fungi and almost always starts in the webbing between the fourth and fifth toes. From there, it may spread to other parts of the foot and, very rarely, to other parts of the body. Other dermatomycoses include jock itch (infection of skin on the inner thighs) and ringworm of the hair, skin, or nails.

Ringworm isn't really caused by worms, of course, though it was once believed to be. The lesions on the skin develop as discrete circles with raised red margins and were assumed to be due to burrowing worms. Today we know better, but the name persists. Medical specialists know ringworms by terms such as *tinea capitis* (head), *tinea pedis* (feet), and *tinea unguium* (nails). The all-too-familiar jock itch is also a form of ringworm: *tinea cruris*. Each of the dermatomycoses is caused by a fungus in one of two closely related genera, *Microsporum* or *Trichophyton,* and each fungus is very specific in its ability to attack skin on just a limited part of the body. Animals can also contract ringworm of skin and hair, and these fungi readily spread to people, especially to children. Fortunately, the diseases usually have no serious consequences and are easily managed with appropriate medications.

Some dermatomycoses, like athlete's foot and jock itch, are products of our modern lifestyle. In more primitive cultures, where shoes and tight-fitting clothes are not the norm, these diseases are virtually nonexistent. However, the warm, moist environments associated with garb worn by more civilized peoples provide ideal places for fungus cultures to flourish. And as any victim of their appetites can attest, they do!

Fortunately, the fungi usually succumb to any of a wide array of over-the-counter, topical fungicides. However, the key to complete cure is continued treatment well beyond the time when itching regresses or lesions heal. Unfortunately, most people stop too soon. The fungi are suppressed but not eradicated and recurrence of these diseases is common.[3]

CANDIDIASIS: YEAST INFECTIONS AND THRUSH

Another mycotic disease, one that occurs with great frequency and generally causes its victims far greater discomfort than the dermatomycoses, is commonly referred to as a yeast infection or candidiasis. The pathogen, *Candida albicans,* is a normal inhabitant of the human mouth and throat, colon, and reproductive organs, where it lives in a delicate competitive balance with bacteria and other microflora of the digestive tract. Under most circumstances, it causes no known disease. However, when people are predisposed by some other factor such as diabetes, old age, pregnancy, and so forth, *C. albicans* can cause symptoms ranging from merely uncomfortable to life threatening.[4]

Skin and mucosal membranes in and around the genitalia seem to be especially susceptible to colonization by *Candida.* Women are particularly susceptible, so much so that it is unusual for a woman to go through her reproductive years without at least one significant yeast infection. For many women, recurrence of the disease one or more times each year causes not only unwanted physical irritation but emotional distress as well. Prolonged use of orally administered antibiotics, birth control pills, or steroids is a significant contributing factor, altering body chemistry and thus tipping environmental conditions against other microbes in favor of *Candida.* A creamy white, curdlike vaginal discharge accompanied by intense itching is the unfortunate consequence. Usually, a combination of changes in dietary habits, clothing, and/or medications, together with administration of drugs designed specifically to suppress *Candida* growth, are sufficient to eliminate symptoms. Yeast infections of male genitalia, known to physicians as balanitis, also occur but are far less common than those in women.

Candida also causes a disease of the mouth and throat in infants, the elderly, and some cancer patients. Of the latter, those preparing for bone marrow transplants seem to be at highest risk for contracting the disease and can expect some added discomfort from it. Oral candidiasis is called thrush, and it presents as a creamy white-to-gray membranous film on the tongue and oral cavity. Infants who become infected usually do so during passage through the birth canal of an infected mother. Once a newborn reaches the age of three days, it becomes immune to infection of the oral cavity until much later in life. In the elderly, diabetes or prolonged exposure to broad-spectrum antibiotics favor development of thrush. In patients of all ages, if thrush remains unchecked it could cause ulceration and swelling of the throat which could, in turn, impede swallowing and breathing.

Candidiasis of the scalp, fingers, lungs, and upper gastrointestinal tract and anus have also been reported, but these diseases are rare. Usually, the fungus remains localized in whatever part of the body it first developed, but systemic infections (where *Candida* is carried throughout the body in blood) have occasionally been reported. For that reason—and for many others—yeast infections should not go untreated.

✦ *More Irritating than You Thought?*

Since the mid-1980s, several physicians have reported that while treating female patients for candidiasis, they seem to have inadvertently—at first—relieved symptoms of other problems. These include premenstrual syndrome, sexual dysfunction—ranging from nymphomania to loss of libido—and depression. They hypothesize that the cause and effect are not just coincidental but that, in fact, some traditionally psychological disorders may be the consequences of above normal populations of *C. albicans.* Dr. W. G. Crook, author of *The Yeast Connection* and one of the pioneers in this area of medical investigation, suggests several possible mechanisms for the unexpected effects of the yeast.[a] They include toxin production by *C. albicans,* yeast-induced nutrient imbalance, and ethyl alcohol fermentation. Critics of Crook's work argue that evidence to support his contentions is wanting. In fact, clinical trials comparing reactions of patients treated with or without the antifungal drug nystatin showed no differences in the test populations. Nonetheless, the debate continues, with a small but vocal cadre of medical professionals convinced that *C. albicans* is responsible for much more disease than it gets credit for.

[a] W. G. Crook, *The Yeast Connection* (Jackson, Miss.: Professional Books, 1986).

SPOROTRICHOSIS

Another mycotic disease of skin, this one characterized by deep-seated, subcutaneous ulcers much different from the ringworms, is sporotrichosis. This disease is caused by *Sporothrix schenckii*, a common inhabitant of organic soil, peat, and rotted wood. Sporotrichosis was first described in the medical literature by B. R. Schenck, who reported a case in the United States in 1898. Shortly thereafter, clinicians in France made the first report of the disease on the European continent, and it is now known throughout the world. The record for the greatest number of cases in the shortest period of time appears to go to South Africa, where over three thousand workers in a Johannesburg gold mine contracted the disease in 1945–46.[5] Fortunately, the disease was properly diagnosed, the mine timbers and miners were treated with appropriate fungicides, and disease incidence plummeted. Today, sporotrichosis seems to be most prevalent among farmers, nursery and greenhouse workers, and home gardeners—the people most likely to be exposed to infested debris.

S. schenckii is introduced into people through wounds; it cannot penetrate intact skin. One common injury sustained by gardeners is a prick from a rose thorn, but any wound—even one caused by metal—could provide a route for entry. Greenhouse workers using infested peat may also contract the disease if they have open sores of any type on their fingers or arms.

Lesions induced by *S. schenckii* are usually restricted to the immediate area of infection where they remain open and ulcerous until proper treatment is administered. In the meantime, lymph nodes at increasingly greater distances from the actual site of infection may become swollen and tender. In rare cases, the disease has been reported to go systemic, causing secondary lesions elsewhere on the skin or on mucosal membranes of the nose or mouth.

Sporotrichosis can be difficult to diagnose because the disease is generally uncommon and not likely to be considered first among the possibilities entertained by most physicians. However, once it has been diagnosed, treatment is straightforward and effective. Where the disease is a known threat, workers are advised to wear gloves to cover existing wounds and reduce the chance for new wounds.

RESPIRATORY DISEASES

Cryptococcosis

There is a wide array of fungi with the capacity to serve as human respiratory pathogens. Many, including the three chosen for discussion here, are not just limited to the lungs but may be disseminated to other parts of the body as well.

First is cryptococcosis, caused by *Cryptococcus neoformans*.[6] The disease has been known since the late 1800s, having been first associated with a cancerlike lesion of a leg bone and subsequently as the cause of skin lesions, meningitis, and pulmonary dysfunction. Exposure to the pathogen and the potential for disease begin when spores of the fungus are inhaled by an unwitting victim. Most otherwise healthy people are apparently resistant to the fungus, but in a suitably predisposed person the spores can begin to grow in the lungs when inhaled. From there *C. neoformans* can enter the bloodstream and be carried throughout the body to cause lesions on the skin and in the bones, abdomen, and, especially, the central nervous system. There it causes cryptococcal meningitis, a usually lethal condition.

As with many other human diseases caused by fungi, crypto-coccosis is most severe in people predisposed by other factors. The disease occurs more often than would be expected by chance in people with leukemia and diabetes, and in patients being treated with steroids. Hodgkin's disease patients are also more likely to contract cryptococcosis. In fact, symptoms of the two diseases are so similar in some respects that one has been mistaken for the other. Also, for some unknown reason, males are more likely than females to get the disease.

People who work in and around areas where there are large quantities of pigeon dung are also at higher risk than others to contract cryptococcosis because the fungus grows well and re-produces abundantly on that substrate.[7] Laboratory results have shown that one gram of basic ordinary pigeon dung can yield up to 50 million spores. Hopefully, designers of buildings in today's big cities will keep those numbers in mind as they exer-cise their visions of form and function of these structures.

Histoplasmosis

Another human respiratory disease is caused by the fungus *Histoplasma capsulatum*. As in the case of cryptococcosis, histoplasmosis—as this disease is called—is commonly associ-ated with exposure to bird feces.[8] Spores of *H. capsulatum* are inhaled, and the fungus begins its life as a human pathogen in the lungs of its victims. As the lungs are colonized, symptoms re-semble those caused by tuberculosis, and without treatment, the disease can be fatal. Fortunately, it rarely is.

Chicken farmers are the highest-risk group for histoplasmo-sis because chicken dung is an ideal substrate to support growth of the pathogen. But urban residents living in areas where high populations of starlings roost are also at risk. As these words are penned, famed singer-songwriter Bob Dylan lies critically ill with a serious case of histoplasmosis that has caused inflammation of the sac surrounding his heart. To many previously uninformed people throughout the world, Mr. Dylan's misfortune has brought an awareness of the serious threats fungi can pose if they are ignored.

Aspergillosis

A third respiratory mycosis, aspergillosis, is caused by the action of one or more of eight different species of molds in the genus *Aspergillus*.[9] *A. fumigatus* is the most common culprit, but other species including *A. flavus, A. niger,* and *A. ochraceous* may be involved. Spores and mycelial fragments of these fungi commonly trigger asthmatic allergic reactions but they may also become invasive, causing areas of dead cells on the lungs that can expand and ultimately be fatal if unchecked.

Repeated exposure to certain species of *Aspergillus* seems to weaken the human body's ability to cope with these pathogens. Thus brewery workers who are constantly exposed to molds on barley develop "malt worker's lung" and farmers who are routinely exposed to moldy hay develop "farmer's lung." Some office buildings with faulty or dirty air conditioners also contain hazardous, spore-laden environments.

SYSTEMIC MYCOSES: COCCIDIOIDOMYCOSIS

Of all the fungus-caused diseases of humans, the systemic pathogens clearly pose some of the greatest threats. One of the most common is coccidioidomycosis caused by *Coccidiomyces immitis*.[10] The fungus grows in desert areas throughout the Western Hemisphere from Argentina to California, and coccidioidomycosis has been reported from all of these regions. In the United States, incidence of this disease in the San Joaquin

Valley of California is so high that it has become known there as "Valley fever."

The "official" name of the disease has a curious history. Ernest Dickson, who did much of the early work on coccidioidomycosis, was a bit of a poet as well as a medical mycologist, and he was compelled to make the name of this disease pleasing to the ear when spoken or sung. Thus, rather than giving it the more logical name of "coccidiomycosis," he added an extra "ido" to give us "coccidioidomycosis." And in that spirit, the following jingle was often presented as part of a tribute to this early work.

Some fungi produce a mycosis
Like blasto- or histoplasmosis
But for musical sake
The one I will take
Is coccidioidomycosis.[11]

Because of generally arid conditions in the southwestern United States, fungal growth and sporulation are somewhat limited there. However, in seasons or years with above average rainfall, fungal development is also more likely, and the potential threat from mycoses becomes higher. When you combine favorable weather for fungal activity with an increasing population of potential hosts as more and more elderly people move to the desert, the stage is set for a possibly serious epidemic of the disease.

Under natural conditions, spores are lifted into the air by wind and dust. However, human activities such as farming and construction, which tend to loosen soil and accelerate wind erosion, also encourage liberation of *C. immitis* spores. Following the Northridge, California, earthquake of 1994, 208 cases of coccidioidomycosis were attributed to the enormous amount of dust (and spores) raised by the quake.[12] Three people died from the disease after contracting it during the upheaval.

The primary route of *C. immitis* into the body is via the inhalation of spores. As with the aforementioned respiratory mycoses, most otherwise healthy people may develop a slight cough upon infection, but their immune systems will otherwise effectively stop the fungus soon after entry, leaving—if anything—little more than a barely discernible lesion in the lung.

However, if the fungus is able effectively to colonize its host, more serious symptoms may present after a seven- to twenty-eight-day incubation period. A patient may then experience symptoms including fever, chest pains similar to a broken rib or heart attack, shortness of breath, coughing, malaise, and fatigue. Brief episodes of anorexia are also common, with weight loss of 20 to 30 pounds over a two- to three-week period. The fungus may also be carried to other parts of the body via the bloodstream, causing disseminated lesions in the skin, subcutaneous tissues, bones (including joints), and guts. Coccidioidomycosis may eventually be fatal, but more often it doesn't progress beyond the very earliest stages. As the medical community becomes more aware of the existence of the disease and techniques for diagnosing it, early detection will surely continue to keep the disease from causing serious illness in most patients.

Control of fungal pathogens of humans is much more difficult than control of bacterial diseases because the chemistry of fungal cells is so much more like that of human cells. As a result, many early efforts to control mycoses with chemicals did so much damage to the healthy cells of the patient that they had to be abandoned. And even some of those used today cause the the patient to suffer excruciating side effects.

The first real breakthrough in therapy for mycoses occurred in 1951, when researchers searching for new chemicals to control fungal diseases of plants came across a chemical that had been discovered almost twenty-two years earlier. The chemical was from a mold, *Penicillium griseofulvum,* and had been virtually ignored since its discovery because the scientist who found it was looking for chemicals to kill bacteria, and this one had no effect on them.[13]

At first, the chemical, called griseofulvin, was only effective in controlling fungus disease of plants, but shortly thereafter it was also determined to alleviate symptoms of fungus diseases of humans and other animals. The results were astounding. A man suffering from ringworm of the scalp for sixty years was completely cured by taking griseofulvin. And an eight-year-old girl who, for her entire life, had been afflicted by a type of ringworm that covered her whole body, including her skin, hair, and nails, began to improve with griseofulvin therapy. Similar stories poured in from all over the world, and word of the success of griseofulvin spread. At one point, enthusiasm for griseofulvin was so high that medical specialists were predicting complete eradication of ringworm of the scalp in just a few more years.

But griseofulvin proved to be a bit of a strange drug. If a patient drank it, it cured infections on the skin and hair but had no effect on mycoses of internal organs. Furthermore, for some mysterious reason it worked best on diseases of the scalp but not quite as well on mycoses of the upper torso, becoming progressively less effective in the lower extremities. Fungus infections of the foot were virtually untouched by it. Nonetheless, griseofulvin was a welcome addition to a meager list of strategies for managing skin-infecting fungi. Two other materials in what might be considered the first generation of antifungal drugs were Amphotericin B and Nystatin. Both of these drugs were produced by organisms known as actinomycetes, and they proved to be effective in many cases where griseofulvin failed. Amphotericin B was particularly effective for the treatment of the deep-seated, systemic mycoses such as coccidioidomycosis, but it was accompanied by such unpleasant side effects that many who used it came to know it as "Ampho the Terrible."

Nystatin was discovered by Elizabeth Lee Hazen and Rachel Brown, scientists who were trying to isolate antibiotics from *Streptomyces noursei*.[14] Because of its promise as an agent against fungi, they named their new drug "fungicidin" but learned later that the word had already been used by someone else to designate another compound. The current name, Nystatin, was then conceived in partial tribute to New York State because it was extracted there and both women were employed by the state's health department.

Newer chemicals focus on disrupting the ability of pathogenic fungi to synthesize cell wall material. In particular, they impede conversion of the chemical lanosterol to ergosterol, an important fungal cell wall component derived from a chemical reaction that does not occur in human cells.[15] This results in drugs specifically targeting fungal cell chemistry, with few if any side effects for the humans who use them. One such compound that has shown good promise for treatment of yeast infections is cilofungin, another by-product of another fungus—this one a species of *Aspergillus*.

In finishing this chapter on mycoses, be comforted by the fact that while there is a vast array of fungi with the potential to cause disease in humans, most will not unless the body is predisposed by other factors. Mycoses are often difficult to diagnose but fortunately are rarely fatal for otherwise healthy people. Thus, patients who wait for diagnoses should not have to worry about life hanging in the balance. And, with most mycoses, changes in lifestyle combined with a growing arsenal of antifungal drugs can usually be used to effect a complete cure.

CHAPTER 8

Medicinal Molds

The preceding chapters and their extended descriptions of fungi as incitants of plant and animal diseases and all the misery associated with them may have led you to believe that you were right about fungi to begin with: they are rotten, disgusting, vile creations, hell bent on mucking up what is otherwise a pretty good life on Planet Earth. Let me assure you that for all the problems the fungi have caused, they have also extended our lives and made them far more enjoyable. The remaining chapters in this book should convince you of that. If not, stop by my office in Cornell's Plant Science Building. We'll chat . . . for as long as it takes.

The subject of this chapter is the fungi that enrich our lives by providing us with a pharmacopoeia that counts antibiotics, cholesterol-reducing drugs, and antitumor agents among its wondrous life-saving stores. In previous chapters, two such groups of drugs—the vasoconstrictors produced by the ergot fungus, and the fungicide griseofulvin from *Penicillium griseofulvum*—received some attention. Here you will learn about many more, some of which defy laboratory synthesis and are available only as they are extracted from fungi grown in culture.

PENICILLIN

The first of these medical marvels is the stuff of which legends are made, and I daresay that not one reader has escaped its influence (fig. 8.1). It was discovered quite by accident in the laboratory of Dr. Alexander Fleming, a medical research scientist at St. Mary's Hospital in London. Fleming was interested in

Fig. 8.1. Conidia of *Penicillium* are produced on a branched, brush-shaped hypha. The spores are blown by wind to new sites.

bacterial pathogens of humans, and in the course of his work he grew cultures of the bacteria—thousands of cultures—in petri dishes containing a nutrient-enriched agar. On that fateful day in 1928, as Fleming slid one plate after another onto the stage of his microscope and then off again, he was visited by a colleague, Professor Merlin Pryce. As Pryce entered the room, Fleming glanced at him briefly, but then resumed his work while carrying on a conversation. Suddenly Fleming stopped, and after a moment's observation said in his usual unconcerned tone, "That's funny. . . ." A contaminating mold was growing on the petri dish he was viewing. Sterile laboratory conditions being what they were in 1928, contamination by molds was hardly a rare occurrence. But on this particular culture, the bacteria surrounding the mold were dissolved. Instead of forming typical opaque yellow masses, they looked like drops of dew.

Immediately, Fleming transferred a piece of the mold to a new test tube because obviously he thought it had some importance. "What struck me," said Pryce, recounting the episode years later, "was that he didn't confine himself to observing, but took action at once. Lots of people observe a phenomenon, feeling that it may be important, but they don't get beyond being surprised, after which they forget. That was never the case with Fleming."[1]

One thing that undoubtedly piqued Fleming's interest in this particular mold was that the bacterium he was trying to grow, the one being killed, was a known pathogen of humans. A few years earlier, Fleming had discovered a chemical in mucus and in tears that could destroy bacteria that were not pathogenic to humans. But this was the first time he had found a chemical—albeit a fungal metabolite—that was apparently able to suppress a pathogenic microbe. Could this possibly be the long-sought-after and hoped-for silver bullet to cure human ills?

Fleming immediately put the rest of his research on hold and dived head first into experiments to learn more about this new mold and its juice. One of the first things he discovered was that the mold was antagonistic to not just one but a variety of human pathogens. And, much to his delight, Fleming learned that the purified juice showed little or no toxicity when injected into test animals.

When it came time to get a proper identification of this special mold, the services of a young Irish mycologist who just happened to be visiting the laboratory were sought. He identified it as *Penicillium rubrum,* and that was the name used in Fleming's first reports of his amazing discovery. Much later, the fungus was determined actually to be *Penicillium notatum.*

As the properties of the mold juice became better known, it occurred to Fleming that the substance ought to have a proper name. He chose the letters p/e/n/i/c/i/l/l/i/n, after the name of the genus of fungi producing it. But how to pronounce this word? Alas! In the true spirit of democracy, the issue was put to a vote of his colleagues. By a count of 7 to 3, we now know it as peni*cil*lin; the minority vote being for the alternative—pen*ic*illin.[2]

Fleming's enthusiasm for his new discovery continued to grow but the progress of his experiments was slowed by his inability to obtain sufficient quantities of purified penicillin for clinical trials on animals or for large-scale experiments in culture dishes. At one point, he employed the services of two young doctors with some extra training in chemistry, and they wrestled for several years with the problem of trying to increase the yield of penicillin, finally giving up in frustration. Much later, historians would record that at the time they quit, they had mastered all but a final, somewhat trivial, step in the purification of penicillin and were just a hair's breadth away from success.[3]

The trouble was that penicillin, the chemical, was just too unstable. It was easy to grow the mold in liquid broth and get an extract with antibacterial properties, but that extract contained other chemical by-products of fungal growth in addition to penicillin, and those other chemicals triggered toxic reactions in test animals. When, by chance, a relatively pure fraction of penicillin was obtained, it lost all activity within a week. These difficulties persisted for ten more years, but finally, in 1939, the task of purifying the drug attracted the attention of Drs. Howard Florey and Ernst B. Chain of Oxford University.

Chain was a chemist, and after innumerable failed attempts to isolate penicillin following traditional protocols, he tried using a relatively new technique—freeze drying—to separate unwanted extraction fluids from the desired product. It worked. A crystalline residue remained, and when Florey tested the substance against bacteria in culture dishes, it killed them. When injected into test animals, it caused no ill effects.

Unfortunately, the scientists scarcely had time to enjoy their success before an event of far greater import overtook them. In June 1940, the Germans began their great offensive across the European mainland. Was England going to be invaded? No one knew, but the Oxford team—which is what Chain, Florey, and their colleagues were now called—decided not to take any chances. They agreed that at all costs they must plan to save the miraculous mold which now held such obvious promise for battling a variety of diseases. In one desperate gesture, they dusted the linings of their clothes with spores of *P. notatum* in the hope that if something did happen to their lab or to them, at least one of them could escape with spores of the precious mold for future work.

As it turned out, the war did not slow the work of the Oxford team as much as initially expected, and by the end of June 1940 they had extracted enough penicillin for a crucial test. Then, fifty white mice were given a lethal injection of a virulent *Streptococcus*. Twenty-five served as controls and received no further treatment. The others were treated with penicillin every three hours over a period of two days and two nights. Florey and his assistant slept in the laboratory, waking every two hours to check on the mice. At the end of sixteen hours, all of the untreated mice were dead, while twenty-four of the twenty-five treated with penicillin remained alive.[4]

The choice of mice for this experiment was especially fortuitous. If Florey had chosen guinea pigs instead of mice, penicillin research may have been stopped dead in its tracks. For some still unknown reason, penicillin is toxic to guinea pigs, and a toxic reaction on the test animals would most certainly have squelched the enthusiasm of the Oxford team.[5]

With their first animal trials behind them, the scientists decided it was time to try their new drug on a human being. At that very moment, a case of such desperate proportions presented itself that a daring experiment was proposed. The patient was an Oxford policeman who was dying of blood poisoning caused by the bacterium *Staphylococcus aureus*. The pathogen had entered his body through a small cut on his mouth, incurred while he was shaving, and had since gone systemic. He had superficial ulcers all over his trunk and limbs and his lungs were failing. The attending physicians regarded his condition as hopeless and agreed to allow treatment with the penicillin.

On February 12, 1941, an intravenous injection of 200 mg of the mold juice was given to the dying man. Thereafter, he received an injection of 100 mg every three hours. By the end of twenty-four hours, the improvement in his condition was startling. His temperature went down, his wounds began to heal, and he began to feel better. He even sat up in bed and began to eat. Unfortunately, the meager supply of purified penicillin was dwindling fast. Some of it was recovered from the man's urine and reused, but two facts became painfully obvious. First, if the penicillin treatment continued, the man would undoubtedly be saved. But second, the treatment could not be continued because the supplies were almost exhausted. Eventually, there was none left and the man died.

The members of the Oxford team were saddened but not discouraged, and they set about to make more penicillin for future clinical tests. The next two patients, whose conditions were also judged to be as desperate as the policeman's, were completely cured. Another, an eight-year-old child, was well on the road to recovery when a blood vessel in her brain ruptured and she died of a cerebral hemorrhage. But the penicillin had done its job.

All that was needed now was a way to make enough penicillin to allow physicians to use it at will. British factories, preoccupied with manufacturing war materials, were unable to meet the challenge, so Florey headed to the United States. There he found his way to the U.S. Department of Agriculture's Northern Regional Research Laboratory in Peoria, Illinois. Among other things, scientists at this lab were trying to find ways to turn organic waste from the processing of agricultural products into something useful. One of those waste products was corn steep liquor, a stinky, sticky goo left over when starch is extracted from corn. The stuff had accumulated in the region to an embarrassing extent, and workers at the lab had experimented with it as a substrate for growing other species of *Penicillium*. With corn steep liquor as the substrate for *P. notatum,* the lab staff quickly obtained an output of penicillin twenty times greater than that obtained in Oxford, and the last hurdle appeared to have been cleared.

Researchers at the Peoria lab also contributed in other ways to the evolution of penicillin as we know it today. For one thing, they initiated a worldwide search for other molds that might produce higher quantities of penicillin. Armed forces pilots traveling to the far reaches of the globe were given the mysterious order to scoop up a bit of soil at each of their landing spots and return it to Peoria as soon as they could. *Penicillium* species were then isolated from these samples and tested for their productivity. The USDA team also hired a young woman who, among other things, was to go to the market periodically and gather samples of all the moldy produce she could find. "Moldy Mary," as she became known, returned one day with a culture of *Penicillium chrysogenum* from a rotten cantaloupe. It proved to be remarkably productive, and many of the strains used today come from that rotten Peoria melon.

Within a few years, techniques for the production of penicillin had been perfected, just in time to save thousands of lives of the Allied Forces fighting in the last stages of World War II. Millions of others since then have either been saved or been spared the anguish of long suffering through illnesses caused by bacterial pathogens. In 1945, Fleming, Chain, and Florey won the Nobel Prize for Medicine for their discoveries. Fleming was recognized for making the initial observations and conducting the first experiments using penicillin; Chain was credited for doing the chemistry that allowed purification of stable forms of penicillin; and Florey was honored for conducting and subsequently supervising clinical trials on use of the antibiotic to cure disease.

From the outset, scientists working on the penicillin project recognized the immense importance of their work to the future of humankind. Though they and various agencies seemed willing to put the promise of personal fame and monetary gain aside in the interest of human welfare, work on the mold still took its personal toll. Florey and Chain, once close friends who walked home from work together each night talking science along the way, had a painful falling out in their later years as their strong personalities kept them from resolving contentious issues. And both felt that Fleming got far more credit than he deserved for his serendipitous place in the drama. Fleming's alleged opening salvo on visiting the Oxford team lab—"I understand you have been working with *my* mold"—set the tone for an uneasy relationship that would evolve between him and the Oxford group. Pharmaceutical companies in both the United Kingdom and the United States who eventually learned to synthesize penicillin derivatives also engaged in prolonged and bitter legal wrangling over rights to the processes. Legal proceedings that had begun in 1959 were not finally resolved until 1980![6]

Despite the occasional down side, however, the drama associated with the discovery and exploitation of penicillin remains one of the greatest episodes in the history of biology, if not in the history of civilized peoples. No doubt some of today's finest scientists were inspired to pursue their chosen careers upon reading of the trials and tribulations of those engaged in penicillin research.

One of the very significant offshoots associated with the discovery of penicillin was that it caused scientists to become acutely aware that mere microbes had the power to make chemicals heretofore unknown to humanity. Furthermore, it was assumed that penicillin was probably not the only one with potential benefit to humans. Thus scientists began to scour the landscape worldwide, isolating every microbe they could find, testing each for active metabolites.

Penicillin was soon followed by griseofulvin, a chemical produced by the fungus *Penicillium griseofulvum* and, strangely enough, toxic to other fungi rather than bacteria. It quickly became and still is an important tool in the fight against human mycoses.[7]

As penicillin-resistant strains of bacteria emerged to challenge medical practitioners, a compound called cephalosporin was discovered. The fungus producing it was a species of *Cephalosporium* isolated from the coast of the island of Sardinia, at a site where a sewer was discharging waste into the Mediterranean Sea. That isolate continues to be the most important source of cephalosporins (e.g., Keflex®) to this day.

At first, metabolites of fungi were the only chemicals of significant medicinal value to be unearthed by the search. Eventually, however, another whole group of antibiotic chemicals produced by filamentous, bacteria-like organisms known as actinomycetes were discovered. Actinomycin, streptomycin, chloromycetin, tetracycline, and chlorotetracycline were all found as a result of investigations triggered by Fleming's observations. While it's likely that microbes producing these other antibiotics would have eventually been discovered anyway, it's equally likely that without penicillin to trigger the search, the others would have become known only precious years later.

Unfortunately, there is a down side to the penicillin story. About 10 percent of the human population is allergic to the drug, and in some people the allergic reaction can result in death. Thus, even though prescription of penicillin to cure a myriad of childhood ills has become commonplace, for each child that first dose must be closely supervised.

The other issue of concern with the now common use of antibiotics is that bacteria, the intended victims of these potent medicines, have begun to fight back. Antibiotic-resistant strains of bacteria have shown up with increasing frequency for two apparent reasons.[8] First, such widespread use of the drugs has exerted a selective pressure on some bacterial populations in favor of tolerant individuals. Second, people taking antibiotics frequently fail to see the treatment to completion. They begin to feel better soon after treatment starts and stop before the prescribed time has elapsed. Thus, low levels of more tolerant cells survive to give rise to the next generation of pathogens. That generation is likely to carry the higher drug tolerance, thus challenging the skills of the medical community and winning the battle far too often.

With the benefit of 20/20 hindsight and knowing about penicillin after the fact, one can find obscure references to a possible role played by penicillin in healing various maladies in ancient times. Lucy Kavaler (in *Mushrooms, Molds, and Miracles*) notes that as long as three thousand years ago, the Chinese put moldy soybean curd on boils and other skin infections. And papyrus scrolls from the sixteenth century B.C. indicate that Egyptians recommended rubbing moldy bread on all sorts of superficial lesions to speed healing. The French used moldy cheese for the same purpose, long before they discovered that the same cheese might actually taste good. In all cases, a prominent group of molds in the mix would have been species of *Penicillium*.

In another noteworthy episode in 1844, it was recorded that a young girl living in Edinburgh was suffering from a wound caused by a road accident. Nothing seemed to be able to alleviate the girl's suffering until the attending physician tried an experimental treatment that proved to be effective beyond all expectations. The girl was so thankful for this wonderful miracle that she asked the physician to write down the name of the treatment. The physician was none other than Joseph Lister, the father of antiseptic surgery. The treatment he wrote down was *Penicillium*. Apparently Lister used a crude mold extract to cure the girl of infection following her wound, but he made no other notes to that effect, and there are very few additional details about his knowledge or use of the therapy.

Before we leave the issue of molds and other microbes and their production of penicillin, let's consider some obvious questions. Why would fungi produce potent antibiotic chemicals like those that have been described? Are these chemicals of any value to the producer? No one knows the answers for sure, but a likely possibility is that antibiotics are produced as part of an effort by the fungus to gain a competitive advantage over the other microbes in the environment in which they live. Most of the fungi and other antibiotic-producing microorganisms live in the soil or in other complex environments with diverse microbial populations—hostile places, to say the least. Any advantage over competitors for scarce organic food materials would probably improve survival, and antibiotic production is one such advantage.

In more recent years, other kinds of drugs produced by fungi have found their way into the human pharmacopoeia. Some of special significance are the cyclosporins produced by several different molds, including *Cylindrocarpon lucidum* and *Tolypocladium inflatum*.[9] Cyclosporin A (Sandimmune®) depresses activity of the human immune system enough to give implanted organs a better chance to become established. Were it not for the discovery of this drug, the science of organ transplants might not have progressed with near as much speed and success as it has. Cyclosporin has also been so effective as a treatment for diabetes that some patients have been able to stop insulin injections altogether. The chemistry behind the effect is not well understood, but the many grateful patients who have been freed from further insulin injections have no complaints about that!

Another important class of drugs to emerge in recent years includes compactin and lovastatin.[10] Compactin is produced by several species of *Penicillium* as well as *Hypomyces*, *Paecilomyces*, and *Trichoderma*. Lovastatin is produced on a commercial scale by a culture of a strain of *Aspergillus terreus*, but in nature it is produced by fungi in at least four other genera. Both drugs and derivatives thereof inhibit cholesterol synthesis by blocking the action of an enzyme, HMG-CoA reductase. Unobstructed, the enzyme mediates the formation of mevalonic acid, the basic building block of the cholesterol molecule. However, if the effectiveness of the enzyme is reduced by the aforementioned drugs, so are cholesterol formation and associated diseases in mammalian systems. Lovastatin, as Mevacor®, and prevastatin, a hydroxylated form of compactin marketed as Pravachol®, are already used extensively for their effectiveness in contributing to reduced incidence of heart disease caused by atherosclerosis. Other derivatives are expected in the near future.

BEYOND THE MOLDS: FLESHY FUNGI FOR MEDICINAL USE

As a changing political climate and improved technology allow for better communication with East Asian cultures, the rest of the world has an unprecedented opportunity to learn about medical treatments practiced for hundreds, if not thousands, of years. One such practice new to modern medicine is the human consumption of fleshy fungi to protect people from certain ills and to cure them of others. Two species seem to have found particular favor in this regard. One is the cultivated shiitake, *Lentinula edodes* (plate 1C), long known for the unique flavor it imparts to many Far East dishes. The other is Ling Zhi or reishi (*Ganoderma lucidum*), a wood-decay fungus grown or collected only for medicinal purposes. Literature on the medicinal values of both species is voluminous, but most of the research has been conducted and published in China or Japan and, until very recently, has been greeted with healthy skepticism in the West. Nonetheless, both Chinese and Japanese people continue to include fungi of all kinds in their diets, and the natives do seem to live a long time with markedly reduced in-cidence of the vascular ills and cancers that plague the "West" of us.

In the case of shiitake, two extracts of the fungus have received the most attention. First is lentinan, a high molecular weight polysaccharide extracted from the cell walls of fruiting bodies or mycelia. The compound is comprised solely of glucose molecules joined together in a triple-helix arrangement. The complex physical structure is believed to be important in its activity.

Lentinan was first isolated for study in 1969, and at the time was found to have antitumor activity far greater than that exhibited by polysaccharides from other mushrooms. It apparently did not act directly against tumor cells, but rather enhanced the immune system of the host in several measurable ways. Since then, it has been found to activate natural killer cells, stimulate transformation of blood lymphocytes into lymphokine-activated killer cells, and enhance natural interferon and interleukin production.[11] In many instances, lentinan is more effective at slowing or arresting tumor growth if it is used in conjunction with other chemotherapeutic agents than if used alone. It also demonstrates some antiviral activity, having completely protected mice from what should have been a lethal dose of influenza virus. In one case, a patient testing positive for HIV but without AIDS showed significantly increased immune system function with a drip infusion of lentinan.

The second component of shiitake to receive considerable attention in laboratory and clinical studies is *L. edodes* mycelium extract (LEM). LEM is a preparation of powdered mycelium extract harvested before mushrooms begin to form. Chemically, it is a far more complex compound than lentinan, described as a protein-bound polysaccharide. Among other chemicals in the mix are at least five sugars (mostly pentoses), nucleic acid derivatives, several members of the Vitamin B complex, ergosterol, and lignin. LEM seems to have greater potential as an antiviral agent than as an antitumor one. Results of *in vitro* tests have shown it to inhibit HIV infection of cultured human cells and enhance effects of AZT against viral replication. In one comparative study, LEM actually was more effective than AZT in reducing giant cell formation. LEM has also shown promise in managing liver disease and improving liver function.

The Ling Zhi mushroom of China and the reishi of Japan are one and the same, both common names for the wood-decaying bracket fungus, *Ganoderma lucidum*. The fungus has a long history in Chinese medicine, with vague references to it extending back as far as two thousand years before Christ. Then, and for about 2500 years hence, it was believed to be the "herb of deathlessness." Anyone fortunate enough to eat it would have a long life, if not immortality.

For most of its history, reishi as a medical treatment has been the domain of Oriental herbalists. In recent years, however, interest in reishi has increased among Western health practitioners. Publication of the first English-language book on the subject, *The Mysterious Reishi Mushroom* by K. Matsumotto, in 1979 brought people in the Western world face to face with this ancient medical therapy.[12] Since then, as biochemical prospecting has become a legitimate scientific endeavor and Western medical practitioners have gained greater respect for their Pacific Rim counterparts, reishi has been the subject of increased scholarly research. Nonetheless, the list of ills cured or ameliorated by reishi is a bit overwhelming and beyond belief to even the most open-minded lateral thinkers. Terrance Willard lists numerous cancers, coronary heart disease, hypertension, bronchitis, hepatitis, arthritis, myasthenia gravis, and muscular dystrophy among the many diseases for which reishi will provide some measurable benefit.[13] The list of active ingredients is equally long and diverse and in need of further study. In addition to *G. lucidum*, other species of *Ganoderma* native to North America, including *G. tsugae* (plate 1D), *G. oregonense,* and *G. applanatum*—the well-known artist's conk—are purported to have some similar medicinal properties. Reishi, however, has a higher concentration of beneficial chemicals per unit weight and it remains the fungus of choice.

Christopher Hobbs presents a long list of other fleshy fungi purported to cure or temper symptoms in a wide array of human ailments.[14] Typical claims are that the fungi boost the immune system, thus slowing tumor growth; improve circulation and heart function; and improve digestion. Some commonly found in North America with beneficial effects demonstrated in human clinical trials include the following:

Mushroom	Common name	Comments
Armillaria mellea	Honey mushroom	See fig. 8.2. One study in China showed reduced hypertension.
Grifola frondosa	Maitake	Encouraging preliminary results shown for treatment of many cancers, hypertension, and hepatitis B.
Grifola umbellata	Zhu ling	Varying degrees of success when extracts are used in combination with other herbal medicaments and/or conventional cancer treatments.
Inonotus obliquus	Chaga	See fig. 8.3. Some success in using extracts for managing lung, breasts, and genital cancers.
Schizophyllum commune	Split gill	When used in conjunction with conventional therapies, significantly prolonged life for patients with various cancers.
Trametes versicolor	Turkey tail	See fig. 8.4. Improved survival rates for patients with one of several cancers.
Wolfiporia cocos	Tuckahoe	When used with metronidazole, nearly doubled cure rate of either metronidazole or tuckahoe decoction alone for viral hepatitis.

Laboratory studies with small mammals suggest that a large number of other fleshy fungi, especially mushrooms, have

Fig. 8.2. Honey mushrooms, *Armillaria* spp.

unique chemicals that may improve the quality and quantity of human life. If only a small portion of those suspected to produce beneficial medicines are found to do so, our store of treatments for many of our most stubborn ills will be greatly increased and diversified.

Of all the fungi with potentially healthful effects, none has attracted more attention in recent years than the slimy, gelatinous life form known as "Kombucha." This "organism" is the product of symbiotic growth of at least two yeasts, *Pichia fermentans* and *Kloeckera apiculata*, and at least two bacteria, *Gluconobacter oxydans* and *Acetobacter aceti*. The latter, *A. aceti*, produces a cellulose membrane that holds the rest of the organisms in a somewhat cohesive mass.[15]

When a small portion (i.e., 4 cubic inches) of a Kombucha culture is transferred to a glass container already containing a quart of sugared green or black tea, the culture not only grows rapidly, but converts the tea to a supposedly flavorful and health-

Fig. 8.3. A sterile, compact mass of
mycelium, characteristic of *Inonotus obliquus,*
protruding from a birch tree.

ful beverage in one to two weeks. When drunk at a rate of about
one and a half cups per day, Kombucha tea will, according to its
proponents, cure people afflicted with AIDS, prevent the development of cancer, lower blood pressure, improve sex drive, and
otherwise turn a dull life into a new adventure. Most of these
claims are substantiated only by anecdotal revelations from devoted users or those trying to sell the cultures to new initiates.
The drink has been popular in various parts of the world for at
least two thousand years, so it might indeed have some beneficial effects.

Medical practitioners in the United States have cast a dim eye

Fig. 8.4. Fruit-bodies of the turkey tail fungus, *Trametes versicolor.*

on Kombucha, publicly decrying its use because they fear the threat from contaminating microbes in the culture. Patients with cancer and AIDS are at special risk because their immune systems are already depressed and possibly unable to cope with accidental inhalation or ingestion of an otherwise benign fungus or bacterium. It is also a concern that many of the molds likely to contaminate Kombucha cultures are producers of life-threatening mycotoxins. Thus the cure could be far worse than the disease.

In concluding the chapter on fungi as producers of chemicals beneficial to human health, I am compelled to tell you about the common mold, *Aspergillus niger.* The fungus is found on rotting food and other bits of organic matter in homes as well as outdoors, and it poses some threat because of its ability to produce aflatoxin and other life-threatening mycotoxins. But *A. niger* also produces an enzyme known as alpha-d-galactosidase, a chemical that, among other things, tends to suppress methane production in the human digestive tract. Obviously, if alpha-d-galactosidase could be harvested, purified, and packaged for large-scale distribution, it would find favor not only among the windy members of the human race but also those who must stand downwind of them. Enter Beano®, a formulation of this important enzyme harvested from large-scale growth of the parent fungus. This unique product made from a fungal metabolite and now found on drugstore shelves throughout North America is yet another testimony to the immense potential for the fungi to improve the quality of our lives.

CHAPTER 9

Yeasts for Baking and Brewing

It was August in a land that would eventually be known as Persia. And it was hot. Far in the future, people would look back upon the year and call it 12,042 B.C. Tamar returned to her tent to continue preparing her family's stores for the coming winter and was immediately panic stricken as her gaze fell on three bowls of wheat meal she had mixed with a bit of water earlier that morning. Their contents should have been poured onto a clay palette and left to dry in the afternoon sun. But these bowls had been forgotten by Tamar in her haste to attend to her ailing son.

Now, five hours later, the contents had expanded to twice their original size and seemed to have come alive in an attempt to escape the confines of the bowls. This was a phenomenon not seen before by the earliest generations of civilized people, so she was convinced that some evil spirit had invaded her flat bread in the hope of sneaking into her body as she ate.

The prospect of finding more grain to replace this lot was bleak, so Tamar decided to make sure the grotesque mass was indeed spoiled before she discarded it. Apprehensively, she took a bite. Much to her surprise, a delightful, new flavor danced across her palate. The bread was much lighter than anything she had made previously, and she relished the ease with which her teeth cut through it. The taste captured her senses as no other food ever had. Eagerly, she took another bite and another and another. And then she rushed out into the plaza to share this miraculous gift from Mother Earth with her neighbors.

That story isn't true. I just made it up. But historians suspect that civilization's first conscious brush with the unique group of fungi known as yeasts probably happened in a similar way. From then on, life would never be the same. What had happened in these bowls?

Sometime during the grinding and mixing of the grain, perhaps when water was added, yeast spores must have found their way into the resultant dough. Because we now know that starch from the grain would not have allowed the yeasts to grow much, there must also have been a source of sugar—perhaps honey. As the yeasts digested the sugar, they grew and multiplied and produced bubbles of carbon dioxide that were trapped in the moist dough, thus giving it its final light texture. The yeast cells also added a unique flavor that made Tamar's serendipitous discovery a culinary marvel. But what about those yeasts? What, pray tell, is so special about them?

Yeasts are like other fungi in that their cells contain true nuclei, their cell walls are of similar chemistry, and at some point in their life cycles, they reproduce by way of spores. However, their reproductive habits and vegetative growth are quite unique.

First, yeasts usually exist only as single cells (fig. 9.1). A few produce mycelium or chains of cells that vaguely resemble mycelium, but a typical laboratory culture is a slimy mass of cells ranging from pale milky to bright red or orange in color. On average, the cells measure 2 to 4 micrometers in diameter—about five times the size of a bacterium. The nucleus within each cell is difficult to see with a conventional microscope.

When yeast cells reproduce asexually, the process is relatively simple. They either bud, or they divide by binary fission. Budding is a process whereby a small part of the wall of the parent spore weakens and enlarges until it has created a second spherical body almost as big as the parent. Then the nucleus divides, a chitinous plate is laid down between the two bodies, other wall materials are deposited on the membrane, and the daughter

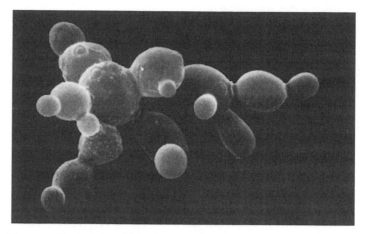

Fig. 9.1. Yeasts are unlike other fungi in that their cells are spherical and reproduce by budding—as seen here in *Saccharomyces cerevisceae*—or by binary fission. (Photo by J. C. DuPreez, University of the Orange Free State, Bloemfontein, South Africa.)

cell is pinched off to grow and bud again. Binary fission, in contrast, occurs when a mother cell grows to almost twice its original size, the nucleus divides, and a cell wall forms between the nuclei to yield two daughter cells.

If yeasts are to reproduce sexually, cells of compatible strains growing in close proximity to one another must be so close that they will grow together. Nuclear fusion follows, then meiosis. For most true yeasts, sexual reproduction is as ascospores borne in membranous sacs. They belong to the Ascomycota, but the sacs are not contained in fruiting bodies. They lie unprotected on the surface of the substrate. A few other yeasts are representatives of the Basidiomycota. The fungi reproduce sexually by way of basidiospores borne on the surface of a basidium, and the yeastlike phase is just one stage in the vegetative growth of the fungus.

Fungi that have two growth phases, one that is yeastlike and one that is filamentous, are called dimorphic fungi, and their evolutionary relationship to true yeasts is uncertain. In most books about fungi, especially fungi that cause human diseases, you may see reference to the "yeastlike growth phase" of a particular fungus that is, in all other respects, clearly different from true, single-celled yeasts.

There are literally hundreds of known species of true yeasts and probably hundreds more yet to be described, but the subjects of most of the rest of this chapter, the culprits in Tamar's historic moment, are all in one genus, *Saccharomyces*. Literally translated, the name means "sugar fungus" and these fungi do, indeed, thrive on substrates with high—but not too high—concentrations of sugar. What's more, if *Saccharomyces* cells are provided with an environment rich in sugar but lacking in oxygen, they do a curious thing. They secrete enzymes that reduce the sugar to two simpler chemicals, carbon dioxide and ethyl alcohol. The process is called alcoholic fermentation.

BAKING WITH YEAST

In making bread, sugar—often in the form of honey or molasses—is added to the flour and water mixture to nourish yeast growth. Then the patient baker moves on to other chores while the yeasts work their magic. And what magic it is! Carbon dioxide bubbles produced as the enzymes work on the sugar are trapped within the dough, causing it to take on an apparent life of its own. It "grows"—rises—to a size three times that of the original mass, only to be punched down by the baker so it may rise again. Then it is baked in an oven. The carbon dioxide lightens and flavors the bread while the other main product of yeast metabolism, ethyl alcohol, evaporates during kneading and baking. In the thousands of years since its discovery, leavened bread has become a dietary staple for people throughout the world. Floured grain and yeast make a nutritious meal whose flavor can be varied a hundred different ways with different grains and different strains of yeast and other additives.

CHAPTER 9

Brewing with Yeast

Although carbon dioxide from yeast-mediated fermentation may be the most important end product for the baker, there are other people in the world who are much more concerned about the other product of the fermentation equation. These folks have their eyes on the ethyl alcohol, and they take great pride in adjusting the fermentation environment to yield beverages with uniquely desirable qualities.

If sugar is fed to *Saccharomyces* in the form of grape juice, the product of alcoholic fermentation is wine.* If sugar is supplied as partially rotted—by another fungus—rice, the product is sake. And if sugar comes from partially germinated barley seeds—brewmeisters call it "malt"—the product is beer. Hops added to the latter give it the flavor modern-day beer drinkers have come to identify with the drink, but that addition is a relatively recent twist to an ancient brew.

Wine is almost as old as civilization itself, and the process for making it—for putting the yeasts to work, if you will—has changed little since those earliest days.[1] To begin, grapes are harvested and the juice is extracted by squeezing, pressing, or stomping. For red wines, the skins are left on during juice extraction and the pigment becomes part of the wine. For white wines, the skins are removed. Inevitably, the juice is contaminated with bits of grape skins, stems, seeds, and other debris, but these are of little concern to the vintner because these "additives" contain chemicals that give many wines their distinctive flavors.

Some naturally occurring yeasts (e.g., species of *Kloeckera, Hanseniospora,* etc.) also find their way into the juice, or "must"

---

* Sorry! Fermentation of juices from other plants may yield palatable drinks but in the strictest definition, wine comes only from fermented grape juice. Fresh juice, at that! Thus, dandelion wine, cranberry wine, and apple wine are twentieth-century misrepresentations of a word coined long ago for a very specific purpose.

in vintner's terms, as it is extracted, but they're welcomed and actually begin the fermentation process as soon as they are immersed. Unfortunately, those wild yeasts can't tolerate alcohol concentrations above about 4 percent, a level hardly acceptable to either vintner or customer.

For higher alcohol levels and to ensure more predictable flavors, a special wine yeast, *Saccharomyces ellipsoideus,* is added to the mix. Typically, strains of wine yeasts tolerate alcohol levels of about 12 percent, and most have been selected after many years of trial and error for the flavors they impart to the wines as well as for their alcohol tolerance.

Unfortunately, yeasts aren't the only microbes likely to grow in fermenting juice. Other fungi, bacteria, and a few minute insects are common cohabitants. Bacteria of particular note—because of their ability to convert ethyl alcohol to acetic acid—are in the genus *Acetobacter.* If left unattended, these noxious intruders can quickly turn a prized Chardonnay into marginally palatable vinegar—an unfortunate turn of events, at best! To counter the actions of *Acetobacter* and other possible contaminants, sulfur is added to the must to kill the hitchhikers and preserve the integrity of the wine. Sulfuring, as it is called, is accomplished on an industrial scale by bubbling sulfur dioxide through the brew; home wine makers do the same thing by adding small amounts of sodium bisulfite in the form of campden tablets. Fortunately, the wine yeast can tolerate slightly higher levels of sulfur than other microbes, and soon after sulfuring is complete, the fermentation begins again.

If there is a lot of sugar in the juice or if extra sugar is added, then the fermentation continues only until the level of ethyl alcohol becomes so high that it actually kills the yeast. In that case, some sugar remains unconverted and sweet wine is the product. Dry wine is made from juice with less sugar to begin with, and the result is more complete utilization of the available sugars.

Any one yeast cell lives only for a few hours, and as the fermentation runs its course, there is constant birth, growth, and death in the teeming ecosystem of the fermentation vessel. Dead yeast cells—lees to vintners—not only cloud the wine but may also mar its flavor and thus must be removed at regular intervals. One way to clarify wine is to carefully pour the mix into new containers, leaving behind the lees that have settled on the bottoms of previous ones. The process is called racking. Negatively charged fining agents, such as charcoal, egg white, or gelatin, may also be added to the wine because they help to speed the settling of positively charged spent cells and other contaminants, thus minimizing the number of necessary rackings.

Several environmental factors must be controlled for fermentation to occur at a predictable rate. One of those is temperature. Not only is there an optimum temperature range for fermentation, but maintaining that temperature is complicated because some fermentation reactions are exothermic—they give off heat. Thus, the mix must be kept in a place that is cool enough to prevent overheating but not so cool as to slow conversion of the sugar or threaten the vitality of the yeast. Few natural places have the constant temperatures that are most conducive to fermentation. Underground caverns are one of them, and this bit of technology, discovered thousands of years ago, still has its place in the making of fine wines today.

Another factor the vintner must monitor closely is acidity. Conditions in the vineyard vary from year to year, and as they do, grapes may yield juice that is either too acidic or too alkaline for optimum fermentation. The juice thus has to be adjusted accordingly. If it is too acidic, the cause is most likely excess tartaric acid—the natural acid in grape skins. Fortunately, this acid precipitates out of solution at low temperatures, and chilling and reracking the wine will settle the tartaric acid crystals at the bottom of the vat.

Coping with wine that is too alkaline can be far more complicated. Records from ancient times indicate that a handful of pigeon dung added to the wine would correct the situation. Thank goodness modern-day commercial wine makers are subject to laws that specify very precisely what additives may go into wine, and pigeon dung is not among them. More acceptable forms of acid are now available.

When fermentation is complete and the wine has been racked for the last time and bottled and sealed, it is usually still not ready for the table. Continued aging allows a small amount of the alcohol to react with certain organic acids to produce chemicals known as esters. Esters have strong, fruity aromas, even in very low concentrations. If given enough time to form, they'll add distinctive flavors, especially to red wines.

The foregoing discussion shows that many different elements work together to make the wine that eventually ends up on the banquet table. While commercial wines produced on a large scale are derived from six or seven standard varieties of grapes, literally hundreds of other kinds of grapes are grown in backyard vineyards around the world. Each has its own unique flavor. Variations in climate (rainfall, temperature, length of season) cause changes in the sugar content of the grapes from year to year and may also determine the composition of the population of native microflora on the grape skins. Strains of yeasts used to produce different wines may also vary from batch to batch and from vintner to vintner. Indeed, some strains are trade secrets guarded with security rivaling that at the doors of Fort Knox. And some wines, not true wines in the strictest definition, are adulterated with added sugar, juices, or even wine from another batch.

There is also the unusual situation where a mold as well as a yeast plays an important role in the nature of the final product.[2] Legend has it that through most of the eighteenth century, when the great vineyards of Germany were still owned by the Church, no one could begin harvesting grapes until they got the official word from the prince-abbot. In one particular year— some say 1716, others 1775, and still others 1783—it seems that the notoriously absent-minded abbot forgot to send out a messenger with instructions to begin the harvest. The monks of Johannesburg waited, patiently at first, but with increasing concern. Finally, frantic with worry as their grapes ripened and passed their prime, the monks dispatched a messenger of their own to get the needed permission. But this man was detained by highwaymen—or a pretty woman—and never returned. A week or so later, a second messenger was sent forth, and he also failed to return. Finally, a third messenger did get through—and came back with approval to begin the harvest.

And so it began, albeit four weeks late. By that time, some of the crop had been attacked by a mold. These grapes were so shriveled that they looked like raisins and were kept separate from the unaffected grapes. But finally, they were still used to make some wine so the monastery could reach its yearly quota.

Much to everyone's astonishment, the shriveled grapes produced the richest wine with the most unique and pleasing flavor the monks had ever tasted. The reason was that the grapes had been rotted by the common gray mold, *Botrytis cinerea* (fig. 9.2). Infection by *Botrytis* had caused the grapes to lose water, thus increasing their relative sugar concentration. In addition, the mold imparted a unique flavor of its own.

Today, grapes in several historic European wine-making districts are purposely held back from harvest until infection by *Botrytis* has elevated them to a desired level of flavor. Special strains of wine yeast have also been selected to complement the effects of mold. The alcohol content of wines made from these ingredients is slightly higher than conventional wines, and the taste is described as "distinctive" but not moldy. *B. cinerea* has become known among vintners as the "noble rot" because of its flavorful impact on grapes and wine made from them. Picolit, Gewürztraminer, and Vouvray are some of the wines made from botrytized grapes. Chateau d'Yquem, otherwise known as liquid gold, is considered by many to be the best.

Sake or rice wine is another drink produced from the combined effects of a mold and a yeast. This popular beverage, originating in the Far East and now drunk throughout the world,

Fig. 9.2. Grapes infected with *Botrytis cinerea,* the noble rot, may look bad but are used to make unique—and expensive—wines. (Photo courtesy of the Department of Plant Pathology, University of the Orange Free State, Bloemfontein, South Africa.)

has rice rather than grape juice as its raw material. The starch in rice is completely resistant to degradation by yeast enzymes and must be converted to sugar first. For this job, another common mold, *Aspergillus oryzae,* is put to work. Mold, yeast, and rice are mixed together in one large vat, and as the mold breaks the rice down into simple sugars, they in turn are reduced by the yeast to ethyl alcohol and carbon dioxide.

In brewing beer, elements of both wine and sake production are employed.[3] Barley is the raw material for this universally loved beverage, but as it comes from the field, it, like rice, is composed largely of starch that is resistant to yeast degradation. Fortunately, as barley seeds germinate, the starch in them is naturally converted into sugar. Barley seeds are moistened and spread out on the floor of a warm, humid room where they can begin to grow. Within hours, however, the experienced brewmeister determines that the conversion has proceeded far enough, the process is stopped by heating, and the partially grown seeds, now known as "malt," are dried and roasted.

To continue brewing, malt is mixed with water and additional sugar, and the mix—now called "wort"—is boiled briefly. After it has cooled to about 90°F, the appropriate yeast is added. Some brewers use strains of *Saccharomyces cerevisceae,* or baker's yeast, while others prefer *S. carlsbergensis.* Both species are closely related but are distinctly different from wine yeasts. Brewmeisters typically add another ingredient to the wort: the dried flowers from a vine known as hops. Two kinds of hops are usually used. One is added as the mix is brought to a boil, and a second—the finishing hops—is added just minutes before the heat is turned off. The yeast does nothing to the hops, but hops add a bitterness that produces the characteristic flavor of beer.

After fermentation is allowed to proceed for a few days or perhaps a week, the wort is siphoned off to a clean container, allowed to ferment a short time more, and filtered. Then it's bottled or kegged with a bit more sugar, and the carbon dioxide released during fermentation in the closed container gives beer its carbonation. Commercial brewers pump carbon dioxide directly into the kegs to get clear beer with a good head.

✦ *Lambic Beer*

One commonly cited difference between brewing beer and making wine is that beer brewers are sticklers for cleanliness while vintners tolerate some extraneous microbes from grape skins in their must. For some wines, in fact, those extras are welcome because they give the wine its unique flavor.

Notable exceptions to the rule of sterility in the beer world

are lambic—or "lambeek"—beers from the Senne Valley in
Belgium.[a] Kriek lambic, with crushed cherries added, and
frambozen lambic from raspberries are two typical brews.
Lambics use no added ale or lager yeasts. Instead, the wort is
fermented in open-air vessels in wooden buildings with whatever yeasts fall out of the air or ride in on the skins of the
fruit. Not surprisingly, the flavor of lambic beer is far removed
from traditional hopped beers, but it is still pleasing to the
palate and commands a high price in the market. Efforts to
brew lambics in other parts of the world have met with limited
success, but the connoisseur still looks to the south of Brussels
for the real thing.

[a] See Butcher, *Ale and Beer.*

People who study the evolution of human cultures would be
remiss if alcoholic beverages, brewed with the unswerving de-
votion of millions of yeast cells, were not placed highly on their
list of important factors. Archaeologists have determined that
from the earliest of times, perhaps as long 25,000 years ago,
wine and beer were drunk by people of all social strata and all
ages.[4] In areas where climate and soil were favorable for growing grapes, wine seemed to be the beverage of choice. Beer was
more popular in cooler or drier climates where the culture of
cereal grains was common. While there is still some disagreement about which came first—wine or beer—there is little
doubt that both were very popular.

In the Middle East, and perhaps elsewhere, alcoholic beverages served several purposes. Some people drank them in mod-
eration with meals to add flavor and to mellow the moment; witness Christ's miraculous transformation of water to wine for a
feast at Cana (John 2:6–10) and the choice of wine to represent
his blood at the Last Supper. Others imbibed these intoxicants
to excess to dull their senses, and still others drank them be-

cause they were the only potable liquids available. Water in rivers and oases was often fouled by sewage from the people and animals living nearby, and it was clearly not fit to drink, and milk spoiled quickly in the heat of the day. But few noxious microbes could survive even modest levels of ethyl alcohol, and the relatively clean liquids rehydrated many a spent soul. Lucy Kavaler relates that by the time of the Pharaohs, mothers concerned about the nutritional value of their children's school lunch sent them packing each day with a supplemental jug of beer.

As civilizations evolved, so did the culture of grapes and grain and the techniques for transforming them into pleasurable food and drink. Efforts of the U.S. government to stem the tide by making intoxicating beverages illegal in 1919 met with such stiff resistance from the public that the edict was rescinded fourteen years later. Today beer brewing and wine making are multibillion-dollar industries. They have been so successful in the United States that the average American consumes about 41 gallons of alcoholic beverages per year: 35 for beer, 3.5 for wine, and 2.5 in distilled spirits. About 50,000 people are employed to sate the nation's appetite for these drinks, and their products are taxed more heavily than most other businesses, making the industry—and the yeasts on which they are built—significant contributors to the U.S. economy.

In the mid-1980s, medical scientists began to publicize results of research indicating that moderate alcohol consumption might actually benefit human health. The focus of their attention was red wine: it apparently reduced heart disease among the French, who have traditionally had diets with the highest fat content of any culture in the civilized world. Based on fat intake alone, the French should have had high rates of coronary heart disease, but research showed that they didn't. Indeed, they had lower rates than the Americans or the British and were comparable to the rates in China or Japan.[5] The cause for the "French paradox," as it is known, continues to be the subject of debate among members of the medical community. Additional research has shown that while the French have generally high levels of "good" HDL cholesterol, the levels are not much higher than those of people in countries with more heart disease. What is different, apparently, is that because the French engage in moderate wine consumption throughout their day, they are better able to sustain consistently high levels of HDL cholesterol. This, in turn, reduces blood platelet aggregation, and thus the chances for clotting and the blockage of circulatory pathways.

Scholars reviewing the older literature for signs of additional medical benefits from alcoholic beverages have not had to look far. Numerous passages in the Bible refer to the healing powers of wine; Plato is known to have extolled its beneficial effects— "No thing more excellent nor more valuable than wine was ever granted mankind by God"—and there is some evidence that Homer used wine to heal wounds. More recently, Louis Pasteur wrote that "wine is the most healthful and most hygienic of beverages."

For all the good that might come from regular, moderate alcohol intake, we know far more about the damage that results from regular, excessive intake. Unfortunately, a certain percentage of the human population simply cannot self-regulate its consumption of alcoholic beverages.[6] For them alcohol has become a sinister crutch they cannot cast away. About 1.5 million Americans are currently in alcohol recovery programs. It is likely that at least as many have yet to realize the trouble they are in. Ethyl alcohol claims about 100,000 lives annually; 20,000 of them are people in the nineteen to twenty-four-year age group who die in alcohol-related accidents. The economic cost to U.S. citizens for all the programs related to the prevention and treatment of alcoholism is estimated at $125 billion.

One can neither praise the yeasts for the joy they've brought nor blame them for the misery they've wrought. All they are trying to do is survive, to perpetuate their own kind. Somewhere along the evolutionary trail, some species acquired the ability to carry out unique chemical reactions, and now humankind must take responsibility for harnessing them for their own use or abuse, as the case may be.

 A Feast of Yeast?

Dissertations on the roles of yeasts in human affairs almost always gravitate toward the contribution of these fungi to alcoholic fermentation. But yeasts are good sources of nutrition in and of themselves.[a] They are high in B vitamins and protein, and are far more efficient at using raw materials than poultry or livestock are. For instance, one person has calculated that one acre of land devoted to the production of carbohydrates could yield 800 pounds of protein in the form of yeast but only 70 pounds in the form of meat or milk protein. Numbers like these are of special interest to leaders of Third World countries who are trying to cope with diminishing arable lands and burgeoning populations. The only limitations seem to be that yeasts contain relatively high amounts of nucleic acids, which can be toxic if eaten in excess, and they are low in the amino acids tryptophan and methionine. Genetic engineering could probably address the latter issue, but if one were to depend solely on yeasts for protein, nucleic acid toxicity could become a problem.

[a] See G. Reed and T. W. Nagodawithsana, *Yeast Technology*, 2d ed. (New York: Van Nostrand Reinhold, 1991).

Edible and Poisonous Mushrooms

If you have an interest in collecting and eating fungi from the wild, you're not alone. Millions of people throughout the world are avid mushroom hunters, and many depend on their collections as important sources of food as well as income. In eastern Europe, especially, mushroom hunting is a favored family pastime, and many a weekend will find families spanning three generations or more wending their way through field and forest, baskets in hand and eyes glued to the ground before them. North Americans are generally more reluctant to enjoy foraging for this unique complement to Mother Nature's fare, for it often means foregoing a round of golf, an afternoon of football watching, or a day at the beach. However, a select few do have the character to make the really tough choices in life, and for these hunters a diverse and delectable array of mushrooms and other fleshy fungi awaits. Each passing year finds more and more people warming to the idea, and now mushroom hunting clubs can be found in most large cities. In fact, wild mushrooms represent such an important source of income for some residents of the western United States that there is genuine concern that mushrooms are being overpicked as people flock to the national forests to reap nature's bounty.[1]

If you want to join the special world of the wild mushroom hunter, then it's important to begin at the beginning and proceed slowly, with caution.

First, you must have the right equipment. A basket or some other rigid container is a necessity—it is important to be able to preserve the structure of each mushroom that you collect until you've had a chance to identify it. You definitely don't want to risk having specimens squashed at the bottom of a soft bag or in your pocket. If carrying a basket doesn't quite suit your self-image, then a container such as a lunch box, tool box, tackle box, or ammunition box will do nicely.

Bring along a notebook and pencil to make notes about the site where you have collected a particular specimen as well as any other pertinent observations you might wish to record. Also have a knife handy for cutting specimens away from wood and for cutting soil-laden stems from familiar mushrooms. And don't forget a trowel for digging mushrooms from the soil, and paper bags for separating specimens.

Each specimen or group of similar specimens must be kept separate from the rest. Do that by wrapping them loosely in wax paper or by placing them in the paper bags. *Do not* place mushrooms in plastic bags. Plastic holds too much moisture, hastening the deterioration of fragile specimens and encouraging growth of potentially toxic bacteria on the surfaces of others.

If you are unfamiliar with the kinds of mushrooms you might expect to find at a particular site, consult a local expert. Many high school and college biology teachers have a rudimentary knowledge of wild, fleshy fungi, and some larger universities and science museums employ people who study only fungi and know them very well. County Cooperative Extension offices of state agricultural departments can also usually steer you toward other local experts in a particular area.

You'll also need at least one and preferably several books to help you identify the fungi you collect. I like the following:

The Audubon Society Field Guide to North American Mushrooms by G. Lincoff (A. A. Knopf, New York); *Mushrooms Demystified* by D. Arora (Ten Speed Press, Berkeley, Calif.); *Mushrooms of North America* by O. K. Miller (E. P. Dutton, New York). These books and many others have excellent color photographs and/or line drawings and thorough descriptions of when and where particular species may be found. Most also have dichotomous keys to the various groups of fungi. In order to use these keys, you'll probably have to acquaint yourself with some new terms, but fortunately most popular books include diagrams to familiarize you with them.

Keep in mind the following while collecting fleshy fungi, especially if you are planning to eat them:

1. *Dig rather than pick.* The stems of some of the most deadly mushrooms rest in below-ground cups known as volvas. If a mushroom with a volva is casually plucked from where it is growing, the volva will likely become detached and remain underground, unseen. To find out if there are any underground structures, dig carefully and lift gently.

2. *Look for evidence of spore color* on surrounding vegetation, caps of adjacent mushrooms, and caps of the mushrooms themselves. When you finally get around to trying to identify your mushrooms with reference books, one of the first things you'll need to know is what color the spores are. Sometimes deposits on surrounding vegetation will give you a clue. Otherwise you will need to wait for several hours to get a spore print indoors.

3. *Keep species (or specimens that look different) separate.* The wax paper or paper bags you brought along are for this purpose.

4. *Don't eat wild mushrooms raw.* No matter how hungry your mushroom hunting trek makes you, do not—repeat, *do not*—eat wild mushrooms raw. Even those listed in your field guide as choice edibles can evoke a toxic reaction if eaten raw. All should be cooked first.

5. *Learn to cope with Latin names.* More and more mushroom field guides supplement Latin names with common ones that may have been invented by the author and perhaps are not used in any other book. Conversely, one author may use a common name for one species while another may use the same common name for a completely different species. Beware!

With the aforementioned equipment, books and advice in hand, what can the intrepid mushroom hunter expect to find? Described below are a few of the more common and easily identified edibles along with some vaguely similar, not so edible counterparts. Think of them as "The Good, the Bad, and the Deadly."

MORELS: *MORCHELLA ESCULENTA*, *M. CRASSIPES*, *M. ANGUSTICEPS*, AND OTHERS (PLATE 2A)

About twenty-eight species of morels grow worldwide, but only six grow commonly in North America. They are not typical gilled mushrooms, but rather are related to the cup fungi. A central, hollow stem and convoluted, puckered—some say brainlike or spongelike—cap distinguishes morels from just about any other mushroom you might find. Most appear in the spring of the year, between mid-April and mid-June in the northern tier of the United States, when oak leaves are the size of mouse ears. Old apple orchards, pine forests, sites with recently dead elms, and recently disturbed (logged, burned, etc.) areas are places where morels are most likely to pop up. In 1994 in Alaska, following an unusual spate of forest fires, morels came up with unprecedented abundance. Collectors reported being able to harvest more than a pound of morels per minute. The market price for a pound of fruit-bodies, which normally ranged between fifteen and thirty dollars, plummeted to one.

As a group, morels are probably the most highly sought-after edible mushrooms. Their subtle meaty flavor is a delightful complement to soups, egg dishes, and creamy casseroles. In recent years, nature's long-kept secrets for growing morels in captivity have been unearthed, and facilities for commercial production of the mushrooms are just beginning to see their first crop. In time, consumers should expect to see the price of these traditionally high-priced delicacies come down.

As is the case with many fleshy fungi, morels tend to come up in the same place for anywhere from three to ten years after the first fruiting. Part of the lure and lore of mushroom hunting is that when a person finds morels, the secret of that location goes to the grave with him or her. One friend of mine was so concerned that some contender might discover his secret place that he would leave home before dawn and drive several miles in an evasive manner to shake any "tails" before he headed for his collection site.

Residents of the state of Michigan have taken morel hunting to new heights by declaring the morel the state mushroom and by hosting morel festivals in several towns. Prizes for the most and biggest specimens are awarded, and merchants with a wide array of mushroom-related goods flock to the scene. So many enthusiasts are drawn to the state from all over North America that morel hunting has mushroomed into an important, albeit short-lived, part of the state's tourism industry.

FALSE MORELS: *GYROMITRA* SPECIES, *HELVELLA* SPECIES (PLATE 2B)

Those who are easily confused by the mushroom world might confuse morel mushrooms with false morels, which are fungi in the genera *Gyromitra* and *Helvella*. False morels are also relatives of the cup fungi and produce fruit-bodies with light-colored, often hollow stems and darker, saddle-shaped (some say lobed or everted or convoluted) caps. They also fruit in the spring in sites where true morels are typically found. However, the various groups of mushrooms are distinctly different and easily separable once a person has had an opportunity to compare the two in the field.

Some false morels are reported to be edible, and some people seek them out with the same zeal that others seek true morels. However, there are also enough reports of sickness and death associated with eating false morels to cause the prudent mushroom hunter to approach them with caution. In at least some of the fruiting bodies, monomethyl hydrazine—the same chemical used by the Armed Forces as a component of rocket fuel—has been detected. Symptoms of false morel poisoning resemble those incurred by armament technicians accidentally exposed to fuel leaks. Despite reports to the contrary, monomethyl hydrazine is apparently not inactivated by cooking, inasmuch as people killed by the mushroom have always eaten cooked specimens. There are even instances where people who never took a bite were poisoned by the fumes produced by a pot of cooking *Gyromitra*. My advice is to let those who think their body chemistry can handle false morels do what they will. But the rest of us are better off not risking exposure.

 Immoral Morels?

Sometimes, people who should know better look the other way because of carelessness or greed. A case in point is the gathering of morels for sale on the open market. In 1977, authorities were perplexed when four patrons of a New York restaurant became ill after eating meals that included morels. Upon further investigation it was determined that the morels used in these particular dishes were not what the package claimed they were. Specimens of toxic false morels were included in the mix.[a] On another occasion, a diner in Detroit ate poisonous early morels, *Verpa bohemica,* that were accidentally included with regular *Morchella,* and he experienced uncomfortable symptoms of liver disease until the toxins were cleared. These episodes prompted a close examination of several hundred shipments of wild, "edible" mushrooms, imported in 1988–89. Of forty-two samples of morels, nine (that's a little more than 20 percent) were contaminated with either early or false morels. Clearly it's safer to collect and identify one's own!

[a] J. S. Gecan and S. M. Cichowicz, "Toxic mushroom contamination of wild mushrooms in commercial distribution," *Journal of Food Protection* 56 (1993): 730–733.

✦

MEADOW MUSHROOMS: *AGARICUS* SPECIES (PLATE 2C)

These are typical gilled mushrooms. They're common in fields, lawns, and pastures and often emerge in whole or partial fairy rings. In the northeastern United States, fruiting usually begins in midsummer and may continue until the first snow-fall in November. The mushrooms emerge from the soil as white "buttons," each with a fragile membrane connecting the margin of the cap to the stem. As each cap expands, the membrane breaks and drapes around the stout stem as a ring or annulus. The gills are off-white at first, but they turn to various shades of pink, then purple, and then dark purple-brown within seventy-two hours. Sizes of fully expanded caps vary with the species, ranging from one to twelve inches. Colors also vary, usually rang-ing from off-white to light brown. The surface of the cap is al-ways dry, never slimy; some caps have scales.

Many species of this genus are edible and have a flavor simi-lar to, albeit stronger than, the commercially grown button mushroom that is also a species of *Agaricus*. The *Agaricus* that have a history of (usually) mild toxicity to humans have some rather distinct features. Several stain yellow when bruised, an-other stains red, and yet another has reddish brown scales on its cap. If one mistakes an edible species of *Agaricus* for a poisonous one, the consequence is likely to be little more than an upset stomach. The greater danger lies in trying to collect meadow mushrooms while they are still in the button stage and are eas-ily mistaken for some highly toxic species in the genus *Amanita*, described below.

DEATH CAPS: *AMANITA PHALLOIDES*, *A. VIROSA* (PLATE 2D), AND OTHERS (PLATE 4A,B)

These species and several others in the genus *Amanita* contain toxins that, if eaten in sufficient quantity, will most cer-tainly kill the unwitting consumer. If you aspire to collect wild mushrooms for your table, read this section several times—care-fully. Then, find the *Amanita* sections in several mushroom-hunting field guides and read those. Distinguishing these mushrooms correctly from all others could be a life-or-death proposition.

Both of these species of mushrooms, as well as almost all others in the genus *Amanita,* are characterized as follows: white spores; gills not attached to the stem; a ring, or annulus, around the stem near the top; and a cup, once a membrane surrounding the button stage, at the base. *Note:* Both the ring and the cup may deteriorate from weather or insect feeding as fruit-bodies age, so examine several specimens. When very young, the mushrooms can be confused with button-stage field mushrooms or young puffballs. However, distinctions among all three should become obvious when a few specimens are slit open lengthwise.

Mature specimens of *Amanita* mushrooms vary greatly in size, with stems from 2 to 6 inches long and caps from 1½ to 7 inches wide. Colors of caps range from pure white (*A. virosa*) to greenish gray (*A. phalloides*) to brown (*A. brunnescens*), and some may be scaly or warty on top while others are smooth.

The most toxic of these mushrooms contains a group of polypeptides known collectively as amatoxins. They damage mammalian systems by blocking enzymes associated with replication of RNA, thus inhibiting the formation of new cells. Unfortunately for the hapless victim, normal maturation and death of existing cells continue without being replaced by new ones. Inasmuch as the toxins tend to accumulate in the liver, damage to that organ is most severe, and the effect has been aptly described as the liver digesting itself.[2]

For a person who has eaten a toxic *Amanita,* there may be no indication of poisoning for six to eight hours. Then, nausea, vomiting, fever, chills, minor tremors, and other symptoms ensue. These may be bad enough to cause the victim to be hospitalized, but they may also simply be passed off as a temporary case of food poisoning. Often, within twenty-four hours the initial symptom will subside and hospitalized patients may be sent home.

Real trouble becomes apparent three to six days later with typical symptoms of liver failure. By then, so much internal damage may have occurred that the hapless victim has little chance for recovery. Those who do are often aided by a liver transplant, massive doses of penicillin G (in Europe only; the latter is not an approved therapeutic strategy in the United States), or decontamination of the intestinal tract with activated charcoal. People who have ingested so little amatoxin that their system can cope with it and thus recover on their own may experience an inordinately high number of other liver ailments during the course of their lives.

Historically, most *Amanita* poisoning has occurred in Europe, where collecting mushrooms for the table is a popular family pastime. However, recent years have brought a marked increase in the number of reported poisonings from North America. In many cases, the victims have been immigrants from Southeast Asia, especially Laos, who presumably confuse a poisonous *Amanita* with a similar-looking edible species from their homeland. If nothing else, these cases of mistaken identity further underscore the need for consultation with local experts before wild mushrooms in new geographical areas are picked and prepared for the table.

Inky Caps: *Coprinus micaceus, C. atramentarius, C. comatus* (Plate 3a,b)

Several members of the genus *Coprinus* are considered by many to be edible and choice. These fungi all have one feature in common: the caps dissolve themselves as part of the spore dispersal process. Thus, though they are tasty, they must be collected and cooked the same day, preferably within minutes or hours of picking.

C. micaceus, the "mica cap," usually comes up in dense clusters of a hundred or more fruit-bodies, usually around old tree stumps. They are relatively small mushrooms, with light brown, fragile caps rarely exceeding $1\frac{1}{2}$ inches in diameter. Thus, large numbers of these mushrooms are needed to make a meal or even to add sufficient flavor to some other food. In view of the tendency of dogs to define their territories by urinating on tree stumps—the same stumps that may sport a crop of *C. micaceus*—my family has lost enthusiasm for this species and opted for more appealing gastronomic delights.

C. comatus, also known as the shaggy mane, is a prolific fruiter on recently installed or disturbed lawns. It occasionally fruits in recently disturbed forest sites as well. Where one specimen is found, there are often dozens more nearby, but each mushroom stands alone; they rarely grow in clumps. The caps are so distinct, with their columnar shape and fragile scales, that it is virtually impossible to confuse them with anything else. Young specimens have off-white gills that quickly become pink, then dark purple-brown, and then black. Stems may have a delicate ring about them early on, but that quickly falls away as the mushrooms age. Mature specimens can be up to 8 inches tall, but they are best picked before reaching full size to catch them before autodigestion for spore liberation begins.

C. atramentarius is considered by many to be the true inky cap. Like *C. micaceus,* it usually occurs in clumps around old tree stumps. However, it's a much larger and more robust mushroom than *C. micaceus* (caps up to 2½ inches diameter, stems ⅓ to ½ inch diameter and up to 6 inches long) and has a grayish brown cap. Although this species is listed as edible and choice in virtually all mushroom field guides, people who eat it are advised not to drink alcoholic beverages for at least 24 to 48 hours before and after eating the mushrooms. That's because *C. atramentarius* fruit-bodies contain a chemical with a mode of action in mammalian systems similar to Antabuse®, the drug used to induce nausea and vomiting in alcoholics who are trying to cope with another fungal product. The poisoning caused by *C. atramentarius* plus alcohol results in such a sudden and violent reaction that many victims end up in a hospital emergency room to ride out their symptoms. If a bottle of beer or glass of wine is part of your daily fare and you're not of a mind to give them up, best find some other wild mushroom to sate your appetite.

(*Note:* Other inky caps do not evoke this reaction and are safe to have with your favorite drink.)

CHANTERELLES: *CANTHARELLUS CIBARIUS* AND OTHERS

Chanterelles are yet another group of wild mushrooms that have found favor not only on dining room tables but also in gourmet restaurants. The fruit-bodies cannot be mass produced in a controlled environment, so all specimens you find on grocery store shelves or in restaurants were hand-picked by somebody who knew what to look for and where.

The funnel-shaped fruit-bodies are a pale to golden yellow color and always come up from the ground, never from tree stumps or roots. Their most distinguishing feature is that they have gills that look like folded membranes rather than the typical sharp-edged gills of other mushrooms. Spore prints from those gills may take more than a day to collect, but they should be pale yellow. Novices should use special care in collecting this mushroom from the field the first time, because there are some common poisonous, but not necessarily deadly, look-alikes. Consult with a local expert if you are the least bit unsure of your identification.

OYSTER MUSHROOMS: *PLEUROTUS OSTREATUS, P. PORRIGENS,* AND OTHERS (FIG. 10.1)

Scientists have known how to grow *Pleurotus* mushrooms under controlled conditions for a long time. However, only in recent years have American consumers become mycologically adventurous enough to try a mushroom with the stem that grows to the side rather than in the middle, as is the case of the oyster mushrooms in the genus *Pleurotus.* Mind you, not all fleshy fruit-bodies with off-center stems are *Pleurotus* or edible,

Fig. 10.1. *Pleurotus ostreatus* fruit-bodies,
typically present on deciduous trees.
(Drawn by Robert O'Brien.)

but those that are, are quite tasty. In the wild, they grow on the
stems of dead trees. Aspen, beech, cottonwood, and tulip poplar
are common hosts for *P. ostreatus; P. porrigens* grows on conifers.
The mushrooms grow in clumps or clusters and have fan-shaped
caps that vary from almost pure white to silvery gray to brown.
Spores from all species are white.

Perhaps the biggest problem with collecting *Pleurotus* is that
the dense clusters of fruit-bodies tend to attract insects and
slugs. Thus, if you do choose to collect these, do so soon after
they appear. Break the clumps up when you get home to make
sure they have no noxious residents, and then cook or dry them
shortly thereafter.

158

HONEY MUSHROOMS: *ARMILLARIA MELLEA*, *A. OSTOYAE*, *A. BULBOSA*, AND OTHERS (FIG. 8.2)

The last of the gilled mushrooms to be discussed in this chapter are the honey mushrooms—*Armillaria mellea* and its relatives. For many years, mycologists and plant pathologists grouped a large variety of vaguely similar mushrooms under the name *Armillaria mellea*. Recently, however, through careful genetic analysis, it has become clear that what was once considered one species is now as many as twelve or more. All have some features in common, but they also have significant differences. From the standpoint of the mushroom hunter, distinction between the various species may be a moot point because all are apparently edible, though some have caused mild indigestion in some people.

Honey mushrooms fruit in clusters of various sizes on tree stumps and at the bases of dead and living coniferous and hardwood trees. The mushrooms vary in size, with stems 2 to 6 inches long and caps 1 to 6 inches in diameter. The caps are brown and sometimes scaly or smooth. The gills are off-white to light brown and relatively firmly attached to the stem, such that the cap and stem are not readily separated. Spore prints are white and can often be found on caps of neighboring mushrooms in a cluster. Stems usually have some vestiges of a ring.

BOLETES: *BOLETUS* SPECIES, *SUILLUS* SPECIES, AND OTHERS (FIG. 10.2A,B)

A final group of stalked mushrooms to be considered here is known as the Boletes because at one time all members of the group belonged to the genus *Boletus*. However, with revisions in taxonomy, the genus has been split into several additional genera, including *Boletellus*, *Gyroporous*, *Leccinum*, and *Suillus*. All are characterized by producing a mushroom on a

Fig. 10.2A,B. *Boletus* sp. showing tubes rather than gills on the underside of the cap.

central stalk, but the underside of each cap contains tubes instead of gills. This gives the overall cap a sort of spongy texture rather than the fleshy or waxy texture of gilled mushrooms. While many boletes are edible and choice, there are some that can cause indigestion in some people, and it is well worth the effort to take a little extra time to identify specimens properly before preparing them for the table. At collection time, note whether the specimens stain either blue or red upon bruising; these features are important to note for proper identification. Many of the blue- or red-staining species are toxic, so newcomers would be wise not to save any of them for the table. Another challenge in collecting boletes, especially in warm, humid climates, is that they are quickly colonized by insect larvae. Unless you need the added protein from maggots in your diet, it's best to harvest these mushrooms soon after they emerge from below ground.

OTHER fungus fruit-bodies are clearly not mushrooms in the traditional sense of the word, but they do produce spores, are common in the landscape, and provide a most tasty addition to any meal. Some are so flavorful and filling that they could easily be a main course. The following are some favorites.

PUFFBALLS: *LYCOPERDON, CALVATIA,* AND OTHERS (PLATE 3C)

Many different species of fungi produce their spores in relatively large, initially closed bodies called puffballs. As puffballs mature, they either form a hole in the top or break open irregularly to release their spores. But before they mature, many species can be harvested and their unique flavor enjoyed with little or no threat of danger. The key to safe collection of puffballs for the table is to make sure that (1) they really are puffballs, and (2) they are still immature enough to possess a desirable flavor. As to the first point, it is possible for a very young *Amanita phalloides* or *A. virosa* that has not yet broken its universal veil to look like a puffball from the outside. It is also possible that a suspect puffball is a member of the poisonous genus *Scleroderma. Scleroderma* species, even when young and firm, have dark purple interiors. In either case, splitting a puffball down the middle with a sharp knife will help to confirm its identity. Resolution of the second issue can also be had by splitting the puffball open with a sharp knife. If the inside flesh, the "context," is still pure white, the puffball is good to eat. However, if it has begun to turn yellow or any shade of brown, that is a sign that it is past its prime and is best left in the field.

Chicken-of-the-Woods: *Laetiporus sulfureus* (Plate 3d)

This fungus, otherwise known as the "sulfur shelf," produces another unmistakable, common, and tasty fungus fruit-body. The bright yellow-orange, fleshy shelves appear on dead or living deciduous trees any time during the summer or early fall. On their undersides, you will see pores rather than gills for spore production. The fungus is a common rotter of several species of deciduous trees and its presence on a living tree is a clue that the tree has sustained some amount of interior decay. What that amount is remains uncertain and requires further testing (see chapter 12), but presence of the fruit-body ought to be noted, nonetheless, if the tree could pose an imminent threat to people or property.

Bearded Hedgehog: *Hericium erinaceus* (Fig. 10.3)

This is another common wood-decay fungus. It grows on a variety of living deciduous trees, especially beech, oak, and maple, and is characterized by producing a roughly spherical fruit-body covered with toothlike or comblike projections. Techniques for growing these fruit-bodies in culture have apparently been perfected inasmuch as packages of them have begun to appear on supermarket shelves, at least in the northeastern United States.

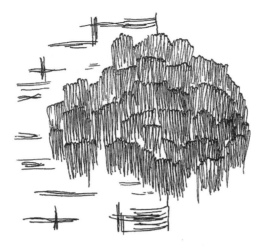

Fig. 10.9. *Hericium erinaceus*, on deciduous trees. (Drawn by Robert O'Brien.)

As I bring this discussion of collecting wild mushrooms for the table to a close, I will add a few more caveats to the list of precautions presented at the top of this chapter.

1. Dig, don't pick. I know—I already said this once. But the value of this piece of advice in preventing a possible fatal poisoning is too great to leave unsaid a second time. Many *Amanita* species. will kill you, and the best way to know whether you may have accidentally collected one is to look for the underground cup.

2. Don't collect mushrooms when they are wet, and do not store them in plastic bags, especially if unrefrigerated. Moisture encourages growth of bacteria which may produce their own array of toxins. I am aware of at least one case where a "mushroom" poisoning was actually due to such bacterial toxins, and I have heard several similar reports from colleagues.

3. Cut all puffballs open before eating them. Puffballs are

safe to eat as long as that's what they are and they have not yet begun to form spores. But you *must* look.

4. Don't feed wild mushrooms to children under five years of age. With virtually all mushrooms as with all other foods, a small percentage of people simply cannot tolerate them. Young children, because of their small body size in relation to the volume they eat, would likely have a more serious reaction than an adult should such an incompatibility occur. It's best to avoid the possibility altogether.

5. Never eat any white-capped mushroom you have not positively identified.

6. Beware of any mushroom with a ring on its stalk.

7. Do not eat any mushroom with a swollen stalk at the base.

If numbers 5–7 don't make sense to you, reread the section on *Amanita*.

TRUFFLES: *TUBER MELANOSPORUM, T. MAGNATUM*

One of the most prized groups of wild, edible fungi grows only sparingly in North America but commonly in western Europe. They are known as truffles, and they have a peculiar growth habit which requires that they infect the roots of certain trees to ensure their survival. The infection is not harmful to the host tree. In fact, it is beneficial, and both partners thrive through their union, known as a mycorrhiza (see chapter 14).

The two kinds of truffles commonly sought for eating purposes are black truffles (*Tuber melanosporum*) and white truffles (*T. magnatum*). The former are most common—although still rare—in Germany and France, while the latter are most likely to be found in northern Italy. White truffles are supposed to be the more flavorful of the two, but, unfortunately, I have not yet had the luxury of serving both up for a gastronomic comparison.

Truffles are unlike any of the traditional mushrooms in terms of growth habit or appearance. They are closely related to the cup fungi and the morels, but they never have an exposed, spore-bearing surface. Instead, the spores are produced within a closed, tuberlike body that vaguely resembles a puffball. It also vaguely resembles a potato, and during the sixteenth century, when potatoes were first being introduced into European culture, they were confused with truffles.

Truffles fruit near enough to the soil surface for their strong odor to attract squirrels and other forest creatures. The fungus depends on these animals to dig up the fruit-bodies and, in the process, to liberate the spores. These same odors help people find truffles—or, more correctly, they help domesticated animals help people to find truffles. For when you want to hunt for truffles, you don't just put on your coat and head out into the woods like you would for a traditional mushroom foray. No, when you want to hunt truffles, you first head for the barn to fetch your prized truffle-hunting pig or dog. Young sows are supposed to be the best. After leashing the animal, you set out on your hunt. When it picks up the scent of a nearby truffle and stops to dig, you jerk firmly on the leash, and finish the rest of the job yourself.[3]

Truffles have an incredibly delightful taste, described by one author as suggesting the flavor of garlic, "but unlike garlic, it does not repeat itself." Others have simply noted that the taste is fantastic, indescribable, and otherwise out of this world. The potency of the aroma is such that a single truffle placed in a closed container with a dozen eggs will permeate the shells of the eggs and leave them with the flavor of truffles when they're later cooked as omelettes or quiches. At our house, with a gift of a slice of a truffle about the size of a U.S. nickel, my wife managed to make three different and tasty dishes. In fact, I was so impressed with that feat that I readily shelled out ninety-six dollars for one and three-fourths ounces of truffles from a specialty shop in New York City. That's about eight hundred seventy-five dollars per pound! It was her Valentine's Day present. I had no money left for a card, so I wrote my affections on the back of the bottle with a grease pencil. She loved it—and me! Oh, those fungi!

With the changing face of the European landscape and especially with the devastation of forests because of development, air pollution, and other factors, the truffle harvest has plummeted from a one-time high of about one thousand tons per year at the beginning of this century to about twenty tons per year today. As the supply has gone down, the price has gone up, and that has attracted the attention of some entrepreneurs who see promise—and profit—in the development of truffle orchards. Oak trees have either been purposely infected with the fungus or infested soil has been spread around the roots of selected trees in the hope of increasing truffle production and doing so in known locations. Oak and truffle orchards have been started in several locations in Europe as well as New Zealand and Texas. One European firm sells truffle-infected seedlings for ten to fifteen dollars apiece to anyone who wants to try starting their own truffle farm.

In addition to their splendid flavor, truffles are sought by some people for their purported aphrodisiacal properties. Most rational people have dismissed such attributions as nothing more than a gimmick to raise the price of the fungi even higher, but the reputation persists. And recently, researchers have found that one component of the odor of truffles is a steroid called alpha-androstenol. This same chemical is found in the saliva and hence on the breath of rutting boars, where it is suspected to serve as a pheromone to attract young female pigs. This may explain the natural talent of young sows for truffle hunting, although another chemical—dimethyl sulfide—has been determined to be the more likely attractant for the animals. Alpha-androstenol is also found in the underarm perspiration of men and in the urine of women, although its role in human sexuality has not been clearly established.

COMMERCIAL PRODUCTION OF
BUTTON MUSHROOMS

For the better part of human history, those folks with a fondness for mushrooms in their meals collected them in the wild. So they had to contend with unpredictable supplies as the seasons changed, as the weather within seasons changed, and as the landscape changed. And, of course, mushroom hunters also had to contend with that little element of risk associated with collecting wild fungi. If one got just a little bit sloppy with identification, the consequences could be disasterous.

It was inevitable, then, that some entrepreneur would recognize the market value of a steady supply of safe, tasty mushrooms and seize the moment to find a way to grow them in captivity. The first records of such come from France in the early 1700s, and they clearly describe cultivation of mushrooms in caves and houses in a manner similar to what is used today.

The industry expanded and eventually found its way to the United States in 1880, with the first commercial production facilities being started in New York City and on Long Island. In 1886, William Swayne decided that Kennett Square, Pennsylvania—about 10 miles southwest of Philadelphia—would be a good place to start a mushroom-growing business because Kennett Square was where many of the horses that were used to power early public transportation in Philadelphia were stabled. Thus, the little town had an abundance of the most important raw material for cultivated mushroom production—horse manure. Others followed Swayne, and Kennett Square quickly became the mushroom-growing capital of the United States. By 1925, 85 percent of the commercial mushrooms of the nation were being produced in Pennsylvania. Since then the mushroom-growing industry has spread to other parts of the country. While Pennsylvania still produces over 50 percent of the nation's crop, the state doesn't have quite the market share that it once did.

In 1996, 318,000 tons (=635 million pounds) of mushrooms were produced in the United States. They ranked fifteenth in commercial vegetable production as determined by weight. However, in monetary value, mushrooms were ranked fifth, behind potatoes, tomatoes, lettuce, and beans, with a wholesale value of $615 million.

The species of mushroom grown most often in the United States, Europe, and Australia and, to a lesser extent, in the Far East is the common button mushroom, *Agaricus brunnescens,* also known as *A. bisporus.* Over the years, certain strains of the common button mushroom have emerged. These have such distinctive flavors that even though they, too, are technically *A. brunnescens,* they have been given special common names. Two of these are cremini and portabello.

✦ *But Are They Any Good?*

One oft-asked question is, "Do mushrooms have any particular nutritional value or do they simply add flavor to things?" The answer is a resounding "Yes, they do have nutritional value." The potential medicinal value of some species was discussed earlier (see chapter 8), but in addition, they contain valuable vitamins and nutrients with little fat or other calories.[a] They are particularly rich in the amino acids—lysine and tryptophan—both of which are lacking in cereal diets, but they have little if any sulfur-containing amino acids—cysteine and methionine. Thus, they could never serve as a sole source of protein. In addition, mushrooms are excellent sources of nicotinic acid and riboflavin, good sources of pantothenic acid, and fair sources of vitamins B1, C, and K.

[a] See E. E. Anderson and C. R. Fellers, "The food value of mushrooms (*Agaricus compestris*)," *Amer. Soc. of Horticultural Sci.* 41 (1942): 301–304.

✦

The fundamental technique of mushroom growing hasn't changed much over the years, but advanced technology has enabled producers to standardize their procedures to ensure more predictable, high-quality crops. And mechanization of many steps along the way has reduced the chance for human error or contamination.[4]

The process begins with growing an initial supply of mycelium, or "spawn." Spawn is made by growing a culture (purchased from a laboratory or saved from a previous crop of mushrooms) on rye or some other grain, to be used to start a larger culture later.

In another part of the facility, a suitably large volume of organic material to support mushroom growth must be produced. Composting a mixture of horse manure, straw, chicken or turkey droppings, and some other minor constituents provides the substrate for further growth. In fact, proper mixing and incubation of compost is arguably the most crucial step in the production of a successful crop. The compost has to be kept at the right temperature and right moisture content for several weeks, so that when it's finally inoculated with the spawn, it has the right balance of other microorganisms and the right level of acidity to allow for maximum growth of the mushroom mycelium.*

When compost has reached a suitable level of development, the previously colonized grain is introduced in a process called "spawning" or "running the spawn." The compost is transferred to beds either in special houses or in underground caves, and the spawn is thoroughly mixed into the compost to make sure colonization is rapid and thorough. This minimizes contamination by outside organisms. Then the whole mix is left to sit for up to several weeks until the compost is thoroughly colonized.

Unfortunately, if the mycelium is left to grow only on the compost, it will produce few if any mushrooms. However, if it is covered with several inches of less nutritious material, such as peat

---

*Rest assured that the manure and poultry litter aren't used straight from the animals. By the time the mix is fully composted and ready to grow mushrooms, it is as clean as virgin soil.

or spent compost from a previous crop, mushroom formation will begin. This overlay process is called "casing," and several days after the compost is cased, the mushrooms start to appear. Several flushes will emerge and be harvested before the compost in a particular bed is spent. Then it is removed, and the bed is refilled with new compost to start the process all over again.

As with any agricultural crop, mushrooms have their fair share of both insect and disease problems, and mushroom growers must be constantly on the lookout for them. Other fungi may overrun compost before it's colonized by spawn, and viruses and bacteria can destroy an otherwise promising crop. At Pennsylvania State University, scientists with backgrounds in entomology and plant pathology as well as mycology are assigned to tackle just such problems, and together their unique team provides solutions for the mushroom industry worldwide. Without their contributions, you can be sure that harvests would be much smaller and more costly.

COMMERCIAL SALE OF WILD MUSHROOMS

Those not inclined to trust their own judgment in identifying wild mushrooms and looking for more variety than that provided by cultivated species have yet another option. That's because wild mushroom picking has become a signicant and lucrative pastime for some residents of the western United States. A survey conducted in 1993 revealed, for the first time, the magnitude of the industry. The 10,400 pickers said they harvested a total of four million pounds of wild mushrooms. Morels, chanterelles, and boletes comprised about two-thirds of the take. Matsutake or pine mushrooms (*Tricholoma magnivelare*) accounted for another 836,000 pounds. The gross value of the U.S industry was conservatively estimated to be $41 million. While the numbers pale in comparison to those for cultivated mushrooms, they still represent a significant exchange of dollars and a yet-to-be-determined impact on the fragile mountain terrain.[5]

✦ *The Bookshelf: "I" Is for Innocent*

Inasmuch as mushrooms have a long history of association with darkness, death, and decay, it only stands to reason that an astute novelist would use the poisonous varieties as the means to a final end for an unwitting victim. Most recently, Sue Grafton did just that with *Amanita phalloides*—the death angel—in her book *"I" Is for Innocent*. What is particularly gratifying is that unlike her few contemporaries who use mushrooms to secure an instant death, Grafton has her victim suffer the prolonged agony that amatoxins actually induce. After this opening exchange with the coroner:

> "The autopsy confirms this. Did you ever hear of *Amanita phalloides*?"
> "Sounds like a sex act. What the hell is it?"

readers are treated to almost two pages worth of reliable information about how, when, and where *Amanita* poisoning could occur.

Why Grafton waited until the ninth book in her alphabetical series (*"A" Is for Alibi, "B" Is for Burglar*, etc.) to hit on this idea is perhaps the greatest mystery to readers of these tomes, but she at least deserves special credit for getting there at all. Robert Ludlum, Tom Clancy, Ken Follet, and Clive Cussler have yet to see the light.

✦

CHAPTER 11

Hallucinogenic Mushrooms

In the autumn of 1927, a New York newspaper colum-
nist and his new bride, Tina, a pediatrician who had emigrated
from Russia as a teenager, were honeymooning at Big Indian, a
resort in the Catskill Mountains of central New York. On that
first beautiful afternoon of their holiday, as they sauntered down
a woodland path, hand in hand and happy as larks, Tina suddenly let go of her husband's hand and dashed off into the forest. She had seen mushrooms coming up on the forest floor, a
vast array of sizes and colors, and she cried out in delight at their
beauty. Not since she had left her family's home near Moscow
ten years earlier had she seen such a wondrous display. As related later by her husband, Gordon:

> She knelt before those toadstools in poses of adoration like
> the Virgin hearkening to the Angel of Annunciation, and she
> began gathering some of the fungi in her apron. I called to
> her, "Come back, come back to me! They are poisonous, pu-
> trid! They are toadstools. Come back to me!"
>
> She only laughed more, and her merry laughter will forever
> ring in my ears. That evening, she seasoned the soup with
> fungi, she garnished the meat with other fungi, and yet others
> she threaded together and strung up to dry for our "winter
> use," as she said. My discomfiture was complete. That night I
> ate nothing with mushrooms in it. Frantic and deeply hurt, I
> was led to wild ideas: I told her that I would wake up a widower.[1]

Of course, the writer did not wake up a widower. In fact, he
awoke to find his new bride just as healthy as she had been the
day before. But that colorful episode in the lives of R. Gordon

and Valentina Wasson vividly illustrated one of the tremendous differences in the cultures in which each was raised.

Valentina, born and raised in Russia, held fungi in high esteem. She had learned about mushrooms from her parents who had learned from their parents and so on. Family outings to collect mushrooms were delightful, eagerly anticipated events. And the Russian vocabulary for mushrooms was seemingly endless. Poets and novelists filled their writings with references to mushrooms, always in an adoring context.

Gordon, on the other hand, was born and raised in New York City and educated at Harvard. His exposure to natural history was limited to the occasional family weekend trips into the countryside, where the few fungi his family might encounter were greeted with disdain. The English-speaking authors and other scholars whom Gordon revered as he progressed through his formal education barely acknowledged the presence of fungi in the worlds of their players. Chaucer and Milton never mentioned them. Shakespeare, Spencer, Shelley, Keats, Tennyson, Edgar Allan Poe, D. H. Lawrence, and Emily Dickinson used the terms "mushroom" and "toadstool" as unpleasant, even disgusting epithets usually linked to death and decay. Clearly, there was nothing in his upbringing to cause Gordon Wasson to conjure up anything but negative images of fungi. Furthermore, his experience seemed to be typical for the vast majority of people raised in cities and towns throughout North America.

The Wassons attributed great significance to the differences in their attitudes toward mushrooms, seeing them as tangible measures of the basic differences between the two cultures that spawned them. They were so absorbed with their discovery that they spent the rest of their lives traveling throughout the world to study the interrelationships between human cultures and mushrooms. They founded what they considered to be a new branch of mycology, "ethnomycology." And to describe the differences between people who love and fear mushrooms, they used "mycophilia" and "mycophobia," respectively.

A prevailing theme in much of the Wassons' writings revolved around a popular theory in psychology that was emerging at about the same time—that deep-seated emotional attitudes acquired in a person's earliest years had a profound impact on one's thoughts throughout life. The Wassons expanded this general notion to conclude that when these deep-seated emotional traits permeate an entire tribe or other group of people and when they differ from one group to another, neighboring group, "then," as they put it, "you are face to face with a phenomenon of the deepest cultural implications whose primal cause is to be discovered only in the wellsprings of cultural history." The Wassons pored over archaeological reports, biblical and mythological tales, and stories passed down through generations of primitive tribes. They became convinced that mushrooms—hallucinogenic mushrooms—had played crucial roles in the evolution of human cultures and religions around the world, and they set out to prove their hypothesis.

They first turned their attention to southern Mexico, where they learned about sixteenth-century Spanish explorers who frequently observed Indians from the Valley of Mexico and south eating inebriating mushrooms. The mushrooms produced hallucinations that the Indians thought were divinely inspired. A Spanish friar described the following Indian experience as if he himself had participated:

> The first thing they ate at the gathering was small, black mushrooms which they called *nanacatl.* These were intoxicating and caused visions to be seen and even provoked sensuousness. They ate these mushrooms before dawn and they also drank chocolate before daylight. They ate these little mushrooms with honey, and when they began to be excited by them they began to dance. Some sang, others wept, for they were already intoxicated by the mushrooms. Some did not want to sing but sat down in their quarters and remained there as if in a meditative mood. Some saw themselves dying

in a vision and wept; others saw themselves being eaten by a wild beast; others imagined that they were capturing prisoners in battle, that they were rich, that they possessed many slaves, that they had committed adultery and were to have their heads crushed for the offense, that they were guilty of a theft for which they were to be killed, and many other visions which they saw. When the intoxication from the little mushrooms had passed, they talked over among themselves the visions which they had seen.[2]

There was no mention of cultivated mushrooms. All were found in the wild and apparently collected with some reverence, including prayer and vigil. The mushrooms were used in religious ceremonies and in festive communal celebrations, sometimes culminating in fierce battles or orgies. This behavior was determined by the civilized Spaniards to be nothing short of barbaric, and those who indulged in it were subjected to brutal punishment. So fearful were the natives that the whole mushroom ceremony was eventually driven underground, remaining there for almost four hundred years.

In 1953, the Wassons set out to find these tribes and to witness the partaking of the mushrooms. Traveling by train, then bus, then mules, and finally on foot, they went from Mexico City to several rural villages in southern Mexico, places rarely if ever visited by non-native people in the past. After numerous frustrating attempts to interview someone who had used the mushrooms, they finally befriended a true *curandera,* a shaman who was paid to eat the mushrooms and interpret the visions for her client. The *curandera*'s visions helped people find lost items or predict the future or perform any of a number of other services that one might expect from a fortuneteller or other medium. In this kind of ceremony, only the *curandero* actually ate the mushrooms and experienced their unusual effects.

The Wassons could observe but not partake of the mushrooms on their first visit but later—they made several trips during the mid-1950s—they were invited to indulge. Gordon Wasson recounted the experience later as follows:

> The sacred mushrooms of Mexico seize hold of you with irresistible power. They lead to a temporary schizophrenia in which your body lies heavy as lead on the mat and you take notes and compare experiences with your neighbor while your soul flies off to the ends of the world and indeed to other planes of existence.
>
> The mushrooms take effect differently with different persons. For example, some seem to experience only a divine euphoria which may translate itself into uncontrollable laughter. In my case I experienced hallucinations . . . visions of palaces, gardens, seascapes, and mountains. . . . With the speed of thought you are translated wherever you desire to be, and you are there, a disembodied eye, poised in space, seeing but not seen, invisible, incorporeal. [Not only are there] visual hallucinations, but all of the senses are equally affected, and the human organism as a whole is lifted to a place of intense experience. A drink of water, a puff of a cigarette, is transformed, leaving you breathless with wonder and delight. The emotions and intellect are similarly stepped up. Your whole being is aquiver with life.[3]

With the assistance from mycologist Roger Heim, they were also able to make some progress on the identity of the magical mushrooms.[4] There were actually several different species, all (at the time) in the genus *Psilocybe* and characterized by having a thin, fragile cap on a slender, ringless stalk with no cup at the base. The gills on the underside of the cap were attached to the stalk at its apex, and the spores were purplish brown. Some of the mushrooms stained blue when bruised or broken. The most commonly found and used species were *Psilocybe mexicana, P. caerulescens,* and *P. cubensis,* the latter sometimes known as *Stropharia cubensis.* For all intents and purposes, this group of mushrooms would have been classed as nondescript little brown mushrooms—LBMs—by all but the most serious of mushroom hunters, and thus had probably grown inconspicuously in the rest of North America for hundreds of years. But the Wassons and Heim and many others who followed them changed all that in a big way.

Subsequent chemical analyses of the mushrooms indicated that there were at least two active ingredients, psilocybin and psilocin. Of the two, psilocin was the more potent, and the best evidence indicated that psilocybin was converted to psilocin in the human body. Both compounds were closely related to the brain hormone, serotonin, and presumably blocked or replaced its function. However, the fundamental chemistry responsible for the vivid hallucinations was a mystery then, and remains so today.

Perhaps the greatest consequence of the Wassons' work was to focus public attention on mushrooms as sources of hallucinogenic drugs and on Mexico as the source of those mushrooms. When Gordon Wasson published his first account of his quest, it was in the May 13, 1957, issue of *Life* magazine. His article, titled "Seeking the Magic Mushroom," and another by his wife ("I Ate the Magic Mushroom") the following weekend in a Sunday newspaper supplement, undoubtedly spurred many adventuresome souls to open their atlases to Mexico and plan the ultimate trip. Quiet rural villages now became magnets for a generation of young people who were long on hair, short on patience, and sporting "Question Authority" stickers, among others, on their backpacks and guitar cases.

IN the summer of 1960, Dr. Timothy Leary, newly appointed director of the Center for Research in Personality at Harvard University, got his first chance to experience the effects of the magical mushrooms while vacationing at Cuernavaca. Leary was particularly intrigued because he had recently proposed a new, existential approach to psychotherapy, an approach actively immersing the therapist in a patient's emotional turmoil rather than remaining a distant counselor. Mind-altering drugs, thought

Leary, might provide the vehicle for a normal person to reach the mental state of the disturbed. Besides that, Leary had been told by his superiors as he assumed his new position that he was "just what we need to shake things up at Harvard." The door was open for unorthodox, even risky, research, and with a supply of mushrooms purchased from a street peddler known only as Crazy Juana, Leary jumped through with both feet. He described his first experience with psilocybin this way:

> I began to feel strange. Like going under dental gas. Mildly nauseous. Detached. . . . Everything was quivering with life, even inanimate objects. I laughed again at my own everyday pomposity, the narrow arrogance of scholars, the impudence of the rational, the smug naivete of words in contrast to the raw rich ever-changing panoramas that flooded my brain. For the next five hours after eating the mushrooms, I was whirled through an experience which could be described in many extravagant metaphors but which was above all and without question the deepest religious experience of my life.[5]

Leary was so enthused by his first hallucinogenic experience that he rushed back to Harvard and crafted plans to use the mushrooms in his research program. Fortuitously, he soon learned that the Swiss pharmaceutical company Sandoz (the same company that had earlier synthesized LSD) could now make pure psilocybin and was willing to supply it to qualified researchers. Leary quickly drafted a request to Sandoz, and within six weeks he had four bottles of pills, more than enough to begin work in earnest. He began holding drug-taking sessions on a regular basis and, together with colleague Richard Alpert and a handful of dedicated graduate students, did some of the first experiments to understand the effects of dosage and place on the psychedelic experience. When the sterile confines of a classroom proved to be unsatisfactory, they sought the placid surroundings of Leary's home and then student residences. Undergraduates were forbidden from participating in Leary's science, and as rumors that the psilocybin sessions turned into wild orgies began to surface, complaints of undergrads being left out became louder and more frequent and were occasionally aired in the student newspaper. Faculty colleagues, engaged in traditional psychological research, were stung by the publicity Leary's program garnered and by his attraction of many of the best and brightest graduate students. Their criticism began in private but soon became public as a reporter from the *Harvard Crimson* eavesdropped on a closed hearing.

Coincidentally, Leary began to experiment with other hallucinogenic drugs—mescaline and LSD. The Harvard campus soon gained national notoriety as the center of hallucinogenic drug research in North America. At a time when recreational use of hallucinogens was sweeping across the country, much to the consternation of state and federal law enforcement agencies, the university found itself in an uncomfortable position. Restrictions on Leary's research were tightened, and relationships between him and former colleagues deteriorated. By 1963, Harvard administrators had had enough of Leary, and he of them. Both he and Alpert were fired, the Harvard campus began to come down from its trip, and state and federal laws were enacted to rid the country of hallucinogenic drugs.

Today, we know there are far more species of psilocybin-containing mushrooms than the half dozen or so discovered by the Wassons and their colleagues in the Mexican countryside. They grow throughout the world, and in the United States are commonly found in cow pastures of the southern states and in fields and forests of the West Coast. Although our current knowledge of their distribution suggests that mild year-round temperatures are required for natural growth and reproduction, this may not be true. A culture of an unidentified but definitely potent species of *Panaeolus* seemed to do just fine in a site near a Maine schoolyard until authorities discovered it. And, *Gymnopilus spectabilis,* the big laughing mushroom, fruits prolifically on stumps and logs throughout the continent.

There may be several or many more species that also have mind-altering powers but are overlooked because of their small size, drab color, and/or difficult identification. However, one should not be tempted by these remarks to think that indiscriminate random sampling of the local mushroom crop might lead to a euphoric commune with nature. Quite the contrary! Many so-called LBMs contain potent toxins that can make one violently ill and may cause death.

In recent years, hallucinogenic mushroom use has been championed by yet another colorful personality, Terrence McKenna. Like Wasson, McKenna lacks the kind of formal scientific education that might otherwise improve his credibility in the eyes of the academic community. After graduating with a bachelor's degree in Shamanism and the Conservation of Natural Resources from the University of California at Berkeley, he spent several years traveling around the globe as a professional butterfly collector. As his physical travels took him to the far reaches of the physical world, McKenna's psychological trips, with frequent use of psilocybin and other psychedelics, took him to the far reaches of a spiritual world. And the two sets of experiences provided McKenna with the grist for a theory about how and why human evolution occurred as it did.[6] He suggests that the relatively rapid transition from apes to humans was mediated by ingestion of hallucinogenic mushrooms. The premise is that as prehistoric peoples foraged in the countryside where they lived, they inevitably happened upon and sampled mushrooms with—unbeknownst to them—hallucinogenic properties. When psilocybin was taken in low dosages, it actually heightened the senses, improving visual acuity and auditory reception. Thus, those who ate hallucinogenic mushrooms were superior hunters because they could see and hear better than their unenlightened counterparts. When game was plentiful, they could easily catch what they needed and have time left over to grow in other ways—cultivating crops, inventing tools, and otherwise expanding their intellectual capacities. When game was scarce, they would survive while those without benefit of drug-induced sensory enhancement might not. McKenna also hypothesizes that hallucinogenic mushrooms tempered primitive peoples' egos so they were more willing to live in a communal environment with sexual freedom and shared child care. Thus, they had more and healthier children. Furthermore, McKenna argues that the root cause of society's ills today is not that we use too many hallucinogens, but rather that we use too few.

SOMA AND BEYOND

As the Wassons' interest in magical mushrooms deepened, they turned their attention, and ours, to hallucinogenic mushrooms in other parts of the world. One of those with a rich and colorful history was the fly agaric, *Amanita muscaria*. This is probably the most familiar, the most drawn, the most photographed, and the most written about of all of the mushrooms.

A. muscaria exists in at least two forms. In the western United States and in all of Europe, it is a relatively large mushroom with a scarlet red cap and white gills and stem. As with other species of *Amanita*, it has a ring around the stem and a cup (volva) at the base. The cap usually has white flecks on top, remnants of an earlier stage of development when the volva encased the whole fruit-body. A second form of the fly agaric has a yellow cap with white flecks. This is the one most common in eastern North America (plates 4A,B).

A. muscaria is a mycorrhizal mushroom (see chapter 14), often found growing in a fairy ring near the base of a host tree. In Europe, it is mostly associated with birch, fir, and larch, whereas in North America it is more often associated with pines. Fairy rings of the yellow fly agarics around the bases of conifers, especially eastern white pines, are very common.

The hallucinogenic properties of this mushroom were first brought to the attention of the Western world in the mid-eighteenth century. It was then that a Swedish traveler, Philip Johann von Strahlenberg, wrote about his journeys in Russia and Siberia. From his pages, we learned for the first time of the Korjak tribesmen of Kamchatka and how they consumed the fly agaric for its intoxicating effect. He wrote:

> Those who are rich among them lay up large provisions of these mushrooms for the winter. When they make a feast, they pour water upon some of these mushrooms and boil them. They then drink the liquor which intoxicates them. The poorer sort, who cannot afford to lay in a store of these mushrooms, post themselves on these occasions round the huts of the rich and [wait for an] opportunity when the guests come down to make water. Then, they hold a wooden bowl to receive the urine which they drink off greedily.[7]

Even reindeer were reported to be attracted to the fungus or to urine that smelled of it. On more than one occasion, a person intoxicated with *A. muscaria* would step outside to relieve himself and be trampled to death by reindeer trying to get at his urine.

The sensation induced by eating *A. muscaria* is apparently quite different from that of the magical *Psilocybe*. Wasson reported the experience of one user this way: "On eating the mushrooms, a period of exaltation ensues in which the chewers of the raw mushrooms shout and rage. Then, they engage in feats of prodigious physical exertion and experience illusions of radical changes in all dimensions, of miraculous mobility attributed to witches and werewolves." And another:

> The usual way to consume Fly Agarics is to dry them and then to swallow them at one gulp, rolled up into a ball, without chewing them. Chewing Fly Agarics is considered harmful, since it is said to cause digestive disturbances. The narcotic effect begins to manifest itself about a half hour after eating, in a pulling and jerking of the muscles. This is gradually followed by a sense of things swimming before the eyes, dizziness, and sleep. During this time, people who have eaten a

large quantity of mushrooms often suffer an attack of vomiting. The rolled up mushrooms previously swallowed whole are then vomited out in a swollen, large, gelatinous form. Even though not a single mushroom remains in the stomach, the drunkenness and stupor nevertheless continue, and all the symptoms of Fly Agaric eating are, in fact, intensified. The nerves are highly stimulated, and in this state, the slightest effort of will produces very powerful effects. Erroneous impressions of size and distance are common occurrences. A straw lying in the road becomes a formidable obstacle, and affected people will make a jump like that needed to clear a barrel just to get past the straw.[8]

Obviously, this mushroom has some powerful effects.

But why is *A. muscaria* called the fly agaric? Ostensibly, it is because flies that feed on the mushroom die soon afterwards. And, indeed, some people in eastern Europe and in the Orient set out dishes with liquid extracts of the fly agaric on their windowsills in the hope of keeping their housefly population in check. Perhaps the fungus does have some insecticidal properties, but if it does they are most certainly limited, for it is not at all unusual to find specimens in the forest that have been riddled by insect larvae and fed upon by other invertebrates—especially slugs. Moreover, on several occasions I have left an *A. muscaria* mushroom on a table top or lab bench for several days only to return to a well-eaten mass of mycelium and a thriving population of maggots that didn't appear to have been poisoned by the fungus in the least.

Wasson offers another explanation for the name. People who have eaten the mushroom exhibit behaviors similar to those of a person or animal going crazy from an incessant swarming of mosquitoes or other insects.[9] Such insect-induced insanity was apparently common among the people and animals in the tundra of Europe. Uncontrollable convulsions, violent jerking of the limbs, and a sensation of one's body being overrun by insects were also symptoms of *A. muscaria* intoxication. Visitors to New York's Adirondack Mountains during black-fly season or to Minnesota's canoe country on a calm, mosquitoey, summer night can well appreciate the feeling. Furthermore, people of the seventeenth and eighteenth centuries still believed that mental problems were caused by animals trapped in one's head; thus the phrases "a bee in her bonnet," "a bug in your ear," "bats in your belfry" to indicate some abnormal brain activity. *A. muscaria* intoxication would most assuredly evoke similar commentary. Explanations along these lines that link the mushroom to flies seem to make at least as much sense as its purported insecticidal properties.

A. muscaria has another special place in cultural history. Wasson and several others believe the mushroom to be Soma, a mysterious life force worshipped since the very beginnings of ancient Hindu culture and a factor in the genesis of modern-day religions.[10] Soma was the sole subject in 120 hymns (in a collection of 1,000) known as the *Rigveda* and is often mentioned in others. While the Soma has not been specifically identified, it has been said to have one foot and a red and white head and is passed from one person to another through urine. These descriptions, among others, are evidence pointing to *A. muscaria*, according to Wasson.

Recent archaeological evidence suggests that shamanic use of *A. muscaria* was not limited to the Eastern Hemisphere.[11] Artifacts from both the ancient Mayan culture and from the Athabascan tribes of British Columbia indicate that it was occasionally eaten by them as well. If humans did indeed migrate from Siberia (the part of the world with the best-documented use of *A. muscaria*) across the Bering Strait to North America, then it is logical that mushrooms, light in weight but heavy in spiritual value, would be carried along on the trip. And some trip it must have been!

Today, human use of *Amanita muscaria* for religious purposes, even among cultures still deemed "primitive," seems to have diminished to almost nothing. Recreational use, at least in the civilized world, is equally unpopular. That's probably just as well, because the few reliable contemporary accounts of *A. muscaria* intoxication describe a most unpleasant journey. While one does apparently experience unusual visions and the senses do reach new limits, most of one's trip is spent being nauseated, in a drunken stupor, or unconscious, and one is always faced with the threat of attack by horrifying creatures. No wonder that those trying to keep drugs out of our veins and minds have not bothered with the issue of the fly agaric: its poison far outweighs any imagined short-term benefits.

CHAPTER 12

Wood Decay

In chapters 1 and 2, you learned about the vital role of fungi in breaking down complex organic molecules into their basic elements, to be used again to create future generations. As long as that decay occurs in a manner that does not threaten human life and property, we generally regard the process as good and stand by politely and applaud. But if it happens in a way that we had not planned, and especially if it happens while those complex molecules are still serving some useful purpose in our lives, then it's not so good. In fact, the consequences can be disastrous.

Decay of wood by fungi, be it wood in standing trees or wood already used in construction, is one such event that has cost many lives and left many other people in peril. When trees fall unexpectedly, when houses crumble while we still own them, and when wooden bridges collapse before we've made it to the other side, the charm of the fungi temporarily loses its luster. Yet even in the face of tragedy, one cannot help but admire the capacity of the fungi to undo some of the greatest creations of humans and Mother Nature. Inasmuch as most people are destined to live lives surrounded by wood in one form or another, it is well to have some basic understanding of what causes it to rot and what, if anything, can be done to slow or stop its progress.

WOOD DECAY IN STANDING TREES

This is a hot topic in the tree care business, because the actions of those who care for trees—especially those who prune them with a poor technique—are believed to have a significant impact on the amount of internal decay that eventually results. The concepts that follow have evolved from the work of many different tree pathologists over the years, beginning in the mid-1800s with Robert Hartig, the "Father of Forest Pathology." Most recently, however, they have been popularized by Dr. Alex Shigo, now retired from the Northeastern Forest Experiment Station of the U.S. Forest Service.[1]

To begin, the prevailing theory—with a few exceptions, of course—is that the wood inside a tree will remain sound as long as the tree remains alive and the bark that is its outer shell is not wounded in such a way that wood within is exposed to open air. Bark is comprised of a unique assemblage of plant cells impregnated with a wide array of chemicals that are toxic to most wood decay fungi. As long as the bark remains intact, the wood is protected. Of course, chances that a tree will survive for any length of time without being wounded are virtually nil. Trees fall on other trees, they're pecked on by birds, they're struck by lightning, they're carved on by misguided romantics, they're hit by cars, they're pruned, and they're otherwise injured with and without malice. They just can't escape, so they have evolved an effective means for coping.

Shigo asserts that after a tree is wounded, the exposed wood is not immediately able to be decayed by fungi. First, it must be colonized by one or more species of bacteria. These microbes are much smaller than fungi and much simpler in structure: single-celled, each cell without a nucleus. They are ubiquitous in the environment and, as determined by assays of wood from freshly wounded trees, are quick to take up residence on the exposed wood. The bacteria have no apparent effect on the structural integrity of the wood, but they do presumably cause slight changes in its chemistry.

Then, one or more of a wide array of common molds settle on the exposed wood. Most of these are related to the ascomycetes, and they are commonly referred to as "pioneer fungi" because of their early appearance. Pioneer fungi also have no apparent effect on the structural integrity of the wood, but in combination with invasive bacteria that preceded them, they will likely stain the wood around the wound.

Only after thorough colonization by the bacteria and pioneer fungi do the wood decay fungi become noticeably active. These fungi, with their ability to degrade cellulose, pectin, and lignin can easily, and often quickly, change sound wood to an amorphous mass of organic rubble. As the succession of organisms proceeds farther into the tree, additional wood is decayed, branches may break, and stems may give way. Decay of root wood could lead to the upending of an entire tree.

Many different species of fungi can rot wood in standing trees. From a taxonomic standpoint, most are basidiomycetes including the mushrooms, fleshy shelves, and rigid brackets. Wood rotters tend to have a limited host range, able to decay only one or a few closely related species of trees. Those that attack many species are usually limited to either conifers or deciduous trees, although a few can even jump that boundary.

Wood decay fungi also seem somewhat to specialize in the part of a tree they attack. Apparently, the chemistry of wood in some parts is sufficiently different from that of other parts to affect fungal growth. Root rotters, such as *Ganoderma lucidum* and *Heterobasidion annosum,* are invariably found only on roots or in the root collar region. *Cerenna unicolor* and *Climacodon septentrionale,* on the other hand, are almost never found on roots but are common higher up the tree. *Laetiporus sulfureus* and *Fomitopsis pinicola* don't seem to have such limitations as they are found on the wood of all but the smallest branches of their respective host trees.

From an even more fundamental perspective, people who study wood decay fungi classify them based on the part of the wood they attack. Some fungi attack lignin first, and only after digesting it do they degrade cellulose and the other major components of the cell. They are known as white rot fungi because they cause partially decayed wood with residual cellulose to be an off-white color. In contrast, brown rot fungi degrade cellulose first and leave lignin virtually untouched. Wood rotted by them has a reddish brown to golden brown color due to the residual lignin. White rot fungi are generally more likely to be found in the wood of deciduous trees, while brown rotters are more frequent in conifers.

It only stands to reason that trees must be able to mount some sort of defense against wood decay fungi or all would be reduced to humus with the first nick in their bark. Indeed, most trees have very effective means for containing invading organisms and are thus able to remain sound and erect for many years. Coincident with the efforts of bacteria and fungi to gain a toehold—hypha-hold?—on the freshly exposed wood, the tree begins to set up defensive barriers of its own. The defense response is called "compartmentalization," and you can expect to hear knowledgeable people in the tree care business refer to the CODIT concept of tree response to wounds. CODIT, an acronym coined by Shigo in the mid-1970s, stands for "compartmentalization of decay in trees."

Compartmentalization is a relatively complex process, and certain parts of the concept are still being debated vigorously. But there does seem to be a general consensus that when a tree is wounded, cells in the vicinity of the wound respond to the potential threat from invading microbes by undergoing physical and chemical changes that make them more resistant to the action of decay fungi. In effect, they form barriers—Shigo calls them "compartment walls"—to the advance of both pioneer organisms and decay fungi. Some of the barriers are more effective than others, so discoloration and decay are more likely to proceed faster in some directions than in others. The advance of invaders above and below the wound is the most rapid, while sideways growth may be considerably slower.

The strongest barrier is invariably the one comprised of a narrow band of wood formed immediately after a tree is wounded.

Even if wood decay fungi get into a tree and rot the wood that is present at the time of wounding, it is unlikely that they will invade wood formed afterwards—unless, of course, there is another wound. In the years after wounding, continued decay of the inner wood with continued addition of sound wood on the outside—protected by the barrier formed right after wounding—results in the hollow trees that are so common in our landscapes and forests.

✦ Heart Rot Fungi

There is another way for hollow trees to develop: through the action of fungi that decay only the heartwood of older trees. Several fungi are specialized for degrading this kind of wood, and in North America they are particularly serious in old-growth coniferous trees in the forests of the Pacific Coast from California to Alaska. Some heart rot fungi don't even need a wound to gain entrance to their hosts; they do it by growing through small branch stubs. There, they not only predispose trees to breakage in strong winds but they also cause a significant loss of wood that might otherwise be used for lumber.

✦

Now, suppose a tree in your front yard was wounded. What would be some of the factors influencing the amount of decay that might occur in that wood?

The first is the species of tree affected. Some species are naturally more resistant to growth of decay fungi than others. In general, black locust, walnut, white oak, cedar, and black cherry seem to be highly resistant to decay. Conversely, aspen, willow, silver maple, and American beech are highly susceptible. Other species vary across the spectrum. When choosing trees for new plantings, especially if they are eventually expected to tower over homes, parks, or city streets, one would be wise to consider susceptibility to decay as an important variable in choosing which species to plant.

A second factor to consider is tree vigor. Barrier formation around wounds is an active process. Trees growing slowly because they are stressed by poor soil conditions, malnutrition, drought, old age, or other noxious factors are slower to defend themselves with adequate barriers. Like people, stressed trees are also less effective in repairing tissue and closing wounds.

A third variable is the size of the wound. Because wounds are the entrance sites of pioneer organisms and decay fungi, it only stands to reason that larger wounds present larger targets for noxious microbes to drop in, and they do. Also, wood decay is an aerobic process; both the pioneer organisms and the wood decay fungi need oxygen to grow. A smaller wound is likely to close more quickly, thus restoring the outer, protective shell and trapping any invading microbes in an environment that is with little or no oxygen. These fungi may not die, but they grow much slower, and the damage they do is usually negligible.

Fourth is the genetic constitution of the tree. As an example, consider cottonwoods, which are notoriously susceptible to decay. If a thousand trees in a cottonwood plantation were wounded, some would incur more decay than others, and some may have no decay at all. That's because there are demonstrable genetic differences among trees within the same species. Given enough time, forest and shade tree breeders will probably exploit those differences by selecting the most decay-resistant individuals to develop lines that will be used as street trees or for timber production.

What can you do after a tree is wounded to reduce the amount of decay that will occur? First, remember that the zone of cells produced immediately after a tree is wounded is highly resistant to invasion by decay fungi. If no further wounds occur, decay fungi may hollow out a portion of the tree, but all wood produced after wounding should be sound. There is no better defense than that. Thus, the best thing people can do to minimize decay is to promote rapid growth and closure of the wound. Watering during periods of drought is crucial, and the tree should also be protected from attack by other pests. For instance, if a recently wounded tree happens to be one of the species favored by a defoliating insect like the gypsy moth, and a gypsy moth outbreak is forecast for the area, it would be prudent to treat the tree with an insecticide to prevent damage by the larvae. This will alleviate added stress associated with defoliation and allow the tree to devote more energy to coping with the wound.

A source of considerable controversy among tree care professionals is whether or not it is wise to to treat new wounds with a wound dressing. Some argue vehemently that such treatments have value, while others are far more ambivalent about the issue. In other words, some people swear *by* wound dressings; others swear *at* them! Research data indicate that wound dressings have little or no apparent effect on reducing the incidence or severity of wood decay in trees. However, latex-based dressings developed in recent years are also unlikely to damage trees. Thus, it appears that they can be safely applied to fresh wounds for cosmetic reasons, but one should not assume that they have any therapeutic value.

Another question of concern to prospective homeowners and to anyone else who takes care of trees in landscapes, parks, and the like is whether or not existing trees have internal wood decay and if so, how much. Not only is knowledge of this information needed to protect oneself and one's family and property from possible damage, but it may also keep a person out of court. Many tree owners have been sued for negligence when their rotten trees have fallen on another person or their property. Where signs of obvious decay were evident, some have been held liable. Of course, the final evaluation of any tree is best left to a professional arborist, but there are things that you can watch for in your daily rounds.

First, look for open wounds or hollows (fig. 12.1). The hol-

Fig. 12.1. Cavities in trees are good indicators of rot and of potentially hazardous
trees.

lows are, in fact, created by decay fungi. When they are seen, the
question then becomes one of how extensive the decay is. That
assessment is best left to a certified professional arborist. He or
she will use one or more instruments to probe into the wood and
measure the extent of decay via differences in electrical con-
ductivity, sound transmission, or analysis of wood color and texture. Then, taking into consideration the crown size, branch
structure, prevailing winds, and other pertinent factors, the arborist will recommend a course of action to lessen any threat of
the tree to life or property.

Second, keep an eye open for fruit-bodies of decay fungi on
the trunk and roots. Some fruit-bodies, like those of *Ganoderma*

Fig. 12.2A,B. Perennial fruit-bodies like those of *Ganoderma applanatum* (A) and annual ones like *Climacodon septentrionale* (B) are signs of decay.

applanatum (fig. 12.2A,B), are perennial and you can expect to find them anytime of the year. This fungus puts on a new layer of growth each year, much the same way that a tree puts on a new layer of wood. And, given the opportunity, these can get to be large enough for a person to stand on.

Most other fruit-bodies are fleshy annuals. They emerge from the tree between mid-July and mid-September, and one must be alert to see them because they may be quickly devoured by insects, rodents, or molds. Some, like *Laetiporus sulfureus* (chicken-of-the-woods) and *Pleurotus ostreatus* (oyster mushrooms) are also prized by mushroom hunters, and more than one valuable bellwether of wood decay has been known to disappear from a residential tree during a clandestine, late-night foray. A general rule of thumb for most tree care professionals is that if a decay fungus fruits on the side of a tree, it has probably caused extensive decay within. However, a thorough evaluation is still advised if pruning or removal of a valuable landscape specimen is contemplated.

A third indicator of potential decay in trees is the presence of seedlings growing in the crotches where two or more large branches are joined. The value of this became apparent to me several years ago while I visited a central New York town that had been ravaged the day before by severe winds. In many trees split by the wind, especially silver maples, wood exposed by the breakage was so rotten that it had the color and texture of rich organic soil. And growing right in that humus was a tree seedling about three feet tall and a quarter inch in diameter. The seedling may have been the same species as the host tree, but just as often it was not. Since then, I have seen and heard reports of many other failed trees with seedlings in junctions of their largest branches and have concluded that these seedlings are indicators worth watching. Just as with trees showing hollows or fungal fruit-bodies, trees hosting seedlings in their branches need immediate assessment by a competent tree care professional to allow for planning the best course of action.

Finally, one must be aware that trees occasionally have significant internal decay while showing no external evidence that such has occurred. The annals of arboricultural tragedies are fraught with stories of branches or stems of seemingly healthy trees breaking off, with no prior indication of a problem. Closer examination, however, showed that many of the trees had extensive decay but no other obvious symptoms. With trees like this, foretelling impending danger is virtually impossible.

DECAY OF WOOD PRODUCTS

Unfortunately, wood decay is not limited to living trees. It also occurs in wood in service—that is, in wood that has been cut and hewn to make houses, fences, bridges, telephone poles, ships, and a wide array of other products. Decay is the most significant problem facing the wood products industries throughout the world, and millions (perhaps billions!) of dollars are spent each year to prevent additional losses and to replace items that have rotted beyond a threshold of safety.[2]

The key factor in determining whether decay will affect wood in service is whether or not the wood gets wet and if so, for how long. Fungi can only rot an already moistened substrate, and if the wood remains dry, decay simply cannot occur. Not surprisingly, wooden ships are the most likely of manmade items to suffer the ravages of decay, and in years past the endless battle to prevent it provided the impetus to seek other materials for shipbuilding. Even the once mighty British Navy was no match for the fungi. During the American Revolution, sixty-six British ships were so rotted during construction that they never left their harbors to join the fray. And the *Queen Charlotte*, built at an original cost of £88,000, rotted so quickly that an additional £96,000 of repairs had to go into it before it ever left port. By 1869, it had sustained another £269,000 in repairs.[3] And you thought inflated defense budgets were a phenomenon unique to the twentieth century!

Wood in continuous contact with moist ground is also highly susceptible to decay. The fungi that rot railroad ties can take their fair share of the blame for the demise of a once thriving railroad industry in many parts of the world. Furthermore, countless millions of dollars are spent annually to treat and replace telephone poles and wood in bridges, playgrounds, picnic tables, and hundreds of other structures.

For most people, the time they are most likely to come face to face with wood decay fungi is when these fungi try to dismantle their houses. Every prospective home buyer should be certain to have his or her intended purchase examined by a professional inspector or building contractor who knows where to look for decay, what to look for, and how to assess potential for more damage. All wooden parts potentially exposed to water need special attention. Those include all wooden elements in contact with the ground or the foundation, all wood around windows and doors, and to whatever extent possible, all wood around sinks, toilets, and showers or tubs. Older houses that have been remodeled and advertise themselves as "energy efficient" deserve special attention because a consequence of "tightening up" houses is that air circulation is reduced, and the moisture generated inside is more likely to stay there.

To prevent decay in new construction, use only sound, dry wood and be sure there is no leakage of water into the structure from the outside. Also, be sure ventilation is good enough to prevent a significant amount of condensation inside. Bathrooms with showers or tubs should be equipped with ceiling fans to ensure that water vapor can be quickly vented. And bathers should *use* those fans!

Places where wood is unavoidably exposed to moisture must either be constructed with decay-resistant wood such as redwood or cedar or with preservative-treated wood. The most effective and least toxic of preservatives is chromated copper arsenate (CCA), and lumber treated with it is plainly evident because the chemical imparts a light green stain to the wood.

Despite its toxicity to fungi, CCA poses no threat to human health when used as directed. However, if the wood is burned, then the individual elements of CCA may be liberated as toxic gases. Thus, people who use treated lumber for any construction project are advised not to burn the scraps but to dispose of them in an acceptable manner.

FOR all the problems wood decay fungi cause people, they serve to sustain or enhance life in other ways. Countless numbers of cavity-nesting birds and animals depend on decay fungi to soften the centers of trees so they can make suitable homes. And thousands of insects either depend on fruit-bodies of wood decay fungi for food or to aid in reducing wood to a palatable substrate. Humans also benefit inasmuch as all commercially produced edible fleshy fungi, except the common button mushroom and its close relatives, are cultivated wood rotters; they include oyster, shiitake, bear's head, and enoki.

More recently, the scientific community has directed considerable resources toward study of the potential use of white rot fungi to solve some pressing environmental problems. These fungi are able to degrade a wide array of otherwise persistent and hazardous materials, including pesticides such as DDT and lindane, little-used wood preservatives (creosote, pentachlorophenol), and other hazardous substances such as dioxin, TNT, and coal tar.[4] Fungi are superior to bacteria for reducing hazardous waste because their enzymes act on a broader spectrum of toxins than those produced by bacteria, and degradation takes place outside of the fungus body where there is little risk of mortality from the toxins. With bacteria, however, the toxins must be absorbed to be degraded, and then degradation must be quick enough to disable them before they kill the cells. Also, because the fungi generate heat as they carry out their metabolic processes, they remain active through the winter, whereas bacteria are more likely to go dormant.

White rot fungi are also being tested as agents to supplement conventional processes for reducing wood chips to individual fibers, a process known in the paper industry as pulping.[5] Historically, wood pulp has been made by immersing chips in solutions of strong acids or bases to degrade the lignin and free the fibers. The slurry is then treated with chlorine to whiten it before it is pressed into thin sheets to be dried as paper. Each step in a typical pulp mill generates thousands of gallons of noxious waste per day, and disposing of it has become a costly undertaking. White rot fungi have promise at both ends of the pulping process. They can be used to pretreat the chips, thus "softening" the wood so its eventual separation requires fewer external chemicals, and they degrade lignin so well that far less chlorine bleach is needed. As environmental regulations tighten, expect to see these fungi employed as key players in the pulp and papermaking industries.

✦ *Dry Rot Caused by* Scrpula lacrymans

Of all the fungi able to decay wood in service, none has attracted as much attention or engendered as much concern as *Serpula lacrymans*—and for good reason. The fungus has been implicated in millions of dollars worth of damage to wood buildings throughout Europe, Asia, Australia, and Japan.[a] The condition it causes, dry rot, is so named because *S. lacrymans* seems to be able to rot wood that is not visibly damp. In fact, the fungus produces specialized aggregations of mycelia, enabling it to carry water and nutrients from one place where conditions for decay are favorable to others where they are not. In this way, the fungus is able to span distances of 15 feet and more across stone, concrete, and other nonnutritive substrates to reach the wood it seeks. There it exudes water to moisten the otherwise dry wood so decay can occur. The only requirements the fungus seems to have are humid air with greater than 95 percent relative humidity, temperatures between 32°F and 82°F, and wood to rot. So pervasive is *Serpula* within older wood structures that detection has become an art in and of itself. In several European countries, specially trained dogs—"rothunds"—are used to sniff out the sinister fungal colonies. Fortunately for North American homeowners, *S. lacrymans* doesn't seem to occur in the Western Hemisphere. A closely related fungus, *Meruliporia incrassata*, causes some—but far less—damage on this side of the world.

[a]D. H. Jennings and A. F. Bravery, *Serpula lacrymans: Fundamental Biology and Control Strategies* (New York: Wiley, 1991).

✦

✦ Bookshelf: Fruiting Bodies and Other Fungi

Although homeowners in many European countries are aware of the threat of rot to their houses, it is doubtful that so many learned so much in so short a time as when Brian Lumley cast *S. lacrymans*—he calls it *Merulius*—as the villain in his award-winning short story, "Fruiting Bodies." A mutant strain of the fungus apparently escaped from tropical lumber washed ashore on the coast of England, and as the story opens, it gained a firm "hypha-hold" on the buildings of Easingham. Sole remaining resident Garth Bentham sums up the salient features of the fungus as if he had just read this chapter:

> "Hard to kill," he said. "And when it's active, moves like the plague! It's active here, now! Too late for Easingham, and who gives a damn anyway? But you tell that friend of yours to sort out his exterior maintenance first: the guttering and the drainage. Get rid of the water spillage, then deal with the rot. If a place is dry and airy, it's OK. Damp and must spells danger!"

Eighteen months later, storyteller Greg Lane returns to Easingham to find Bentham but instead . . .

> Oh, Jesus—all that sat there was a monstrous grey mushroom! It was a great fibrous mass, growing out of and welded with mycelium strands to the settee and in its center an obscene yellow fruiting body. . . .
>
> On nerveless legs, I backed away . . . into what had once been a piece of furniture. . . . Soft as a sponge, the thing

collapsed and sent me sprawling. Dust and (I imagined) dark red spores rose up everywhere.

Our hero survives but forever after he wonders, as he should, about those spores he inhaled.

Of added interest is that this story is one of a collection of short stories entitled "Fruiting Bodies and Other Fungi." Yet only the first story has anything to do with fungi! Clearly the publisher of this book knew which words and pictures would catch the eyes of would-be buyers. Another enlightened soul emerges from the ranks!

✦

CHAPTER 13

Interactions of Fungi and Insects

In previous chapters, insect interactions with fungi—some casual, some seemingly with more purpose—have been mentioned. Fungi attract insects through smell, taste, or luminosity; insects serve as vectors of some plant-pathogenic fungi; and insects feed on mushrooms and other fungal fruit-bodies, often destroying their appeal as food for humans. But there are some instances where insects and fungi have coevolved to weave a much more intricate web of influence on each other's lives.

FUNGUS MATCHMAKERS

If you have read this book from the beginning, you already know that some fungi produce their spores in matrices that are either smelly enough or tasty enough to attract insects. Some may even utilize the complex chemistry of bioluminescence to lure the nocturnal crowd. For the fungi mentioned earlier, the insects serve largely to spread spores to new substrates where they can, in turn, develop into new colonies. But for some fungi, insects play an even more vital role. They transfer fungus spores of one mating type to a colony of a second compatible mating type, thus enabling eventual sexual recombination and reproduction.

Rust fungi are particularly noteworthy in this regard. Many of the various species have one time in their life cycles when they produce minute spores, or spermatia, in nectar. The nectar attracts insects who inadvertently pick up the spores as they probe the fluid for its tasty contents. As they continue to forage, the insects will carry the spermatia to another droplet of rust nectar on the same or a different leaf, where they are—again inadvertently—deposited. At the same time, spores from that nectary are likely to be picked up and spread to yet another in a process that continues as long as the insect is on the go. Spermatia cannot infect host plants, but they can fuse with specialized hyphae of the fungus that also grow in the nectar droplets. This fusion leads to the introduction of a second mating type with compatible nuclei, which, in turn, leads to fertilization and eventual production of races of rust. Without the insects, this event, so vital to the ability of the fungus to adapt to new hosts and different environments, would be much more haphazard.

Most rust fungi seem to be content with the attractive powers of their nectar to draw the insects they need. However, some also cause the leaf tissue on which they grow to turn bright yellow in spots around the colony. This obvious contrast with the surrounding green leaf tissue may also serve to catch the compound eye. But the grand champion of devious fungi must be *Puccinia monoica*, a parasitic rust fungus on wild mustards (*Arabis* sp.) in the mountains of the western United States.[1] This pathogen, like other rusts, produces its spermatia in nectar. But that is only a small part of the story. The fungus also invades the actively growing cells of its host plant and causes subsequent growth to be grossly different from uninfected relatives. Diseased plants are twice as tall as they should be and have twice as many leaves. Furthermore, the infected leaves are in the form of a dense rosette at the top of each stalk, they are bright yellow, and they are covered with a sticky, sweet-smelling, spore-laden exudate. The entire growth looks so much like a large yellow flower that botany students—and even some professors—have mistakenly collected it as a new species. The "pseudoflowers" attract a wide array of insects—far more than the number or variety drawn to healthy mustard plants—to ensure cross-fertilization of the fungus. Unfortunately, they may be so effective at drawing pollinators that they do so at the expense of neighboring plants that also depend on those insects for their reproduction. Ecologists are still trying to quantify the magnitude of the problem while mycologists are licking their chops.

Fungus Cultivators I: Leaf-Cutter Ants

Three large groups of insects are notable in their interactions with fungi in that they not only eat fungi but they also purposely cultivate them to ensure a continuous food supply. In Central and South America, the insects are ants in several different genera, most notably—and the subject of the following discussion—the genus *Atta*.[2] They are known as leaf-cutter ants or parasol ants, the latter name derived from the way the ants look as they march single file across the landscape carrying pieces of leaves over their heads (fig. 13.1).

A colony of leaf-cutter ants begins when a winged female—a queen—carrying a wad of mycelium of an all-important fungus from a previous colony finds a suitable place to set up a new home. Then she spits the wad of mycelium onto a piece of plant material, and as soon as the fungus begins to grow, she lays eggs on it. Egg laying continues at the rate of about fifty per day for the next three months, most of the eggs also serving as food for the female. However, a few survive each day, and these hatch to become at first larvae and eventually workers. Gradually, the population of workers builds until by the end of the second year, a nest may have up to seventy-five different entrances, and by the end of the third over a thousand. Eventually, a colony may be comprised of up to five to seven million individuals.

Leaf-cutter nests are completely underground—to depths of 18 feet—and within them may be one thousand or more interconnected chambers, each about the size of a grapefruit. Here eggs are laid and distributed to appropriate chambers, larvae hatch and feed on the cultivated fungi, and workers tend both larvae and fungus cultures to ensure continuation of both species.

The caste system is alive and well among the attines, as worker

Fig. 13.1. Leaf-cutter ant in typical form as it carries a leaf piece back to its home.

ants become one of four sizes, each with its own assigned mission in the colony. The largest, the soldiers (about three-fourths of an inch long), are solely involved in guarding the colony, protecting it against intruders and patrolling the trails. The next smaller individuals, the maxima (about one-third of an inch long), are most numerous, and they forage out into the nearby landscape in search of plant tissue, especially leaves. These they cut into irregularly shaped pieces up to one-half inch in their longest dimension and then carry them back to the colony. There, still smaller workers, the media (about one-sixth of an inch long) reduce the plant debris to still smaller pieces and move it into the chambers. The smallest ants, the minima (one-sixteenth of an inch long), receive the leaf pieces, clean them, inoculate them with bits of fungus mycelium, and tend both the fungus gardens and the larvae.

Identification of the fungus cultivated by leaf-cutter ants has proven to be an elusive task, for it never seems to produce spores. Rather, it is transferred as mycelium from one colony to another. However, most experts agree that the fungus is a basidiomycete—related to the mushrooms—and have settled on the name *Attamyces bromatificus.* Free-living cultures have never been found; the fungus is always associated with leaf-cutter ant colonies.

While there is little question but that the ants benefit by cultivating the fungi, there is some disagreement among scientists as to just what that benefit is. At first, it was believed that the ants depended solely, or almost so, on *Attamyces* for food. More recently, however, it has been observed that adults seem to be able to get almost all the nutrition they need from plant sap exuded as they cut and transport the leaves. What little fungus tissue they eat may simply supply some essential amino acid. The larvae, however, depend entirely on the fungus to digest the leaves, and they, in turn, digest the fungus. Conversely, the fungi need the ants to provide them with food in the form of leaf fragments.

As the colony grows and the number of ants reaches the hundreds of thousands or millions, the need for plant tissue to feed to the fungus also grows. In fact, in tropical rain forests of Central and South America, leaf-cutter ants are the dominant herbivores, consuming up to 17 percent of total leaf production by surrounding vegetation. They utilize a wide range of host plants, including many food and fiber crops, and in many areas they have actually become agricultural pests. In those instances, the ants have had to contend with new adversaries: farmers equipped with the latest in pest-busting machinery and chemicals. There may be temporary setbacks, but when it comes to betting on an eventual winner, I'll put my money on the ants.

✦ Ants and Fungi: Serving Much More

Though leaf-cutter ants may destroy desirable plants, their activity benefits many other forms of life and does much to enrich the diversity of species in tropical lands. Numerous arthropods, including springtails, mites, and other ants, live in the nests, and some snakes and lizards lay their eggs there. The latter find the constant temperature in the underground chambers to be just right for incubating eggs, and the ants, for their trouble, cultivate their fungus on the egg shells. Ant-eating animals such as army ants, toads, armadillos, and tamanduas depend on the ants for food. Even native people find the plump, egg-filled queens a delectable snack.

✦

Fungus Cultivators II: Termites

While Atta ants are busy cultivating fungi in South America, another group of insects is busy doing the same thing in Africa. But in this case they are not ants, they're termites. And they are not just any termites, for most species harbor populations of protozoans in their guts to break down plant material so the elements can be used for growth and reproduction. Termites in the family Microtermitinae get no such help. They pass plant material through their bodies once, to get what they can from it, and use their feces—containing undigestible debris from the first passage—to grow cultures of fungi in the genus *Termitomyces*.[3] This secondary digestion, then, takes place outside the termites' bodies, and when complete the fungi become a second source of nutrients. In many respects, the lives of the Eastern Hemisphere termites are like those of the Western's leaf-cutter ants, but with some significant differences.

To begin, some species of fungus-cultivating termites build mounds consisting of fecal matter and fungus mycelium above their underground nests. The mounds vary in size and shape depending on the termites involved, and "chimneys" up to thirty feet tall are common in many parts of the African bush (fig. 13.2). Inside, the mounds are constructed in a honeycomb-like manner, with numerous air-filled shafts that help to dissipate heat during the hot season and retain it when outside temperatures are too cool for fungus growth. Each mound contains a

Fig. 13.2. Termite mounds like these are common sights throughout the African continent. Inside, fungi are being cultivated to feed the busy colony.

queen and a king, and—perhaps—hundreds of thousands of workers.

Termites carry bits of wood, leaves, fruit, and other organic debris to their mounds but often not in the orderly caravan that characterizes leaf-cutter ant foraging. When they get their loot home, they eat it near the entrance to the mound—only going in afterwards to defecate. The fungi then grow exclusively on the resident workers' fecal matter, and not on large volumes of raw plant tissue. All stages of termites—larvae and most adults—readily eat the fungus; only the king, queen, and soldiers eat the salivary secretions exuded by the workers.

Termitomyces are mushroom producers, but for some reason the termites prevent the mushrooms from forming in active mounds. However, when they sense an impending rainstorm, they may take bits of mycelium out of their mounds and spread them on the ground nearby. Several days later, the mushrooms appear and shed their spores, presumably with the opportunity to cross-fertilize with other cultures from other mounds. Then the termites reappear to collect fungus tissue that may be genetically mixed through simple growing together of fungal hyphae, which is then cultured in a new mound or in a new part of an old one. Abandoned mounds also produce crops of mushrooms for several years after the termites have left, and these are considered by the African people to be rare delicacies.

Like leaf-cutting ants, fungus-growing termites have become pests because of their continual collection of plant debris to nourish their fungal cultures. They occasionally threaten cultivated crops, but have a more devastating effect on wooden structures, where their food collection can result in a maze of galleries that leave the wood with little strength. Use of conventional insecticides has been a successful measure, but more recently pest managers have considered using fungicides in the mounds to arrest growth of the *Termitomyces*. If that strategy worked, it might provide a more directed and, perhaps, more environmentally friendly alternative.

Fungus Cultivators III: Ambrosia Beetles

The third example of insects that transport fungus spores or mycelium from one place to another with every intention of eating the developing cultures is not quite so elegant as the association exhibited by termites and leaf-cutter ants. Nonetheless, these insects are just as dependent on their fungal partners for growth and reproduction as the aforementioned ones. And the fungi involved have precious few alternatives for spore dispersal other than by the insects that intend to eat them.

The insects are wood-boring beetles, most in the family Scolytidae, usually found in trunks of living trees stressed by adverse environmental conditions (drought, air pollution, defoliation, etc.) or in recently cut or wind-thrown trees.[4] Winged adults—usually females—land on the bark of such trees and begin to bore through it into the tree. Once a short tunnel has been prepared, the female emerges from the tree, copulates with an available male, and then returns to her tunnel to resume excavation. As she progresses, she also lays eggs on the tunnel walls and inoculates the wood with fungi she has carried from a previous home. The fungi, in the form of spores and mycelium, will have been transported by the beetle in specialized body cavities known as mycetangia.

When the eggs hatch, the developing young larvae are incapable of eating the wood around them. However, they can and do eat the fungi, which by this time have grown to form a continuous thin mat on the tunnel walls and are called "ambrosia," meaning "food of the gods." The fungi, in turn, use their enzymes to digest some of the wood. Most are ascomycetes, and their action does little to affect the strength of the wood. However they do cause a visible stain. Eventually, full-grown larvae pupate and emerge as adults with a supply of fungi in their mycetangia, which they inoculate in the next generation of galleries to nourish the next generation of larvae. Because of their obvious role as food for the larvae, the fungi have become known as ambrosia fungi and the insects as ambrosia beetles.

Insects as Fungus Food

For every insect species that survives long enough by eating fungi to reproduce and thus continue its species, there is at least one fungus—and probably hundreds more—that survives by eating insects. In fact, if you are in a building with windows as you read this book, it is very likely that a good example

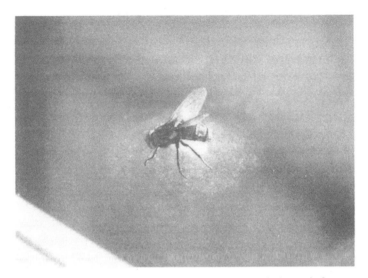

Fig. 13.3. *Entomophthora muscae* claims another victim as it fastens a fly to a window pane and surrounds it with a halo of spores.

of such parasitism is close by. So get out of your chair and take a short walk. Look carefully at those windows. Any signs of insects? How about flies? Every place has flies! Don't concern yourself with the live ones; look for those that are dead. In fact look for those that are dead and stuck to the glass. Got one? Good! Now look closer. On the glass around the carcass, do you see what might be called a cloudy halo? Well, that halo, my friend, is a mass of spores from the fungus that killed that fly (fig. 13.3). The fungus is most likely *Entomophthora muscae*, and other species in the genus also kill aphids, some caterpillars, and grasshoppers. The fungus obviously does not have a significant impact on the fly population, because there are still plenty to go around. Yet is is one of several fungi being studied as possible biological control agents for houseflies and their relatives both in houses and barns.[5]

Sexually Transmitted Disease for Flies?

Before you leave that fly, take one more look. Are legs and wings outstretched? They should be. Is the rear end up in the air? It should be, too. This is because *E. muscae* usually leaves its victims in a position that resembles a female fly ready to mate. And any unsuspecting male that happens by will be hard pressed to ignore such an overt gesture. Alas! All the visitor will get is exposure to the pathogenic fungus and a substantially shortened life. What a scoundrel that fungus is!

✦

Another entomopathogenic fungus has a special place in the history of biology because from it came the first solid evidence that an infectious agent could cause disease. This was the first substantive challenge to the concept of spontaneous generation and the strongest support to date for the germ theory of disease. The disease was called muscardine disease and it was killing silkworms in Europe with such a vengeance that the future of the silk industry there was in jeopardy. Agostino Bassi, an Italian lawyer turned farmer, not only determined that death of the worms was due to the chalky powder on their corpses but he also identified that powder as a mass of fungus spores. The fungus, *Beauveria bassiana,* was eventually named in his honor and it has since received considerable attention from people looking for alternatives to chemical pesticides. A commercial preparation of spores, sold under the trade name Mycotrol, is used for control of potato beetles, and the fungus has proven to be effective for control of several other insect pests, as well.[6]

✦ *Bassi: Credit Where It Is Due*

The significance of Bassi's work on muscardine disease seems to have been lost among those who record the history of biology. As the transition from support of the concept of spontaneous generation to that of the germ theory of disease evolved, names like Pasteur, Lister, and Koch came to the fore. But their work associating living organisms with disease was done in the 1870s. Bassi had things figured out forty years earlier. Unfortunately, because his patients were insects and his pathogens fungi, he never got the credit he deserved. Perhaps with belated efforts such as this one, another neglected student of mycology will find his rightful place in the annals of microbiology.

Another group of fungi known to prey on insects is the genus *Cordyceps*.[7] If you have read previous chapters in this book, that name may sound familiar, because it's a bit like *Claviceps,* the fungus that causes ergot. Both names mean "club head" and both fungi look vaguely similar. *Claviceps* develops a resting body known as a sclerotium in the head of a grass such as rye or wheat or barley. The sclerotium germinates in spring to give rise to stalks with swollen, spore-bearing "club" heads. *Cordyceps,* on the other hand, develops a sclerotium in the body of the insect it has killed. In spring that sclerotium gives rise to club heads of its own. Spores from *Cordyceps'* club heads, however, are intended to infect more insects.

Early scientists called *Cordyceps*-infected larvae "vegetable insects," and there were great hopes that these fungi could be used as natural controls of some insect pests. That has not been realized, but of greater interest these days is the purported medicinal value of this strange fungus that grows from the cadavers of insect larvae. Contemporary curiosity stems from an episode at the Chinese National Games in Beijing in 1993 that caused at least some skeptical Western medical specialists to do a double take.[8] There, Wang Junxia knocked 42 seconds off of the world record in the 10,000 meter race, and she and her teammates set several other world records with impressive performances. At first, meet officials suspected illegal drug use by the athletes, but the women's coach assured challengers that his charges had done nothing more than train hard and drink a stress-relieving tonic made from a "caterpillar fungus." Further investigations revealed that the fungus, *Cordyceps sinensis,* had been a standard prescription in Chinese medical practice for over a thousand years, used for a wide array of conditions including keeping the lungs fit, strengthening the kidneys, building up the marrow, and controlling hemorrhage. It was also a tranquilizing medicine as well as a treatment for anemia, malignant tumors, chronic coughing and asthma caused by senility, and spitting of blood from chronic tuberculosis. While all of this is reminiscent of claims made by traveling medicine men in the developing American West, the rapid rise of Chinese track and field athletes in recent years is cause for more investigation. I doubt that we have heard the last of this strange fungus and its magical powers.

◆ *Are You Standing on the Next Frontier?*

Articles in the popular press, and even those in scientific journals, lead one to believe that discovery of new chemicals from microbes is most likely to occur in exotic, far-away places, most likely in the Tropics. But that's not true! In 1996, students in a field mycology class at Cornell found one such rare and valuable specimen while on a collecting trip in a woodland just a few miles from Ithaca in upstate New York. The fungus was another insect pathogen, and the students didn't recognize it for what it was at the time. But closer examination later that night confirmed it to be only the fifth collection in recorded history of the sexual stage of a fungus that produces cyclosporin A. That piece of land has now been set aside as a biodiversity preserve. All the people who do not have the resources to travel to the far reaches of the world in search of new things are heartened to learn that many discoveries can still be made right in their own backyards.

◆

Finally, among fungus pathogens of insects, consider the situation faced by scientists studying gypsy moths in Connecticut in

1989. By way of background, gypsy moths are native to the Orient and were accidentally introduced to the North American landscape in 1868–69. This followed a tragic accident that enabled the moths to escape from a laboratory in Boston where they were being studied for potential silk production. Since then, gypsy moths have spread throughout much of the northeastern United States and southeastern Canada, and have defoliated and killed millions of deciduous trees in forests and landscapes. In any given locale where gypsy moths live, populations may be relatively small and tolerable in most years. However, there are occasional "epizootics" of such magnitude that highways are made slippery by squashed caterpillars and deciduous trees over many hectares are stripped bare in mid-June when they should be flush with leaves. Many of those trees die, especially if they have been defoliated in the previous year, as well. In years following such episodes, the gypsy moth population crashes as a lethal virus disease—also introduced from the Orient in the early 1900s and always present in small amounts—builds to extraordinarily high levels and kills most of the insects.

One feature of cadavers of virus-killed caterpillars is that they tend to hang on the trunks of trees in inverted V's. This feature is used by scientists monitoring gypsy moth populations to track the progress of the disease. But in 1989, field scouts in Connecticut noticed an unusually large number of dead larvae hanging straight up and down on the sides of trees rather than in V's. That these larvae were in a site where a population explosion had not recently occurred was cause for additional scrutiny. Upon closer examination of the atypical carcasses, there was clear evidence of fungus mycelium growing from them, and the possibility was raised that a second disease—this one caused by a fungus—also threatened the gypsy moth's welfare. With a bit of laboratory sleuthery, the role of the fungus was confirmed. It was one that had not been described previously and was soon named by the USDA scientists at Cornell as *Entomophaga maimaiga*.[9]

Although discovery of this very effective biocontrol agent for one of the most devastating forest pests of the twentieth century was welcomed with open arms, it also raised some challenging questions. One of those was: "Where did the fungus come from?" Since gypsy moths were native to the Orient and populations there were probably kept in check by some other parasite or predator, that seemed to be a logical place to look. Sure enough, a trip to Japan yielded several dead gypsy moth larvae that proved to be infected with the same fungus. But how did it get to the United States?

The answer to that question remains clouded, but one intriguing hypothesis is that the disease has been in the country for eighty years or more. Records show that experimental work was done at Harvard with an unidentified "gypsy fungus" collected from Japan in the early 1900s. In those experiments—all conducted outdoors with the gypsy moths in screened cages— failed to yield encouraging results for the investigator. When the colony was eventually killed by the virus disease, the work was abandoned. A suspicion now is that the fungus actually did survive even though its effect on the caterpillars was too low to be noticed. Furthermore, it is highly likely that because the experiments were done outdoors, the fungus was able to escape the wholly inadequate confines of the cage and take up residence in the surrounding landscape. Thereafter, researchers reason, the fungus gradually increased in number and range, but for many years was simply not recognized for what it was—perhaps because the population was still very low or perhaps because it was confused with virus-induced mortality. Finally, in 1989—a year with unusually wet spring weather favorable for fungi of all kinds—the population of *E. maimaiga* literally exploded. Thus, eighty years after it was begun, the experiment became a success.

Other hypotheses entertain other scenarios and none have been proven conclusively. The good news, however, is that in the meantime, *E. maimaiga* seems to have played a significant role in reducing gypsy moth populations throughout much of the northeastern United States.

Symbiotic Relationships of Fungi with Plants

Ecologists define symbiosis as a condition where two organisms live in close proximity to each other, usually in a mutually beneficial relationship. There are many instances where fungi are partners in symbiotic relationships with plants.

MYCORRHIZAE AND OTHER ENDOPHYTES

One of the most significant symbiotic associations of plants and fungi was first discovered in the mid-1800s by scientists who were trying to determine how terrestrial plants without chlorophyll got the food they needed to stay alive. The focus of the attention was on plants in the genus *Monotropa*, known in North America as Indian pipes (fig. 14.1). At the outset, it was assumed that the only way a plant without chlorophyll could possibly survive was if it were parasitic on the roots of other plants. But when Indian pipes were dug up, it was quite obvious that their short, stubby roots had no such direct contact with other plant roots in the vicinity. Indian pipe roots did, however, have a white sheath of a matted and somewhat woolly substance.[1]

Eventually, it was determined that the roots of *Monotropa* were infected by a fungus. Furthermore, mycelium of the fungus ramifying through the soil—digesting, absorbing, and transporting various nutrients and water back to the plant—was what kept *Monotropa* alive. And from these observations, the word "mycorrhiza" (*mycos* = fungus, *rhiza* = root) was coined. The relationship was truly a mutualistically symbiotic one because each partner benefited from the other, and both fared better than either would if left to grow on its own.

Fig. 14.1. *Monotropa uniflora* is a seed plant
without chlorophyll that depends entirely on
mycorrhizal fungi to supply it with water, nutrients, and food materials.

One of the many interesting features about mycorrhizae that
has become apparent in the years following early work with
Monotropa was that most species of perennial plants have mycorrhizal relationships. This was by far the rule rather than the
exception.

The fungi that participate in mycorrhizal relationships represent the entire spectrum of the kingdom, with common and
important representatives from all the major groups. However,
the most conspicuous ones are those that fruit in the form of

mushrooms. In fact, many of the edible and poisonous genera mentioned in chapter 10, including *Amanita, Boletus* and related genera, *Cantharellus* (chanterelles), and *Tuber* (truffles) are mycorrhizal partners with trees and other forest plants. Theoretically, one could carefully follow the right hyphal strand from the stem of one of these fruit-bodies through the soil to the root that the fungus has partnered with. There, one would likely find a short, stubby, multiply branched root piece less than one-eighth inch long protruding from a larger, woody root. Many people mistakenly assume that these are the root hairs they learned about in their elementary science classes, but this is not the case. Root hairs are much smaller and grow only at the very tip of an elongating root. Mycorrhizae are far more abundant.

Upon closer examination—I'm talking really close, with a microscope—the general structure of these mycorrhizae becomes apparent. Each short multiple-branched "root" has a central core of plant tissue, but it is completely enclosed in a dense mat of fungus mycelium. Some hyphae penetrate the root tissue but they stay between the root cells, never actually breaching the cell walls. Technically, these are called "ectomycorrhizae," and they are common on most conifers as well as some deciduous plants.

In contrast, there are many more endomycorrhizal partnerships that are characterized by complete absence of the mycelial sheath and by hyphae that readily penetrate right through host plant cell walls. In fact, these are considerably more difficult for the inexperienced eye to identify because there is little or no outward indication that a fungus partner is present. Only by examining properly stained thin sections of the roots with high magnification does one actually see the hyphae. The most important fungus partners forming endomycorrhizae are Zygomycota in the genus *Glomus,* and they occur on a wide array of deciduous trees and shrubs as well as many food crop plants.[2]

Mycorrhizae are not just idle curiosities to challenge the patience and visual skills of those who want to see them. Rather, they are important contributors to plant growth and development. In fact, they are so important that it is almost impossible to find normally mycorrhizal plants free of them. Experiments comparing mycorrhizal plants with nonmycorrhizal ones must be done in chambers or greenhouses with filtered air, and test plants must be grown from seed in sterile soil. With those strict precautions in place, scientists have shown that mycorrhizae greatly increase the absorptive surface area of a host plant's root system, thus increasing its ability to absorb water and to withstand drought. Mycorrhizal plants are also better able to obtain mineral nutrients from the soil and to tolerate environmental extremes, including high soil temperatures and unusually high or low soil acidity. Finally, mycorrhizae seem to offer some protection from soil-borne pathogens including other fungi and microscopic plant-parasitic roundworms known as nematodes.[3]

Plants aren't the only benefactors in the mycorrhizal partnership, however. The fungi also come out ahead. The plant host serves as a refuge from hostile soil conditions (especially cold and drought), and it supplies needed food materials. In one case, measurements of carbohydrate dispersal showed that the fungus partner used up to 25 percent of the food manufactured in its host tree leaves to sustain its own growth. Despite that, the tree grew better than it would have without the mycorrhizae!

Because mycorrhizae are so ubiquitous in our world, we rarely get the opportunity to see how ecosystems would fare without them. But there is one place where both plant and fungus partners have been destroyed through the thoughtless actions of people. Attempts to repair the damage have fallen far short of expectations, so fragile is the environment that has been affected. Unfortunately, the ruined region is getting bigger rather than smaller: it is the tropical rain forests of Central and South America.[4]

Imagine the sense of power that must have coursed through the veins of European explorers as they set foot on the coast of Central America in the 1500s. Not only were they able to subdue the native peoples with relative ease, but before them lay a land with lush vegetation on obviously fruitful soil. Surely by clearing a few acres of those trees, one could grow enough crops to feed, well, an army!

So the trees were cut, the brush was cleared, and the land was plowed and planted. But the crops that followed showed nowhere near the growth or yield that had been expected, and to the perceptive naturalist the reason was obvious. The tropical forest was not like forests of temperate climes. In many sites, there was no thick layer of leaf litter and no rich bed of organic soil. Instead, the forest floor was covered with a relatively thin (less than 4 inches deep) layer of debris in the form of rotting leaves and fruit, and below that was a dense mat of fungus mycelium. Pick out a strand of that mycelium and follow it for a ways and you would find it firmly connected to the rootlets of a large tree.

Nutrient cycling in the tropical forest was relatively quick and very efficient. When plant debris—be it leaves, branches, fruit, or whole trees—fell to the ground, some was devoured by insects but most was decayed by fungi that were thoroughly colonizing the surface of the forest floor. Although plant root systems could never possibly recover enough of the elements so vital to their growth before they were washed away by the next rain, the mycorrhizal fungi could and did. Because they were there to exercise their chemical jaws and snap up the liberated elements, they had become key players in evolution of the virgin rain forest, the most complex and varied ecosystem on our planet.

When the trees and shrubs were removed, the fragile understory mycelia were starved for carbohydrates and baked by the tropical sun. There was no rich bed of organic soil upon which to grow food crops, and yields were disappointing at best. Of greater concern, perhaps, was the startling realization that correcting the mistake was going to take a long, long time. There was little that people could do to speed the process; they just had to wait for the plants and the fungi to come back on their own, if they could.

In recent years, people who monitor populations of mushrooms in several west European countries have become concerned that human-caused destruction of mycorrhizae may not be limited to distant lands.[5] Rather, they have noticed a dramatic decrease in the number of wild mushrooms—many, mycorrhizal types—being collected on forays and sold in markets. Some say this is because collectors have been picking too many for market, thus depleting nature's supply. But populations of poisonous mushrooms have also declined, and there is no reason why those would be overharvested—or harvested at all, for that matter.

One of the leading students of this subject, the Netherlands' Eef Arnolds, wonders out loud whether air pollutants may be contributing to the decline of these formerly common fungi, but he is even more suspicious of the possible deleterious role of nitrogen contamination from nearby agricultural fields. Excess nitrogen in the soil does stifle fungal growth, and if enough of that should happen, it could eventually lead to the reduced vigor of overstory trees as well. Inasmuch as some European forests are now suffering from a striking and unexplained decline, the notion of an unthrifty mycorrhizal population contributing to the problem draws more attention than it might otherwise have.

In addition to the fungi that decay live plants or form mycorrhizae with their roots, scientists have relatively recently discovered that some plants harbor one or more other species of fungi that affect plant growth in yet another way. Collectively, these fungi are called "endophytes" because most of their vegetative bodies are within their host plants, and the effect they confer on their hosts is presumably beneficial.[6] This is in contrast to pathogens that might also be called endophytes but are more often called parasites because of their destructive nature.

At the top of the list of endophytes that receive close scrutiny by the scientific community are members of the genus *Neotyphodium*. These fungi, which live entirely within grasses except during a brief sporulation phase, first attracted attention when they were found to be responsible for the toxicity of some grasses to livestock.[7] The problem began when farmers and ranchers in the southeastern and midwestern United States reported that some of their livestock, especially females, got sick after eating tall fescue grass. Tall fescue is a hardy, pest-free, drought-tolerant grass that had been used with considerable success as forage in Europe. When it was introduced to the United States, perhaps accidentally, in the early 1900s, it thrived here—especially during droughty times when other grasses collapsed. And because of its tenacity, it was widely planted across the country. But something was obviously wrong with the North American plantings because the illness they caused was far more common and severe than anything recorded in Europe. The births of foals by pregnant mares were delayed by a month or more, and the young were so large that if they were still alive they inevitably had to be taken by Caesarean section. Then the mothers produced inadequate milk to nourish them. Some cattle lost limbs to dry gangrene. And all were more sensitive to other diseases because of a general reduction in vitality.

You may recognize the aforementioned symptoms as being similar to those caused by the ergot fungus, *Claviceps purpurea*— and for good reason. Species of *Neotyphodium*—natural endophytes found in fescues—produce ergovaline, ergosine, and ergonine, some of the same toxins produced by *Claviceps*. But in fescues, the fungus actually improves the health of the plant because it uses very little of the plant's resources for its own nourishment, and the alkaloids it produces are powerful deterrents to feeding by insects. In fact, growers of fescue turf grass seed, especially for golf courses and other high-maintenance sites, are now taking extra pains to ensure that the seed they sell is infested with the fungus. It enables landscape managers to reduce pesticide use significantly. In the meantime, livestock producers want seed that is fungus free.

Experience with *Neotyphodium* has prompted scientists to look elsewhere in the plant kingdom for endophytic fungi, and they're finding them. Not all have an obvious purpose but the possibilities are intriguing. Consider the endophytes of oak leaves with the potential of being pathogens. They remain dormant until "activated" when the leaf is attacked by a sedentary insect. The fungi then kill a small portion of the leaf surrounding the insect, the insect dies for lack of live leaf tissue to feed on, and there is no further damage from either![8]

LICHENS

There is another large group of organisms that results from the union of fungi with plants, and traditionally the organisms have had top billing as classic examples of mutualistic symbiosis: two organisms living together, each benefiting the other. The plants involved are algae, and the fungi are ascomycetes, relatives of the cup fungi. The products of the partnerships are lichens.*

Many lichens live in places that are virtually inhospitable to other organisms and they are able to do so because of their unique partnership. The fungus mycelium absorbs water and uses its enzymes to extract nutrients from the substrate—even from rocks. And the alga, via photosynthesis, provides carbohydrates. However, recent observations raise questions about just how "mutually beneficial" the relationship is.[9]

Upon closer examination, it has been found that the algal partner only constitutes 5 to 10 percent of the total biomass of a lichen. The rest is mycelium. And while the fungus partner can live only in the presence of the algal partner, at least some of the algal partners can grow alone without the fungus. Furthermore, microscopic examination reveals that hyphae of fungi actually

* Lichens are also formed through a symbiotic relationship of fungi with blue-green algae—microbes that are more closely related to bacteria than algae, but that do have chlorophyll and can make their own food.

penetrate the algal cells and form absorptive structures similar to those formed by pathogenic fungi. Thus, biologists are now inclined to think that the fungus in the lichen is really parasitizing the alga—holding the alga hostage, if you will—and using the products of algal photosynthesis to insure its own survival.

Despite these technicalities, however, lichens remain unique entities in the living world. One recent estimate is that there are about twenty thousand species. They are highly variable in shape, size, and color and are typically classified as either flat and firmly attached to their substrates (crustose), scaly (squamulose), leafy (foliose), or fruticose (upright or hanging, bushy or in sparse strands).[10]

Reproduction for a lichen could be a bit of a challenge if it had to depend on wind-blown fungus spores landing in the vicinity of a compatible alga. Some of this probably happens, but far more often a more reliable strategy is employed. Many lichens produce flakes of combined fungus and alga (soredia) in a powdery mass on the upper surface of the lichen body. Others produce fragile, upright pillars (isidia) containing cells of both partners. These fragments, be they soredia or isidia, are dislodged with ease and are blown about much like fungus spores. If they land in a favorable spot, they can begin a new colony.

One of the remarkable things about lichens is that they are able to survive where little else will grow. They cling to just about anything and can tolerate temperature extremes from near absolute zero to the blazing heat of the Sahara Desert. Lack of water also does not seem to faze them. One species that grows on rocks in the Atacama Desert of Chile can go for ten years with only fog for moisture. Others are not in quite such hostile sites, but they tolerate far harsher conditions than other living things their size. In the worst of times, lichen growth is understandably slow. A colony in the Arctic was estimated to be expanding at a rate of about 2 inches per thousand years.[11] Typically, though, growth is more likely to be on the order of 40 to 160 inches per thousand years. While it is doubtful that lichens will ever be the zucchinis of the fungus world, their growth is inexorable. Some colonies are estimated to be more than 4,500 years old.

Because lichens have no roots or other absorptive organs, except for sparse hyphal growth, they are far more dependent on the atmosphere and on rainfall for their nutrition. The consequence of this is that lichens are highly sensitive to perturbations in the chemistry of rain and air.[12] Thus, they have become valuable indicators of the occurrence of atmospheric pollution. Both acidic precipitation and elevated levels of sulfur dioxide kill many species of lichens, and many cities in developed countries have become lichen deserts because of the poor quality of their air.

As sources of food, lichens have little appeal to most humans even though their nutritional value rivals that of wheat or oats. But through the course of history, it was inevitable that since lichens grew in places where hardly anything else did, people would eventually try to eat them. Indeed, natives of boreal or subarctic regions have used them as supplemental sources of carbohydrates in times of famine. And in the deserts of the Middle East, the manna lichen (*Aspicilia esculenta*) may have been the foodstuff that fell from above to save the Old Testament children of Israel from certain starvation.[13] Even George Washington's troops are said to have used an extract of boiled lichens to thicken their soup as they huddled around the fires at Valley Forge and plotted their next move.

Aside from these few exceptions, most lichens contain various and sundry acids that limit their use by humans. They are far more important as sources of animal food, particularly in the Arctic regions. Deer, reindeer, and a host of other mammals native to these remote parts of the world supplement their diets of willow twigs and sedges with lichens during the winter. In fact, under severe winter conditions, lichens may constitute as much as 95 percent of the total diet of reindeer. They are so hungry that they quickly head for the sound of the nearest chainsaw, hoping to find a bountiful feast of lichens in the crown of the downed tree. Those who get there before the tree is cut through may be killed when it falls. To prevent this, loggers now first cut some lichen-laden branches from the crown and move them away from the trees to divert the starving reindeer. Lapps practice controlled grazing and even harvesting of reindeer mosses in northern Scandinavia. In subarctic Canada, vast areas are covered with lichen fields that have considerable potential use as caribou pastures.

Unfortunately, the use of lichens as food by reindeer has not been all that good for the health of the native peoples. This issue came to the fore in 1965, when a study was launched to learn more about the effects of radioactive fallout from nuclear bomb tests. The plan was to sample people from all over the world, with Lapps serving as the control group. After all, it was assumed, where else but in the frozen tundra could one find people whose innards were so unspoiled by the poisons of progress?

But when the results were in, much to the surprise of all, the Lapps' tissues had fifty-five times more radioactivity than those of the Finns living farther south, and up to one-third of the maximum amount permissible according to the standards of the time.[14] Further investigation revealed that radioactive caesium and strontium were being inadvertently concentrated by lichens, which were then eaten by reindeer, which were then eaten by people. Fortunately, above-ground testing of nuclear bombs stopped soon thereafter, but with little consolation to the people who had been unwittingly exposed for so long.

The nuclear reactor explosion in Chernobyl in 1986 further demonstrated the capacity of lichens to concentrate radioactive fallout. Within eight months of the accident, meat from reindeer in Norway and Sweden that had fed primarily on lichens had over ten times the legal limit of measurable radiation. In some areas, it exceeded the limit by twenty times. The reindeer were slaughtered and the carcasses were sold to mink and fox farms. Be forewarned if you are offered a "hot" deal on a fur coat from Russia![15]

At the other end of the climate spectrum, sheep in the Libyan deserts are reported to graze on a type of lichen that grows on rocks. Apparently the sheep find the lichen much to their liking and consume it with gusto—but suffer premature loss of teeth through abrasion from chewing it.

Although lichens hold little promise as contributors to modern-day diets, they may have a brighter future as sources of medicines to treat human ills.[16] Over half of all species tested have been found to have some antibiotic activity, but so far they have been found to be generally less effective than antibiotics from other sources. One notable exception is usnic acid, used in a burn ointment sold as Usno®. It is purported to be superior to penicillin in its ability to prevent secondary bacterial infections. Another lichen extract has caused the regression of tumors in mice. As chemical prospectors continue to scour the world, other valuable chemicals are likely to be discovered in lichens.

In the meantime, a more lucrative market for lichen extracts exists—in the manufacture of perfumes. Essential oils are extracted from over 8,000 tons of lichens harvested from various sites in Europe each year, to be used as fixatives and base odors in the final product.

Lichens have a place in our cultural history because for many years they were used to dye woolen fabrics. From the early 1300s until well into the 1800s an active dye industry existed in southern Europe. Lichens were collected as raw material and then dried, beaten into a fine powder, then boiled in a mixture of water and urine. The basic dyeing agent was extracted as a paste and used in coloring wool various shades of purple, red, or brown. To this day, Harris tweeds, manufactured in Scotland, are still dyed with native lichen dyestuffs that impart a unique, musty odor.[17]

As I review the preceding pages describing symbiotic relationships, I can't help but continue to be impressed with the demonstrated ability of the fungi to fill a niche that will ensure their survival. But they aren't selfish about it; they're willing to pay their way, to contribute to the ultimate welfare of their partners, and to leave a legacy of community spirit. Just like the people who write books about them!

I don't know how many other authors have faced the dilemma I'm facing as this work draws to a close, but it is indeed difficult for me to decide just where and when to stop writing. The scientific community, spurred by new enthusiasm for the potential uses of fungi in industrial processes—including synthesis of pharmaceuticals—and introduction of new technologies for studying all aspects of fungal biology, brings us into a time of rapid and profound transition. Thus, even though I *must* close—already being eight months past my publisher's deadline—I find myself planning changes to current chapters and additions of new ones for the second edition. Areas of inquiry that we will hear more about as the twenty-first century dawns include the following.

Taxonomy of Fungi. The art of describing and naming fungi was the cornerstone of mycology even before mycology was defined as a unique part of biological science. It has been so ever since, and students of mycology—including amateur mushroom hunters—have spent a good deal of time trying to come to grips with dichotomous keys and the terminology they engender. But new advances in the study of interrelationships between fungi, based on their nucleic acid sequences rather than on physical characteristics, have revolutionized the science. In the over one hundred presentations on fungal taxonomy that I have heard at professional meetings in recent years, only a handful of the speakers have had reason to illustrate the fruit-bodies of their subjects. One wonders whether they have, indeed, ever seen them. Instead, the screen is lit with an endless procession of agarose gels on which segments of DNA or RNA have been separated by electrical current according to size and shape.

There is little question but that the future of fungus taxonomy will continue in this vein, becoming ever more distant from the physical features of fruit-bodies and ever more mechanized. In fact, it may become so much so that mushroom identification will involve placing a drop of mycelial extract on a pretreated wafer and looking for certain patterns of spots rather than making traditional spore prints and peering through the microscope to compare structural details.

Plant Diseases. The same revolution in biotechnology that has changed methods of fungal taxonomy has also changed our ability to study plant pathogens. Now we can identify specific chemicals that enable some fungi to be pathogens, and we know something of the genes that make those chemicals. Similarly, we know which genes in plants make them susceptible to fungal attack. Engineering of disease-resistant plants has already begun, and once public concern about eating such engineered produce is allayed, I suspect many more crops will be designed with fungus-disease resistance and with other desirable characteristics.

Mycoses. While most of the future of our association with fungi promises to be bright, it also seems that we will continue to battle fungus diseases in humans for a long time. The problem, of course, is that as we have made progress in treating many other human diseases, we have done so by using drugs that depress our immune systems. At such a point, an array of normally benign fungi become serious pathogens in their own right. Prevention or treatment of these secondary agents, because of their similarity to mammalian cells, is not likely to be resolved soon. Instead, one might expect better success with advances in primary treatments to shorten the time of depressed immunity.

Drugs from Fungi. In chapter 8 I alluded to a vast array of possible benefits to human health from both molds and fleshy fungi. Although at present many of the claims that these fungi actually do what they are purported to do are anecdotal, I expect them to receive considerably more credible scientific attention in the years to come. I suspect that we have seen just the tip of a very large iceberg with respect to the discovery of drugs from molds to manage bacterial diseases, hypertension, mycoses, and a wide array of other human ills, and the coming years will see the discovery of many more. Even the ergot fungus is being cultivated on rye by some pharmaceutical companies hoping to discover valuable new alkaloids.

Among fleshy fungi, the merits of eating shiitake mushrooms are likely to be high on the priority list for further study. This is partly because they have a long history of health benefits in the Far East, and some of the claims are strengthened by reliable experimental data. Also, shiitake growing is relatively easy and utilizes wood waste in the process. If the mushrooms do improve the quality of life, it should be a relatively simple matter to grow enough to make them readily available to all who seek to use them. Also, their culture should be amenable to genetic manipulation with contemporary biotechnological techniques if that promises to improve their worth. Studies of other fleshy fungi are likely to follow suit, but the pace of those studies may weigh heavily on the success or lack of it with shiitake.

There is also increased interest in lichens as sources of drugs that can prevent both plant and animal diseases. So far, few microbes have been found to cause disease in lichens, and that suggests that they must have an array of protective chemicals worthy of further investigation.

In a continuing search for new sources of pharmaceuticals, expect to see increased attention paid to identifying and assaying microbes from the tropical rain forest. Despite the discovery of a valuable drug-producing fungus just 9 miles from Cornell

University, the lure and lore of the tropics are likely to garner a greater percentage of private and public research dollars.

Yeasts and Yeast Technology. In recent years, biologists have reported success in decoding the entire complement of DNA in *Saccharomyces cerevisiae*. This is the first organism of any kind with true nuclei in its cells for which this feat has been accomplished. Now that it has been done, however, the task of determining just what the various parts do is made easier, and one can expect rapid advances in designing yeasts to make new chemicals and mediate other chemical reactions. Yeast-based products such as wine, beer, and bread may be supplemented with entirely new flavors, and yeasts themselves may be engineered for improved palatability and use as protein sources, especially in burgeoning Third World countries.

Wood Decay Fungi. In the Acknowledgments section at the front of this book, I mentioned that I completed this project while at the University of the Orange Free State in South Africa. That experience enabled me to mingle with scientists who had considerably different interests than my close colleagues in the United States. From that experience I came away most impressed with the scope of research programs that are in place to learn how use of white rot fungi can lessen the damage done by conversion of wood to pulp for paper and other products. Pretreatment with white rotters lessens the need for chlorine bleach, reduces the amount of water needed, and allows the pulping process to take place at a lower temperature. Although implementation of all of these advancements on a commercial scale may be some years off, there seems to be little doubt that they will eventually be used, with the rest of our environment the clear winner.

Pest Management and Fungi. The apparent outstanding success of *Entomophaga maimaiga* in suppressing gypsy moth larvae, together with the commercialization of other less well publicized fungi to control other insect pests, seems to have renewed interest in the use of fungi as biocontrol agents. Research at both public and private laboratories is likely to continue, and the prospect of seeing more success stories on the horizon is bright. In addition, it seems that with each month that passes, another report of the discovery of an endophytic fungus that helps to protect a particular plant against insect attack appears in the literature. These fungi are already being exploited in the turf-grass industry, and their eventual use in other crops—especially intensively managed ones—seems inevitable.

Symbiotic Association of Fungi with Plants. After years of research on the effects of mycorrhizae on plant growth, scientists have made several commercial formulations of especially promising fungi available for application to roots of new transplants and established trees. Their value when used at transplant has already been demonstrated, and they are likely to become standard additions to afforestation programs. If, when added to the root systems of established trees, they perform as well as the developers hope they will, they could also become useful tools in caring for landscape specimens.

Most certainly, the next five to ten years will see the fungi playing markedly increased roles in our lives. For the most part, I suspect these will improve our lot, but the occasional mycotic infection or plant disease or poisonous mushroom or moldy ear of corn will serve to remind us just how vulnerable we are to the oft-neglected fungus world.

NOTES

CHAPTER 1. CLASSIFICATION AND NAMING

1. R. Villemet, "Essai sur l'histoire naturelle du champignons vulgare," *Nouveaux Memoires de l'Academie de Dijon,* 2d ser. (1784), 195–211, cited in B. J. Coppins, and R. Watling, "Lichenized and Non-lichenized Fungi: Folklore and Fact," *Bot. J. Scotl.* 47: 249–261.

2. R. H. Whittaker, "New concepts of kingdoms and organisms," *Science* 163 (1969): 150–161.

3. C. Woese, "Archaebacteria," *Scientific American* 244(6) (1981): 98–102.

4. J. Ruiz-Herrera, *Fungal Cell Wall: Structure, Synthesis, and Assembly* (Boca Raton, Fla.: CRC Press, 1992).

5. R. DeZeeuw, "Notes on the Life of Persoon," *Mycologia* 31 (1939): 369–370.

6. H. M. Fitzpatrick, "Curtis Gates Lloyd," *Mycologia* 19: 153–159.

CHAPTER 2. WHAT FUNGI DO AND HOW THEY DO IT

1. A. H. R. Buller, *Researches on The Fungi,* vol. 1 (New York: Longman, 1909); E. Haindl and J. Monzer, "Elongation growth and gravitropic curvature in the *Flammulina velutipes* (Agaricales) fruiting body," *Exp. Mycol. 18* (1994): 150–158; and J. Monzer, E. Haindl, V. Kern, and K. Dressel, "Gravitropism of the basidiomycete *Flammulina velutipes:* Morphological and physiological aspects of the graviresponse," *Exp. Mycol.* 18: 7–19.

2. A. H. R. Buller, *Researches on the Fungi,* vol. 3 (New York: Longman, 1924).

3. D. A. Glawe and W. U. Solberg, "Early accounts of fungal bioluminescence," *Mycologia* 81 (1989): 296–299; and D. J. O'Kane, W. L. Lingle, D. Porter, and J. Wampler, "Localization of bioluminescent tissue during basidiocarp development in *Panellus stipticus,*" *Mycologia* 82 (1990): 595–606.

4. C. T. Ingold, *Dispersal in Fungi* (Oxford: Clarendon Press, 1960).

5. C. M. Christensen, *The Molds and Man* (Minneapolis: University of Minnesota Press, 1965).

6. R. Duran, *Ustilaginales of Mexico* (Pullman: Washington State University Press, 1987).

7. H. J. Brodie, *The Bird's Nest Fungi* (Toronto: University Toronto Press, 1975).

8. B. D. L. Fitt, H. A. McCartney, and P. J. Walklate, "The role of rain in dispersal of pathogen inoculum," *Ann. Rev. Phytopathology* 27 (1989): 241–270.

9. P. H. List and B. Freund, "Geruchstoffe der Stinkmorchel, *Phallus impudicus* L. 18. *Mitteilung über Pilzeinhaltstoffe. Planta Med.* suppl. (1968),

123–132, cited in C. J. Alexopoulous, C. W. Mims, and M. Blackwell, *Introductory Mycology,* 4th ed. (New York: John Wiley & Sons, 1996).

10. A. H. R. Buller, *Researches on Fungi,* vol. 4 (New York: Longmans, Green, and Co., London, 1934).

11. C. T. Ingold, "Sphaerobolus: The story of a fungus," *Trans. Br. Mycol. Soc. 58* (1972): 179–195.

12. N. P. Goldberg, M. C. Hawes, and M. E. Stanghellini, "Specific attraction to and infection of the cotton root cap cells by zoospores of *Pythium dissotocum. Can. J. Bot.* 67 (1989): 1760–1767.

CHAPTER 3. FUNGI AS PATHOGENS OF FOOD CROPS

1. R. N. Salaman, *The History and Social Influence of the Potato* (New York: Cambridge University Press, 1985).

2. K. Neill, *Illustrated History of the Irish People* (Dublin: Gill and MacMillan, 1979).

3. E. C. Large, *The Advance of the Fungi* (London: Jonathan Cape, 1958).

4. G. L. Carefoot and E. R. Sprott, *Famine on the Wind* (New York: Rand McNally, 1967).

5. C. Poirteir, *Famine Echoes* (Dublin: Gill and MacMillen, 1995).

6. C. Woodham-Smith, *The Great Hunger* (New York: Harper and Row, 1972).

7. W. D. Griffin, *The Irish in America* (Dobbs Ferry, N.Y.: Oceana Publications, 1973).

8. Carefoot and Sprott, *Famine on the Wind.*

9. Ibid.

10. W. E. Fry et al., "Historical and recent migrations of Phytophthora infestans: Chronology, pathways, and implications," *Plant Disease* 77 (1993): 653–661.

11. Carefoot and Sprott, *Famine on the Wind.*

12. P. A. M. Millardet, "Concerning the history of the treatment of mildew and rot with copper sulphate," *J. Agr. Pratique* 2 (1885): 801–880, cited in F. J. Schneiderhan, transl., *Phytopathological Classics,* no. 3 (St. Paul, Minn.: American Phytopathological Society, 1983).

13. Large, *Advance of the Fungi.*

CHAPTER 4. FUNGI AS AGENTS OF CATASTROPHIC TREE DISEASES

1. H. Merkel, "A deadly fungus on the American chestnut," *N.Y. Zool. Soc. Ann. Rept. 10* (1904): 97–103.

2. G. L. Carefoot and E. R. Sprott, *Famine on the Wind* (New York: Rand McNally, 1967).

3. W. A. Sinclair, H. H. Lyon, and W. T. Johnson, *Diseases of Trees and Shrubs* (Ithaca, N.Y.: Comstock Publishing, 1986).

4. E. Exum, "Tree in a coma," *American Forests* 98 (1992): 20–25.

5. C. R. Burnham, "The restoration of the American chestnut," *American Scientist* 76 (1988): 478–487.

6. U. Heiniger and D. Rigling, "Biological control of chestnut blight in Europe." *Ann. Rev. Phytopathology* 32 (1994): 581–589.

7. Robert Frost, "Evil Tendencies Cancel?" in *Collected Poems* (London: J. Cape, 1943).

8. F. W. Holmes, *Dutch Elm Disease—The Early Papers: Selected Works of Seven Dutch Women Phytopathologists* (St. Paul, Minn.: APS Press, 1990).

9. Ibid.

10. W. A. Sinclair and R. J. Campana, eds., "Dutch elm disease: Perspectives after 60 years," *Search Agr.* 8 (5), New York State Agricultural Experiment Station, Cornell University, Ithaca, N.Y.; and C. M. Brasier, "Ophiostoma novo-ulmi sp. nov. causative agent of the current Dutch elm disease pandemics," *Mycopathologica* 115 (1991): 151–161.

11. L. M. Hanisch, H. D. Brown, and E. A. Brown, *Dutch Elm Disease Management Guide*, USDA Forest Service Bulletin 1, Washington, D.C.

12. Sinclair and Campana, "Dutch elm disease."

13. Hanish, Brown, and Brown, *Dutch Elm Disease Guide.*

14. R. J. Stipes, "Glitches and gaps in the science and technology of tree injection," *J. Arboriculture* 14 (1988): 165–172.

15. E. B. Smalley and R. P. Gurics, "Breeding elms for resistance to Dutch elm disease," *Ann. Rev. Phytopathology* 31 (1993): 325–352; and F. S. Santamour and S. E. Bentz, "Updated checklist of elm (*Ulmus*) cultivars in North America," *J. Arboriculture* 21 (1995): 122–135.

16. Sinclair, Lyon, and Johnson, *Diseases of Trees.*

17. Ibid.

18. G. W. Hudler, M. T. Banik, and S. G. Miller, "Unusual epidemic of tar spot on Norway maple in upstate New York," *Plant disease* 71 (1987): 65–68.

19. M. L. Daughtrey and C. Hibben, "Dogwood anthracnose: A new disease threatens two native Cornus species." *Ann. Rev. Phytopathology* 32: 61–73.

CHAPTER 5. ERGOT OF GRAIN CROPS

1. "Bread of madness infects a town," *Life* magazine, September 10, 1951, pp. 25–27.

2. M. V. Wiese, ed., *Compendium of Wheat Diseases,* 2d ed (St. Paul, Minn.: APS Press, 1987).

3. Z. Rehacek and P. Sajdl, *Ergot Alkaloids: Chemistry, Biological Effects, Biotechnology* (New York: Elsevier Science Publishing, 1993).

4. F. J. Bove, *The Story of Ergot* (New York: S. Karger, 1970).

5. J. G. Fuller, *The Day of St. Anthony's Fire* (New York: Hutchinson, 1969), and G. Barger, *Ergot and Ergotism* (London: Guerney and Jackson, 1931).

6. M. Matossian, *Poisons of the Past* (New Haven: Yale University Press, 1989).
7. G. Barger, *Ergot and Ergotism* (London: Guerney and Jackson, 1931).
8. Ibid.
9. Matossian, *Poisons of the Past,* and L. R. Caporael, "Ergotism, the Satan loosed in Salem?" *Science* 192 (1976): 21–26.
10. Wiese, *Compendium of Wheat Diseases.*
11. Bove, *The Story of Ergot.*
12. A. Hoffman, *LSD, My Problem Child* (New York: McGraw-Hill, 1980).
13. M. A. Lee and B. Shlain, *Acid Dreams* (New York: Grove Weidenfield, 1985).
14. R. Crockett and R. A. Sandison, *Hallucinogenic Drugs and Their Psychotherapeutic Use* (Springfield, Ill.: Thomas Publishing, 1963).

CHAPTER 6. MYCOTOXINS: TOXIC BY-PRODUCTS
OF FUNGAL GROWTH

1. J. G. Heathcote and J. R. Hibbert, *Aflatoxins: Chemical and Biological Aspects* (New York: Elsevier, 1978).
2. I. F. H. Purchase, *Mycotoxins* (New York: Elsevier, 1974).
3. D. L. Eaton and J. D. Groopman, *The Toxicology of Aflatoxins: Human Health, Veterinary and Agricultural Significance* (San Diego: Academic Press, 1994).
4. B. N. Ames, R. Magaw, and L. S. Gold, "Ranking possible carcinogenic hazards," *Science* 230 (1987): 271–280.
5. R. C. Croy and E. A. Crouch, "Interaction of aflatoxin and hepatitis b virus as carcinogens in human populations," pp. 87–102 in G. A. Bray and D. H. Ryan, eds., *Mycotoxins, Cancer, and Health* (Baton Rouge: Louisiana State University Press, 1991).
6. Purchase, *Mycotoxins.*
7. A. Z. Joffe, *Fusarium Species: Their Biology and Toxicology* (New York: Wiley and Sons, 1986).
8. G. C. Bergstrom, Cornell University, personal communication, 1997.
9. S. Seagrave, *Yellow Rain* (New York: M. Evans and Co., 1981).
10. J. Robinson, J. Guillemin, and M. Meselson, "Yellow rain: The story collapses," *Foreign Policy* 68 (Fall 1987): 100–117.
11. T. Whiteside, "Annals of the Cold War: The yellow rain complex," *New Yorker* 66 (1991): 52–62.
12. P. E. Nelson, A. E. Desjardin, and R. D. Plattner, "Fumonisins: Mycotoxins produced by Fusarium species: Biology, chemistry, and significance," *Ann. Rev. Phytopathology* 31 (1993): 233–252; and J. P. Rheder, W. F. O. Marasas, P. G. Thiel, E. W. Sydenham, G. S. Shephard, and D. J. VanSchalkwyk, "Fusarium moniliforme and fumonisins in corn in relation to human esophageal cancer in Transkei," *Phytopathology* 82 (1992): 353–357.
13. B. J. Wilson and R. R. Maronport, "Causative fungal agent of leucoencephalomalacia in equine animals," *Vet. Rec.* 88 (1971): 484–486.

CHAPTER 7. MYCOSES: FUNGUS DISEASE IN HUMANS

1. J. W. Rippon, *Medical Mycology* (New York: W. B. Saunders, 1988).
2. C. W. Emmons, C. H. Binfor, and J. P. Utz, *Medical Mycology* (London: Henry Kimpton, 1971).
3. Rippon, *Medical Mycology*.
4. Ibid.
5. Ibid.
6. Emmons et al., *Medical Mycology*.
7. W. J. Weber, *Health Hazards from Pigeons, Starlings, and English Sparrows* (Springfield, Ill.: Thompson Publications, 1979).
8. P. Negroni, *Histoplasmosis: Diagnosis and Treatment* (Springfield, Ill.: Thompson, 1975); and H. C. Sweany, *Histoplasmosis* (Springfield, Ill.: Thompson, 1960).
9. J. Batten, "Clinical aspects of Aspergillus infection in man," in R. DeHaller and F. Suter, eds., *Aspergillosis and Farmer's Lung in Man and Animals* (Berne, Switz.: Hare-Huber, 1974).
10. D. A. Stephens, "Coccidioidomycosis," *New England J. Medicine* 332 (1995): 1077–1082.
11. L. Ajello, *Coccidioidomycosis—Current Clinical and Diagnostic Status* (New York: Symposia Specialists, 1977).
12. E. Schnieder et al., "A coccidioidomycosis outbreak following the Northridge, California, earthquake," *JAMA* 277 (1997): 904–908.
13. Rippon, *Medical Mycology*.
14. M. Wainwright, *Miracle Cure: The Story of Penicillin and the Golden Age of Antibiotics* (Oxford: Basil Blackwell, 1990).
15. N. S. Ryder and H. Mieth, "Allylamine antifungal drugs," pp. 158–188 in M. Borgers, R. Hay, and M. Rinaldi, *Current Topics in Medical Mycology* (New York: Springer-Verlag, 1992).

CHAPTER 8. MEDICINAL MOLDS

1. A. Maurois, *The Life of Sir Alexander Fleming, Discoverer of Penicillin* (New York: E. P. Dutton, 1959).
2. J. C. Sheehan, *The Enchanted Ring: The Untold Story of Penicillin* (Cambridge, Mass.: MIT Press, 1982).
3. Ibid., and M. Wainwright, *Miracle Cure: The Story of Penicillin and the Golden Age of Antibiotics* (Oxford: Basil Blackwell, 1990).
4. T. I. Williams, *Howard Florey: Penicillin and After* (Oxford: Oxford University Press, 1984).
5. Sheehan, *Enchanted Ring*.
6. Ibid.
7. Wainwright, *Miracle Cure*.
8. S. B. Levy, *The Antibiotic Paradox: How Miracle Drugs Are Destroying the Miracle* (New York: Plenum Press, 1992).

9. J. F. Borel, "The history of cyclosporin-a and its significance," pp. 5–17 in D. J. G. White, ed., *Cyclosporin A* (New York: Elsevier, 1982).

10. S. M. Grundy, "HMG-CoA reductase inhibitors for treatment of hypercholesterolemia," *New England J. Medicine* 319 (1988): 24–32.

11. S. C. Jong and C. Birmingham, "Medicinal and therapeutic value of the shiitake mushroom," *Advances in Applied Microbiology* 39 (1993): 153–185; and C. Hobbs, *Medicinal Mushrooms* (Santa Cruz, Calif.: Botanica Press, 1995).

12. K. Matsumoto, *The Mysterious Reishi Mushroom* (Santa Barbara, Calif.: Woodbridge Press, 1979).

13. T. Willard, *Reishi Mushroom, Herb of Spiritual Potency and Medical Wonder* (Issaquah, Wash.: Sylvan Press, 1990).

14. Hobbs, *Medicinal Mushrooms.*

15. G. W. Frank, *Kombucha: Healthy Beverage and Natural Remedy from the Far East,* trans. A. Tynedale (Steyr, Germany: Ennstahler, 1995).

Chapter 9. Yeasts

1. H. W. Allen, *A History of Wine: Great Vintage Wines from the Homeric Age to the Present Day* (London, 1961); and H. Johnson, *Vintage: The Story of Wine* (New York: Simon and Schuster, 1989).

2. F. P. Kuno, *The Great German Wine Book* (New York: Sterling Publishing, 1983).

3. A. D. Butcher, *Ale and Beer: A Curious History* (Toronto: McLelland and Stewart, 1989).

4. B. Bower, "Ancient site taps into soldier's brew," *Science News* 146 (1994): 390; and S. H. Katz and F. Maytag, "Brewing an ancient beer," *Archaeology,* July/August 1991, 24–33.

5. S. Renaud and M. de Lorgeril, "Wine, alcohol, and the French paradox for coronary heart disease," *The Lancet* 339 (1992): 1523–1525; and R. Beaglehole, R. Jackson, and R. Scrogg, "Alcohol consumption and risk of coronary heart disease," *British Medical Journal* 303 (1991): 211–216.

6. A. Fleming, *Alcohol, the Delightful Poison* (New York: Delacorte, 1975).

Chapter 10. Edible and Poisonous Mushrooms

1. M. Lipske, "A new gold rush packs the woods in central Oregon," *Smithsonian* 24 (1994): 35–46; W. E. Schlosser and K. A. Blatner, "The wild edible mushroom industry in Washington, Oregon, and Idaho," *Journal of Forestry* (March 1993): 31–36; and R. F. Rowe, "The commercial harvesting of wild edible mushrooms in the Pacific Northwest region of the United States," *The Mycologist* 11 (1997): 10–15.

2. D. R. Benjamin, *Mushrooms: Poisons and Panaceas* (New York: W. H. Freeman, 1995).

3. R. Walsh, "Seeking the truffe," *Natural History* 105 (1996): 20–23.

4. P. B. Flegg, D. M. Spencer, and D. A. Wood, *The Biology and Technology of the Cultivated Mushroom* (New York: John Wiley & Sons, 1985).

5. Schlosser and Blatner, "Wild edible mushroom industry," and Rowe, "Commercial harvesting."

CHAPTER 11. HALLUCINOGENIC MUSHROOMS

1. R. G. Wasson and V. Wasson, *Mushrooms, Russia, and History* (New York: Pantheon Books, 1957).

2. Ibid.

3. Ibid.

4. R. Heim and R. G. Wasson, "Les Champignons hallucinogens du Mexique," Museum of Natural History, Paris, France, cited in R. G. Wasson, "The hallucinogenic mushrooms of Mexico: An adventure in ethnomycological exploration," *N.Y. Acad. Sci. Trans.* 21 (1959): 325–339.

5. T. Leary, *Flashbacks: A Personal and Cultural History of an Era* (New York: G. P. Putnam and Sons, 1983).

6. T. McKenna, *True Hallucinations* (San Francisco: HarperCollins, 1993).

7. F. J. Von Strahlenberg, *An Historico-Geographical Description of the North and Eastern Parts of Europe and Asia* (London, 1736), cited in R. G. Wasson, *Soma—Divine Mushroom of Immortality* (New York: Harcourt, Brace, Jovanovich, 1968).

8. R. G. Wasson, *SOMA—Divine Mushroom of Immortality* (New York: Harcourt Brace Jovanovich, 1968).

9. Ibid.

10. Ibid.

11. D. R. Benjamin, *Mushrooms: Poisons and Panaceas* (San Francisco: W. H. Freeman, 1995).

CHAPTER 12. WOOD DECAY

1. A. L. Shigo and W. E. Hillis, "Heartwood, discolored wood, and microorganisms in living trees," *Ann. Rev. Phytopathology* 11 (1973): 197–222; and A. L. Shigo, *Tree Decay, An Expanded Concept,* USDA Forest Service Information Bulletin 419, Washington, D.C.

2. J. Singh, *Building Mycology* (New York: E. and F. N. Spon, 1994).

3. J. Ramsbottom, "Dry rot in ships," *Essex Naturalist* 25 (1937): 231–267.

4. R. T. Lamar, J. A. Glaser, and T. K. Kirk, "White-rot fungi in the treatment of hazardous waste," pp. 127–143 in G. F. Leatham, ed., *Frontiers in Industrial Mycology* (New York: Chapman & Hall, 1992); and D. L. Illman, "Hazardous waste treatment using fungus enters marketplace," *Chemical and Engineering News* 71 (1993): 26–29.

5. T. Kirk, R. R. Burgess, and T. W. Koning, Jr., "The use of fungi in pulping of

wood: An overview of bio-pulping research," pp. 99–111 in G. F. Leatham, ed., *Frontiers in Industrial Mycology* (New York: Chapman & Hall, 1992).

CHAPTER 13. INTERACTIONS OF FUNGI AND INSECTS

1. B. A. Roy, "Floral mimicry by a plant pathogen," *Nature* 362 (1993): 56–58.
2. B. Holldobler and E. O. Wilson, *The Ants* (Berlin: Springer-Verlag, 1992); L. R. Batra and S. W. T. Batra, "The fungus gardens of insects," *Scientific American* 217 (1967): 112–120; and C. R. Huxley and D. F. Cutler, *Ant-Plant Interactions* (New York: Oxford Scientific, 1991).
3. M. M. Martin, "The evolution of insect-fungus associations: From contact to stable symbiosis," *American Zoologist* 32 (1992): 593–605; W. A. Sands, "The association of termites and fungi," pp. 495–524 in K. Drishna and F. M. Weesner, eds., *Biology of Termites* (New York: Academic Press, 1969); and T. G. Wood and R. J. Thomas, "The mutualistic association between macrotermitinae and Termitomyces," pp. 69–92 in N. Wilding, N. M. Collins, P. M. Hammond, and J. F. Webber, eds., *Insect-Fungus Interactions* (San Diego: Academic Press, 1989).
4. R. Beaver, "Insect-fungus relationships in the bark and ambrosia beetles," pp. 121–143 in ibid.
5. H. C. Evans, "Mycopathogens of insects of epigeal and aerial habitats," pp. 205–238 in ibid.; and Y. Tanada and H. K. Kaya, *Insect Pathology* (New York: Academic Press, 1993).
6. Tanada and Kaya, *Insect Pathology*.
7. E. B. Mains, "North American entomogenous species of Cordyceps," *Mycologia* 50 (1958): 169–222.
8. D. C. Steinkraus and J. B. Whitfield, "Chinese caterpillar fungus and world class runners," *American Entomologist* 40 (1994): 234–239.
9. A. E. Hajek, R. A. Humber, and J. S. Elkinton, "Mysterious origin of *Entomophaga maimaiga* in North America," *American Entomologist* 41 (1995): 31–42; and T. G. Andreadis and R. M. Weseloh, "Discovery of *Entomophaga maimaiga* in North American gypsy moth," *Proc. National Acad. Sci. USA* 87 (1990): 2461–2465.

CHAPTER 14. SYMBIOTIC RELATIONSHIPS OF FUNGI WITH PLANTS

1. M. C. Rayner, *Mycorrhiza: An Account of Non-Pathogenic Infection by Fungi in Vascular Plants and Bryophytes* (London: Wheldon and Wesley, 1927).
2. A. H. Fitter and J. W. Merryweather, "Why are some plants more mycorrhizal than others? An ecological enquiry," pp. 26–36 in D. J. Read, D. H. Lewis, A. H. Fitter, and I. J. Alexander, eds., *Mycorrhizas in Ecosystems* (Wallingford, U.K.: CAB International, 1992).
3. L. C. DuChesne, "Role of ectomycorrhizal fungi in biocontrol," in F. L.

Pfleger and R. G. Linderman, eds., *Mycorrhizae and Plant Health,* pp. 27–45 (St. Paul, Minn.: APS Press).

4. D. P. Janos, "Mycorrhizae influence tropical succession," *Biotropica* 12 (1980): 56–64.

5. E. E. Arnolds, "Decline of ectomycorrhizal fungi in Europe." *Agricult. Ecosyst. Environ.* 35 (1991): 209–244, and P. Lizon, "Decline of macrofungi in Europe: An overview," *Trans. Mycol. Soc. ROC* 8 (1993): 21–48.

6. K. Clay, "Fungal endophytes of grasses: A defensive mutualism between plants and fungi," *Ecology* 69 (1988): 10–16; and G. Carroll, "Fungal endophytes in stems and leaves: From latent pathogen to mutualistic symbiont," *Ecology* 69 (1988): 2–9.

7. J. A. Stuedemann and J. S. Hoveland, "Fescue endophyte: History and impact on animal agriculture," *J. Prod. Agric.* 1 (1988): 39–44.

8. H. Butin, "Effect of endophytic fungi from oak (*Quercus rober* L.) on mortality of leaf inhabiting gall insects," *Eur. J. For. Path.* 22 (1992): 237–246.

9. R. Honegger, "Functional aspects of the lichen symbiosis," *Ann. Rev. Plant Physiol. and Plant Molec. Biol.* 42 (1991): 553–578.

10. M. E. Hale, *The Biology of Lichens* (London: Edward Arnold, 1983).

11. F. Bremmer, "In praise of the lowly lichen," *International Wildlife* 21 (6) (1991): 30–33

12. D. H. S. Richardson, *Pollution Monitoring with Lichens* (Sough, U.K.: Richmond Publishing, 1992).

13. Hale, *The Biology of Lichens.*

14. D. H. S. Richardson, *The Vanishing Lichens* (Vancouver, B.C.: David and Charles Ltd., 1975); and Y. Tuominen and T. Jaakola, "Absorption and accumulation of mineral elements and radioactive nuclides," pp. 185–223 in V. Ahmadjian and M. E. Hale, eds., *The Lichens* (New York: Academic Press, 1973).

15. Bremmer, "In praise of the lowly lichen."

16. S. D. Sharnoff, "Lowly lichens offer beauty and food, drugs and perfume," *Smithsonian* 15 (1984): 134–143; and D. H. S. Richardson, "Medicinal and other economic aspects of lichens," in M. Galun, ed., *Handbook of Lichenology,* pp. 93–108 (Boca Raton, Fla.: CRC Press, 1988).

17. Hale, *The Biology of Lichens.*

INDEX

Pages in **bold** are illustrations